MAR 2 3 2005

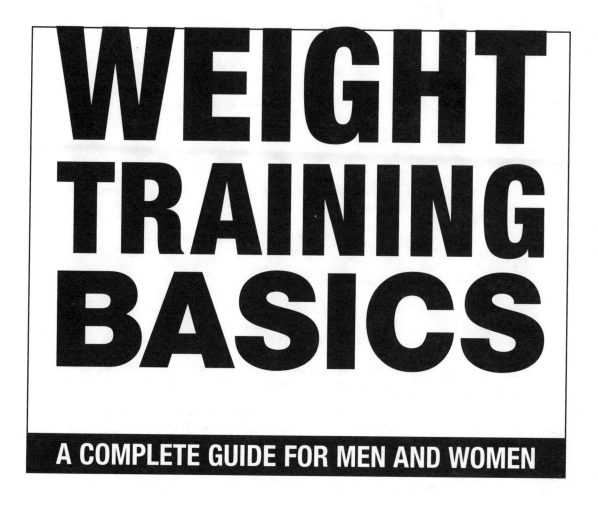

WEIGHT TRAINING BASICS

A COMPLETE GUIDE FOR MEN AND WOMEN

Also by Thomas D. Fahey, Ed.D.

Weight Training Basics. New York: McGraw-Hill, 2005. In press (trade book)

Exercise Physiology: Human Bioenergetics and Its Applications. New York: McGraw-Hill, 2005.
(co-author with G. A. Brooks and K. Baldwin; 4th edition)

Fit and Well. Mt. View, CA: McGraw-Hill, 2005.
(co-author with Insel and Roth, Stanford University; 6th edition)

Specialist in Sports Conditioning. Santa Barbara: ISSA, 2003. (course for personal trainers)

Youth Fitness Trainer. Santa Barbara: ISSA, 2003. (course for personal trainers)

Fitness for Kids and Teens. Santa Barbara: ISSA, 2003.

Strength, Quickness, Speed: Improving Performance in Power Sports. Santa Barbara: ISSA, 2003.
(includes videotape; co-author with Larry Burleson and Richard Trimmer)

Basic Weight Training for Men and Women. Mt. View, CA: Mayfield Publishing Co., 2004.
(5th edition; first edition entitled *Basic Weight Training*)

Superfitness for Sports, Performance, and Health. Boston: Allyn and Bacon, 2000.

Phosphatidylserine (PS): Promise for Athletic Performance. New York: Keats Publishing Co., 1998.
(co-author with Edmund Burke)

Basic Golf. Mt. View, CA: Mayfield Publishing Co., 1995.

Weight Training for Women. Mt. View, CA: Mayfield Publishing Co., 1992.
(co-author with Gale Hutchinson)

Steroid Alternative Handbook. San Jose, CA: Sport Science Publications, 1991.

Athletic Training: Principles and Practice. (T. Fahey, Ed.) Mt. View, CA: Mayfield Publishing Co., 1986.

What to Do About Athletic Injuries. New York: Butterick Publishing, 1979.

Good-Time Fitness for Kids. New York: Butterick Publishing, 1979.

The Good-Time Fitness Book. New York: Butterick Publishing, 1978.

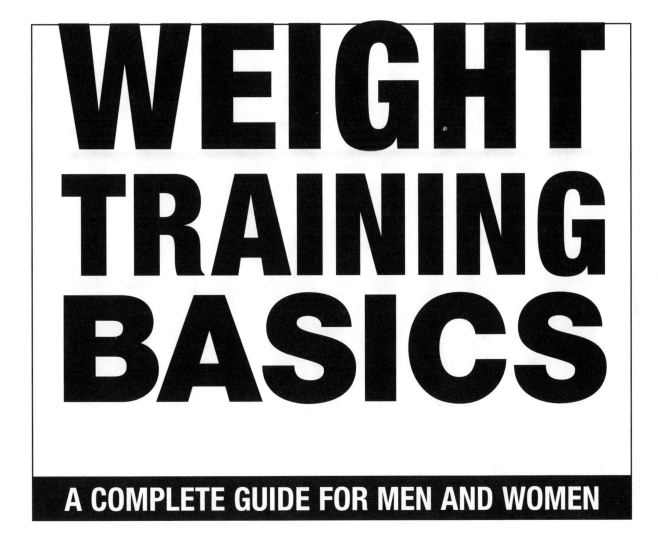

WEIGHT TRAINING BASICS

A COMPLETE GUIDE FOR MEN AND WOMEN

THOMAS D. FAHEY, Ed.D.

McGraw·Hill

New York   Chicago   San Francisco   Lisbon   London   Madrid   Mexico City
Milan   New Delhi   San Juan   Seoul   Singapore   Sydney   Toronto

The McGraw·Hill Companies

Library of Congress Cataloging-in-Publication Data

Fahey, Thomas D. (Thomas Davin), 1947–
    Weight training basics : a complete guide for men and women / by Thomas D. Fahey.
        p.   cm.
    Includes bibliographical references and index.
    ISBN 0-07-144647-8
    1. Weight training.   I. Title.

    GV546.F26   2005
    613.7'13—dc22   2004021949

1 2 3 4 5 6 7 8 9 0   VLP/VLP   0 9 8 7 6 5

ISBN 0-07-144647-8

Interior photographs by Taylor Robertson

McGraw-Hill books are available at special quantity discounts to use as premiums and sales promotions, or for use in corporate training programs. For more information, please write to the Director of Special Sales, Professional Publishing, McGraw-Hill, Two Penn Plaza, New York, NY 10121-2298. Or contact your local bookstore.

This book is printed on acid-free paper.

CONTENTS

ACKNOWLEDGMENTS

I have been fortunate to make my passion for sport my life's work. Competing as a high school, college, open, and masters athlete has granted me the practical knowledge that has enhanced the formal training in physical education and exercise physiology that I received at both the University of California, Berkeley, and San Francisco State University. I am indebted to my mother and father for instilling in me a love of sport. My undergraduate instructors at San Francisco State—including Frank Verducci, Allen Abraham, Vic Rowen, and Arner Gustafson—taught me to look at sport as a science. My college coach Bob Lualhati has been an inspiration to me for my entire adult life. He taught me to be a lifelong student of sport and to never make excuses. My friend, mentor, and coauthor Dr. George Brooks, from the University of California, Berkeley, taught me the meaning of excellence. Steve and Elise Blechman, owners and editors of *Muscular Development* and *Fitness Rx* magazines, have allowed me to express my ideas to millions of their readers. I learned about sports from some truly gifted athletes and coaches, including John Powell, Brian Oldfield, Carl Wallen, Dave Mackenzie, Dan John, Bob Fritz, Art Burns, Jim McGolderick, Yuri Sedykh, and Ben Plunknet. It has been a pleasure working with colleagues who appreciate the meaning of sport, including my lifelong friend Rich Schroeder, my coach as a masters discus thrower Larry Burleson, Dick Trimmer, Bill Colvin, and Steve Henderson. Finally, this book would not have been possible without the expertise of the production staff at McGraw-Hill.

Weight Training: The Key to a Leaner, Stronger Body

"There are two kinds of people—those who think they can and those who think they can't. . . . They're both right."
—Henry Ford

What activity cuts fat, builds muscle, boosts metabolism, reduces the risk of heart attack, strengthens bones, and improves sex appeal? Weight training will do this and a lot more. Young people, older adults, and children are taking up weight training faster than any other activity—and for good reason. You will see substantial improvements in your body within a few months with just a little effort.

The ultimate couch-potato gadget is the electric easy chair that lifts people from their seat so they don't have to stand up on their own. Most people who are physically fit can't relate to being so weak that they can't get up from a chair. Yet, millions of Americans are so deconditioned that they have trouble performing even simple tasks.

Bodybuilders like Steve Reeves (Hercules), Arnold Schwarzenegger (movie star and governor of California), Jack La Lanne (legendary fitness expert) and Charles Atlas (mail-order strength-training guru) epitomized fit-

ness in the minds of most Americans for most of the past century. These men looked healthy and muscular, and people wanted to look like them. That all changed with the advent of aerobics.

The popularity of books such as *Aerobics* and *Total Running*, published in the '60s and '70s, pushed weight training into the background. They emphasized the importance of endurance exercise that developed cardiorespiratory capacity. While they sometimes recognized the value of muscle-building exercises, clearly strength training took a backseat to running, walking, swimming, and cycling.

The aerobics craze created a backlash against weight trainers. Lifting weights was looked on as an activity people did to avoid doing real exercise. Skinny people who looked like distance runners bragged about how many miles they ran. If you didn't run at least 30 miles a week, many people thought you were sedentary. Weight trainers were almost ashamed to be seen on the street!

Fortunately, things have come full circle—strength training has regained its position in the pantheon of beneficial exercises. Scientists and millions of people around the world discovered that weight training makes you lean, fit, and sexy; revs up your metabolism; cuts body fat; shields you from heart disease and stroke; protects your muscles and bones from deterioration; and boosts your self-esteem. For older people, strength training may be more effective in promoting health and independent living than any other activity. Almost all health experts now see weight training as a health-promoting activity—something that most people should include in their fitness programs (see Table 1.1).

Most men and women lose a little strength and muscle mass every year after about age 30. By age 75, about 25 percent of men and 75 percent of women can't lift more than 10 pounds. While aging contributes to the loss of muscle mass and strength, inactivity causes most of the loss. Well-controlled studies of weight training among middle-aged and older adults show that these people gain strength at the same rate as younger people. You are definitely not over the hill when you hit 30!

THE BENEFITS OF WEIGHT TRAINING

For nearly 100 years, scientists thought that the heart's capacity to pump blood to the tissues determined fitness. Cardiovascular capacity is certainly important, but fitness is more complicated than that. Muscle power capacity and muscles' resistance to fatigue are also important. Resistive exercises, such as weight training and plyometrics ("bounce" exercises), build muscle power better than any other techniques.

Building muscle power is important to both athletes and nonathletes. Football players, discus throwers, and golfers perform better and fatigue more slowly with stronger, more powerful muscles. Also, stronger muscles mean fewer injuries.

Strong, powerful muscles are equally important for the smooth and easy performance of everyday activities, such as carrying groceries, lifting boxes, and climbing stairs, as well as for responding to emergency situations. They help keep the skeleton in proper alignment, prevent back and leg pain, and provide the support necessary for good posture. Strength and power mean freedom to the average person. If you lose your balance when taking a shower, you recover quickly if

Table 1.1 CHANGES TO THE BODY FROM WEIGHT TRAINING

Change	Effect
Increased muscle mass	Tighter, firmer-looking body and stronger muscles
Increased size of fast- and slow-twitch muscle fibers	Increased strength and power
Increased blood supply (high-repetition program)	Increased delivery of oxygen and nutrients to the cells and increased elimination of wastes from the cells
Increased fuel storage in muscles	Increased resistance of muscles to fatigue
Ability to use more motor units during muscle contraction	Increased strength and power
Improved coordination of motor units	Increased strength and power
Increased strength of tendons, ligaments, and bone	Lower risk of injury to these tissues

SOME MAJOR HEALTH BENEFITS OF REGULAR EXERCISE

- Reduces risk of premature death (all causes)
- Reduces risk of coronary artery disease
- Lowers blood pressure
- Lowers body fat
- Lowers blood fats
- Increases high-density lipoproteins (HDL) (protective substance)
- Reduces platelet stickiness (platelets are a type of blood cell)
- Reduces effects of stress
- Improves glucose tolerance (related to a type of diabetes)
- Encourages healthy living habits
- Reduces the risk of some types of cancer
- Improves mental health
- Prevents or delays osteoporosis (bone loss)
- Prevents or improves symptoms of arthritis
- Prevents muscle and nerve deterioration

---

you're strong and powerful, but fall and risk breaking your hip if you are weak and slow. The stronger person can walk up hills while on vacation, lug groceries easily from the car to the house, and push a car to the side of the road when it runs out of gas. Sedentary people remain on the sidelines while life passes them by.

Weight Training Enhances Metabolic Fitness

In 1996, the U.S. surgeon general released a report on physical fitness and health. The report stated that exercise is the single most important lifestyle habit contributing to good health.

Based on considerable research, several recommending organizations—including the American College of Sports Medicine, the surgeon general, the Centers for Disease Control and Prevention, and the American Heart Association—made a distinction between physical activity as it relates to health and as it relates to physical fitness. Low levels of exercise, practiced almost every day, reduce the risk of degenerative diseases and enhance metabolic health; yet, they do not contribute to improved physical fitness.

Weight training contributes to both types of fitness. Weight training makes your cells run more efficiently. It

---

BENEFITS OF WEIGHT TRAINING

- Increases strength and power of muscles
- Improves ability to perform daily tasks
- Enhances performance in sports
- Enhances appearance
- Improves self-esteem
- Reduces risk of injury
- Improves back health
- Improves metabolic fitness (insulin metabolism, blood pressure control, blood lipids, and blood clotting control)
- Reduces body fat—particularly abdominal fat
- Speeds the movement of food through the gastrointestinal tract
- Prevents sarcopenia (muscle loss)
- Prevents osteoporosis (bone loss)
- Prevents arthritis
- May reduce the risk of coronary artery disease, stroke, and some cancers
- In women, builds strength without bulk
- Increases sensitivity to testosterone
- Provides a fun activity with observable progress
- Promotes socialization if you train at a club

improves insulin sensitivity in the cells by increasing the amount of chemicals that help transport blood sugar in the cells' interiors.

Problems with insulin metabolism cause a host of health problems called *syndrome X* or *metabolic syndrome*. Insulin resistance—due to lack of exercise, poor diet, and genetics—leads to high insulin secretion, high blood pressure, obesity (particularly the more dangerous abdominal obesity), and blood fat abnormalities. Weight training helps combat many of the factors associated with syndrome X. A chief example is that weight training helps promote a better ratio of "good" high-density lipoproteins (HDL) to "bad" low-density lipoproteins (LDL) cholesterol.

Weight training also reduces abdominal fat, which is particularly dangerous in promoting heart disease, diabetes, and high blood pressure. Weight training helps you lose abdominal fat metabolically rather than through spot reducing. You can't do hundreds of sit-ups and lose your gut without affecting total body energy balance. Weight training induces subtle changes in metabolism, such as preventing insulin resistance, thereby helping your body avoid storing fat in the abdomen.

Weight Training Helps Control Body Fat

Exercise alone is insufficient for long-term weight loss, but combining diet and exercise improves your chances of losing weight and keeping it off. Weight training helps preserve lean body mass (fat-free weight), increases total energy output, and speeds fat use after exercise. Weight training increases energy output nearly as much as aerobics does—if you train intensely. It also increases the amount of calories you burn while digesting food. Above all, it increases the amount of calories

you burn during and after exercise—mainly by increasing fat-free mass. Fat-free mass is principally composed of muscle—the most important tissue determining the calories you burn (metabolize).

Metabolism includes all the chemical reactions that occur in your body. Every time you exercise, make new proteins, break down foods you eat, or repair injured tissues, your body uses energy that contributes to metabolism. Muscles are hotbeds of metabolism. They make up about 45 percent of your body weight—more than any other tissue. Muscles use a large amount of energy when they contract. During exercise, metabolism increases by more than 10 times above rest. World-class endurance athletes can increase their metabolism by more than a whopping 20 times above rest.

Even at rest, muscles use a lot of energy because they are highly metabolic tissues. This means that your metabolic rate is higher if you have more muscle. More muscle makes it easier to burn calories and create a negative energy balance that metabolizes fat. Weight training can also help you maintain your muscle mass when you're trying to lose weight, helping you to avoid the significant drop in resting metabolic rate associated with weight loss. So, when you lift weights, you will find it easier to lose fat, maintain your new healthier weight, and look great at the same time.

Muscles continue to increase metabolic rate even when you stop exercising. Lifting weights, particularly when you train intensely, increases muscle temperature, which increases calorie use after exercise. The increased temperature helps to raise metabolic rate above normal resting levels. Just as a car burns more gas when it runs at a high rpm rate when idling, your body's metabolism runs at a faster rate after exercise and helps you burn more calo-

Caution: While weight training may reduce the risk of heart attack, stroke, high blood pressure, and diabetes, you should not try to treat these health problems by yourself. Rather, exercise should be part of a coordinated wellness plan undertaken after consulting with your physician.

Caution: Spot reducing doesn't work–you cannot reduce fat over specific muscles through exercise. You can lose fat only by expending more calories through exercise and metabolism than you take in through diet.

WEIGHT TRAINING: THE KEY TO A LEANER, STRONGER BODY

ries all day. Greater muscle mass helps stoke your metabolism during and after exercise. Greater metabolism is the key to losing weight and mastering your metabolism.

Weight loss through low-calorie dieting alone makes you lose muscle mass and decreases the efficiency of fat metabolism. This makes continued weight loss more difficult and makes it easier to regain the weight. The overall energy expenditure, mainly determined by the frequency and duration of exercise, is more important than exercise intensity for controlling body fat. Most research studies suggest that a good exercise program for losing body fat should include both endurance and resistive exercises, practiced at least three times per week, with an energy expenditure of approximately 1,500 calories per week.

Weight Training Prevents Muscle Loss with Age (Sarcopenia)

The World Masters Games are held every four years in a major city around the world. Representatives from many countries compete in more than 20 sports. A notable entrant in one of the Games was Ben Levinson, a 103-year-old man from Los Angeles. He set the world record of 10 feet 1 inch in the shot put (eight-pound, eight-ounce) for men over 100 years of age. He began training for the event when he was 100.

During an interview with Jay Leno on the "Tonight Show," he said that training for the shot allowed him to throw away the cane he used to help him walk. In a typical workout, he walks for 20 minutes at 2.5 miles per hour and does 20 repetitions (number of times exercise performed) for 8 to 10 weight-training exercises. He demonstrated his shot-put technique during the show and threw an amazing four feet farther than his world record. His example shows that almost anyone

can improve muscle strength at any age. Almost all weight-training studies of people 40 to over 80 years of age show that on a percentage basis, older people gain strength just as fast as 20-year-olds do.

Good muscle strength helps people live healthier lives. A lifelong program of regular strength training prevents muscle and nerve degeneration that can compromise the quality of life and increase the risk of hip fractures and other potentially life-threatening injuries. After age 30, people begin to lose muscle mass and strength. At first, they may notice that they can't play sports as well as they could in high school. After more years of inactivity and strength loss, people may have trouble performing the simple movements of daily life—getting out of a bathtub or automobile, walking up a flight of stairs, or doing yard work. Poor strength makes it much more likely that a person will be injured during the course of everyday activities.

As people age, motor nerves become disconnected from the portion of muscle they control. Muscle physiologists estimate that by age 70, 15 percent of the motor nerves in most people are no longer connected to muscle tissue. Aging and inactivity also cause muscles to become slower and therefore less able to perform quick, powerful movements. This occurs because fast-twitch motor units are converted to less powerful slow-twitch motor units. Weight training helps maintain motor nerve connections and the quickness of muscles.

Weight Training Prevents Bone Loss (Osteoporosis)

Most of us think of bone loss disease as something that mainly concerns older women. Think again. The seeds of osteoporosis are sown during adolescence and early adulthood. Lifetime

Caution: Failing to maintain good muscle mass throughout life can result in falling, loss of mobility, and premature death.

exercise habits, to a large extent, determine the depth of the problem during aging.

In osteoporosis, bone mass is so low that even minor trauma can cause fracture—most commonly in the hip, spine, and wrist. It is a major public health problem that affects more than 25 million Americans, 80 percent of whom are women. It is linked with more than 1.5 million fractures a year. Because osteoporosis is a symptom-free disease, it can progress undetected for decades. As the population ages, the incidence of osteoporotic fractures will increase. Prevention includes maximizing bone density during childhood and young adulthood, estrogen supplements at menopause, dietary calcium and perhaps vitamin D supplements, and regular weight-bearing exercise throughout life.

For women, peak bone mass occurs between 15 and 20 years of age. After that, bone building and breakdown remain in balance until menopause. Then, bone breakdown accelerates, resulting in a gradual loss of bone mineral mass. Men lose bone mass as they age but at a much slower rate than women do.

Bone responds to stress and disuse by reducing tissue in areas where it is no longer needed and increasing it in areas that are subjected to stress. Weight training causes exercise-induced bone growth, while inactivity promotes bone loss.

One of the best strategies for preventing postmenopausal osteoporosis is to build bone mass when you're young. Do this by lifting weights, doing aerobic exercise, and including at least 1.2 grams of calcium in your diet every day. Regular exercise, particularly high-stress activities such as weight training, running, and gymnastics, promotes a higher lifetime peak bone density and lowers your fracture risk.

Until recently, physicians thought that estrogen replacement therapy was critical for preventing postmenopausal bone loss. However, newer studies have shown that hormone replacement therapy after menopause increases the risk of heart attack and stroke. Weight training is a natural way to prevent bone loss after menopause. Factors to consider include:

- **Bone mass changes only in bones loaded (forces compressing or pulling on bone) during exercise.** Lower-body exercise will strengthen leg bones but will not strengthen bones in the upper body.
- **Bone growth requires bone stress.** Non-weight-bearing exercises, such as swimming, have no effect on bone mass.
- **Use it or lose it—gains in bone mass are reversible.** You will lose gains in bone mass when you stop training.
- **People with the lowest bone mass will improve most from a weight-training program.**
- **Genetics limit your capacity to increase bone mass.** Gains in bone mass level off as you reach your genetic ceiling.

Prevention is the best method of dealing with osteoporosis. As discussed, a valid lifetime strategy is to maximize bone mass before menopause through diet and exercise and maintain bone mass after menopause with estrogen, diet, and exercise. Bone mass at menopause is a significant predictor of long-term bone health. Weight training is a major player in beefing up your bones.

Weight Training Can Prevent Arthritis

Carl Lewis, the great Olympic track-and-field athlete, revealed that he has severe degenerative arthritis caused by his years of sports performance. A fair question for the nonathlete is "Will

Caution: Discuss hormone replacement therapy with your doctor before taking any such supplements.

Caution: Women should "bank" bone while they are young by doing weight-bearing exercise; eating a diet rich in calcium, vitamins D and K, iron, folate, fruits and vegetables, and phosphorus; and ensuring good hormone health.

weight training put so much stress on my joints that I will get arthritis?"

The risk of developing arthritis increases when people play sports involving high levels of impact, such as football, or torsional loading of the joints, as in skiing. People who continue playing sports after joint injuries are also at higher risk. The famous Framingham study (a study that examined the health habits of people who live in Framingham, Massachusetts) found that people at increased risk of developing arthritis of the knee included those who were obese, smokers, and former athletes in high-impact sports.

Studying cartilage degeneration with loading is impossible in humans. So, scientists use animals for this purpose. In one study on hamsters, animals forced to be sedentary had lower proteoglycan content in the cartilage and a lower synovial fluid volume—factors critical for cartilage strength and nutrition. These changes are associated with cartilage abnormalities, such as pitting and fissuring. Conversely, daily exercise prevented early cartilage degeneration and maintained normal joint cartilage. Thus, it appears that moderate exercise may enhance joint cartilage health, while high-stress exercise may cause damage and deterioration.

Weight Training Enhances Self-Image

Weight training leads to an enhanced self-image by providing stronger, firmer-looking muscles and a toned, healthy-looking body. Men tend to build larger, stronger, shapelier muscles. Women lose inches, increase strength, and develop greater muscle definition. Because weight training involves measurable objectives (pounds lifted, repetitions accomplished), a person can easily recognize improved performance, leading to greater self-confidence.

WOMEN AND WEIGHT TRAINING: SHAPING WITHOUT BULK

The image of the incredible muscle development of women bodybuilders, weight lifters, and throwers makes many average women shun weight training. Few women want to have tree trunk legs, bowling ball calves, or bulging biceps. These concerns are not justified. In fact, intense weight training helps lose fat, burn calories, and make muscles look firm, lean, fit, and sleek. Behemoth women strength athletes often get that way because they have more male hormones than normal or they take muscle-building drugs, such as anabolic steroids or growth hormone. Weight training will not build large muscles in most women.

Scientists began studying the effects of weight training in women more than 30 years ago. Every one of the studies showed that women do not build large muscles from weight training. Rather, they lose fat and gain only some muscle. Weight training makes women look smaller, firmer, and toned —not larger and bulkier. Muscle is denser tissue than fat. When you lose fat and gain muscle, you lose bulk because dense muscle tissue takes up less space than less-dense fat.

Muscle stokes your metabolic furnace, helping you use more calories. Most studies show that women who weight-train while dieting maintain muscle mass and prevent the decrease in metabolic rate that accompanies weight loss. Women who lose weight and either don't exercise or do only aerobics look drawn and flabby because they lose muscle. Muscle is what makes you look healthy, toned, and fit.

Men have bigger muscles than women because men have higher levels of testosterone in the blood. Testosterone levels are more than 10 times higher in men than women. Young

Caution: Most women do not gain bulky muscles when they lift weights. Muscle is less dense than fat, so they lose rather than gain inches. Women should train intensely with weights to get the most benefits.

men (18 to about 40 years old) have between 400 and 1,000 nanograms of testosterone per 100 milliliters of blood, while women have 30 to 150 nanograms (10^{-9} grams; very small units). Women produce another "male" hormone called androstenedione that can be converted to testosterone. Scientists from Drew Medical College, in Los Angeles, have shown that muscle growth depends on blood levels of testosterone—the higher the level of the hormone, the more muscles grow.

Women have low levels of testosterone, so they don't gain much muscle tissue when they train with weights. Rather, they train their nervous system to use existing muscle. The muscle they gain makes the upper and lower body look firmer, leaner, and shapelier.

Some women have high levels of testosterone and androstenedione and will gain muscle faster than normal. If you are a woman with larger muscles than other women, you might have high testosterone levels. However, even if you are one of these rare people, gaining muscle and strength will make your body look better.

INJURY PREVENTION

Increased muscle strength provides protection against injury because it helps people maintain good posture and appropriate body mechanics when performing everyday activities such as walking, lifting, and carrying. Strong muscles in the abdomen, hips, lower back, and legs support the back in proper alignment and help prevent low-back pain, which afflicts more than 85 percent of all Americans at some time in their lives. Weight training also makes the tendons, ligaments, and joint surfaces stronger and less susceptible to injury.

BUILDING BLOCKS OF A STRONGER, FITTER YOU: WEIGHT TRAINING, AEROBICS, WEIGHT CONTROL, DIET, AND MENTAL PREPARATION

You are reading *Weight Training Basics* because you want to be lean and healthy. You are unique because you watch what you eat, lift weights, and get plenty of cardiovascular exercise. You are part of only 12 percent of the population that exercises vigorously. Fifty percent of Americans don't get enough exercise, and 25 percent don't do any exercise at all. Among high school students, participation in daily physical education classes decreased by nearly 50 percent in the last 10 years. The problem is most severe among young women and gets worse in both sexes throughout the teen years. By college age, young men and women approach the exercise levels of the adult population. Lack of exercise is the main reason that more than 60 percent of Americans are overweight and 22 percent are obese. The following building blocks can help you get a good start on improving your physical fitness:

- **Be active every day.** Move instead of watching TV, surfing the Internet, or vegging on the couch. Exercise at least 30 minutes a day—at least 60 minutes a day if you have a weight problem.
- **Exercise vigorously—greater than 60 percent of maximum effort—if you want to improve fitness.** Engage in a variety of activities, including weight-training, cardio, stretching, and muscle endurance exercises.
- **Eat a healthy diet.** Eat a variety of foods, emphasizing fruits, vegetables, whole-grain products, and lean meats. Avoid simple sugars, saturated

and trans fats, excessive amounts of alcohol, and desserts.

- **Take care of obvious health problems.** See your physician regularly for checkups. Get treated for known problems, such as high blood pressure and high blood fats. Stop smoking. Do back-pain-prevention exercises if you have a back problem.

- **Enjoy life.** Americans work hard trying to make it in a competitive society. Take time to enjoy your friends and family.

Caution: If you don't want to exercise, see your doctor to determine if your body can withstand the effects of an inactive lifestyle.

2

How Muscles Contract and Grow

"It is hard to fail, but it is worse never to have tried to succeed."
—Theodore Roosevelt

The structure of your weight-training program determines the way your body and muscles respond. Develop an attractive body by building muscle size and symmetry and minimizing surface fat. Improve performance in power sports such as tennis, golf, football, soccer, and volleyball by building strong muscles that can react quickly and forcefully. Prevent back pain by building stable core muscles (the muscles of the abdomen, hips, and back) that have good endurance.

People interested in developing more attractive bodies and people interested in improving performance in sports require completely different training programs. There are optimal training programs for each. People often mistakenly do the wrong kinds of programs: power athletes do bodybuilding programs, and bodybuilders do exercises that do not help them reach their goals.

Until recently, scientists knew relatively little about the best ways to increase muscle strength and size. People were on their own—whatever seemed to work was put into practice. Scientists did not have the tools to study the way muscles grow; the technology wasn't available. That all changed in the 1960s and '70s, when the development of the electron microscope, muscle biopsy techniques, and radioactive tracers allowed scientists to look inside the muscle and study its physiology and biochemistry.

Today, scientists know a lot about the way muscles get stronger and increase in size. New technologies and the opening up of the sports medicine laboratories in the former Communist eastern bloc have added immensely to our knowledge. Apply our knowledge of muscle physiology and sports medicine and you will make gains far greater than you ever thought possible.

MUSCLE STRUCTURE AND THE NERVOUS SYSTEM

Muscle contractions make possible many of the events of daily living, including physical work conducted on the job, athletic activities on the playing field, and graceful movements in the performing arts. These fantastic feats of strength and endurance are possible because of the conversion of chemical energy to mechanical energy in muscle.

Muscles convert energy in foods to mechanical and heat energy. When you train, you are attempting to improve the capacity of this system—you hope to make it faster and more efficient.

Skeletal Muscle Structure

Muscles cause movement by pulling on the skeleton. When a muscle contracts (shortens), it moves a bone by pulling on the tendon that attaches the muscle to the bone.

Muscles consist of individual cells, or fibers, connected in bundles. A single muscle is made up of many bundles of muscle fibers, called fasciculi, covered by layers of connective tissue that hold the fibers together. Connective tissue runs from end to end of muscle (i.e., from the tendon of origin to the tendon of insertion) and exists within muscle tissue surrounding the fibers and giving rise to muscle bundles.

Individual muscle cells are subdivided into myofibrils and myofilaments. Thin and thick myofilaments interact to cause contraction. Bundles of myofilaments are called myofibrils. When your muscles are given the signal to contract, protein filaments within the myofibrils slide across one another, causing the muscle fiber to shorten. Weight training causes the size of individual muscle fibers to increase by increasing the number of myofibrils. Larger muscle fibers mean a larger and stronger muscle. The development of larger muscle fibers is called hypertrophy.

Under a magnifying glass or a light microscope, skeletal muscle fibers have a striped (striated) appearance. Actin and myosin, the two main proteins of contraction and the principal components of the myofibrils, cause the strip-

ing within the cell. The thin actin filaments are attached to the Z line. The Z line forms the foundation for shortening in muscle. The sarcomere—made up of the contractile proteins lying between two Z lines—is the basic functional unit of the muscle. Contraction occurs when actin (A) combines with myosin (M), triggered by a chemical reaction within the muscle cell.

The Motor Unit

A motor unit consists of a motor nerve and its associated muscle cells, or fibers. All muscle fibers are turned on by at least one motor nerve; a nerve impulse turns on the muscle fibers and makes them contract. One motor nerve may be connected to as few as 3 and as many as 1,000 muscle fibers. When the motor unit fires, all of the muscle fibers in the unit contract to their maximum capacity.

Muscle fibers are classified as fast-twitch or slow-twitch according to their strength, speed of contraction, and fatigue resistance. To achieve greater precision, muscle physiologists further classify human muscle fibers by their biochemical characteristics as well as their strength, power, speed, and endurance, as follows: Type I (slow-twitch; slow oxidative—SO), IIa (fast-twitch; fast oxidative glycolytic—FOG), and IIx (fast-twitch; fast glycolytic—FG). The complexity of muscle fiber typing is confusing, so, to simplify things, we will limit the discussion to slow-twitch and fast-twitch fibers.

Slow-twitch fibers are relatively fatigue resistant, but they do not contract as rapidly or strongly as fast-twitch fibers. Fast-twitch fibers contract more rapidly and forcefully than slow-twitch fibers but fatigue more quickly.

Most muscles contain a mixture of slow-twitch and fast-twitch fibers. The type of fiber that acts depends on the type of work required. Endurance activities such as jogging tend to use slow-twitch fibers, whereas strength and power activities such as sprinting use fast-twitch fibers. Weight training can increase the size and strength of both fast-twitch and slow-twitch fibers, although fast-twitch fibers are preferentially increased.

The body turns on (recruits) motor units when it needs muscle force—to lift a weight, throw a ball, or put weight on the edge of a ski. The number of motor units recruited depends on the amount of strength required: you use more motor units picking up a large weight than a small weight. Weight training improves your ability to recruit motor units—a phenomenon called muscle learning, which increases strength even before muscle size increases. Muscle learning is an important means for gaining strength during childhood and in women because low testosterone levels make it difficult to gain significant muscle size.

MUSCLE STRENGTH: SIZE, NEURAL ACTIVATION, ELASTIC ENERGY, AND SKILL

Weight training builds muscle strength because it increases the size of muscle fibers and improves the body's ability to recruit motor units to exert force. Optimal muscle performance requires good muscle size, coordination between the muscles and nervous system, efficient use of the muscles' elasticity, and skill development. Each factor depends on the others for peak muscular development. Muscles develop best when contracted at high tensions. Developing the neural and elastic properties of muscle, in addition to muscle protein, will ultimately result in faster and more impressive gains in sports performance. So, get all three systems working for you!

Hypertrophy or Hyperplasia?

For more than a hundred years, scientists have argued whether strength training increases muscle fiber number (hyperplasia) or only muscle fiber size (hypertrophy). Most studies show that strength training makes muscle fibers larger, not more numerous. However, there is some proof that muscle fibers can increase in number under certain circumstances. Also, some extremely strong people may be born with more muscle fibers than others. Generally, though, it is muscle hypertrophy that makes muscles bigger and stronger.

Increasing Muscle Size

Muscle fibers get bigger by increasing the number of myofibrils; in other words, muscles increase in size by adding protein. Proteins are composed of combinations of basic building blocks called amino acids. Strength and muscle size increase as myofibrils are added to the muscle. The more myofibrils added to the muscle, the greater the increase in strength and size.

CRITICAL ELEMENTS FOR MUSCLE HYPERTROPHY

- Muscle tension (force) and duration of tension
- Anabolic hormones: testosterone, growth hormone, IGF-1, insulin
- Amino acids
- Carbohydrates (postexercise)
- Calories (energy balance)
- Genes: myostatin, muscle growth factors

Protein Synthesis. As the muscle continues to receive increased demands, the activity of the cells' protein-making machinery increases. Scientists think that a chemical messenger system may trigger protein-making genes to increase muscle size.

The nucleus is the control center for protein production in muscle cells. Most cells in the body contain a single nucleus. Muscle cells, however, contain many nuclei, giving them a high capacity to produce new proteins. Proteins are made from amino acids on cell structures called ribosomes. The protein-making genes in the nucleus send messages to the ribosomes telling them exactly how to arrange the amino acids to form a specific protein. The cells also manufacture enzymes, a type of protein involved in cell function and physical performance. Many factors influence protein production in muscle, including muscle tension, hormones, amino acid concentration, nutritional status, and rest.

Muscle Tension. Muscle tension is the most important factor in promoting muscle hypertrophy. Muscle tension speeds the movement of amino acids into the muscle and triggers the nucleus to build new muscle. Greater movement of amino acids into the muscle speeds the rate of protein synthesis. In other words, optimal muscle growth depends on triggering tension receptors in the cell and on accelerating the rate at which amino acids enter the cell. Any training program designed to stimulate muscle growth should attempt to maximize the intensity and duration of muscle tension.

Hormones. The four most important hormones in promoting protein synthesis in muscle are testosterone, growth hormone, insulin-like growth factor (IGF-1), and insulin. These hormones influence muscle cell nuclei and their messengers to speed the production of muscle proteins. Insulin also speeds the movement of amino acids into the muscle cell. This action is critical for muscle growth—the more amino acids transported into the muscle cell, the greater the rate of muscle hypertrophy.

Other hormones cause protein breakdown. The most important of these are the corticosteroids, produced by the adrenal glands (hormone-secreting glands that lie on top of each kidney). The adrenals produce corticosteroids, such as cortisol, during times of stress. These hormones increase after a hard workout or during periods of overtraining. When you have overtrained, your blood level of corticosteroids will rise and your level of testosterone will fall. You are in a catabolic state—gains in muscle size are impossible.

Scientists recently discovered a chemical called myostatin that keeps muscles from growing too large. Geneticists have already developed myostatin blockers that they have used to increase muscle size in beef cattle. How long will it be before gene techniques are used by bodybuilders and power athletes?

Amino Acid Concentration and Nutritional Status. Rapid movement of amino acids into muscles requires an ample supply of amino acids in the blood and muscles. Usually, this is not a problem because most people take in enough protein in their diets to supply the muscles with plenty of amino acids. However, during times of heavy training, extensive soft tissue injury, or overtraining, amino acid concentration may not be adequate. Energy intake is also essential. If you do not take in enough calories, your body will break down its own structural proteins for energy.

Rest. Muscles hypertrophy during recovery from weight training. Repeated training without adequate recovery slows muscle growth and prevents intense training. Rest, therefore, is an integral part of the weight-training program. Rest should be planned and not used as an excuse not to exercise.

Anabolic-Catabolic Cycles. As any body-builder or weight lifter can tell you, training does not lead to continuous gains in muscle size. Muscle size increases for a while and then levels off, and sometimes regresses. One reason for this is protein turnover—the constant buildup and breakdown of structural proteins. If you provide the optimal training environment for the muscles (i.e., good muscle tension during training and ideal concentrations of anabolic hormones and amino acids), then your muscles will grow. You are in an anabolic, or growing, phase. If training and nutritional considerations are not optimal, then training gains will be less, or you may actually lose ground.

The goal of the training program should be to stay anabolic and avoid catabolic periods. Optimize tension in the workout by using cycles. Intense workouts increase muscle size. You must be adequately rested to train intensely. If you exercise at maximum effort every time you go into the weight room, you will never recover enough to train intensely. Quality of the training stimulus is the key to maximizing protein synthesis in muscle. Design your program so that you set yourself up for intense workouts.

Delayed-Onset Muscle Soreness (DOMS). DOMS is muscle soreness that you feel one to three days after a workout. In the past, scientists thought that lactic acid buildup or muscle spasms caused muscle soreness. Now we know that sore muscles are caused by cell damage.

Heavy workouts can cause damage to the fibers and calcium storage depots within the cells. Calcium is a chemical trigger that causes muscles to contract. Unfortunately, high concentrations of calcium cause muscle breakdown. Following muscle damage, calcium leaks into the muscle and causes the muscle proteins to break down. This causes pain and muscle inflammation. After a few days, the muscles form protective proteins that temporarily shield the muscle from further damage and soreness. If you skip too many workouts, you lose these protective proteins and become susceptible to more muscle soreness. Scientists think that muscles hypertrophy and increase strength in response to muscle injury.

The Nervous System, Muscle, and Strength

Muscle fibers receive the signal to contract from nerves connected to the spinal column under the direction of signals from the brain. As noted earlier, these nerve-muscle combinations are called motor units. Powerful muscles, such as the quadriceps in the legs, have large motor units—each motor nerve is connected to many muscle fibers. Smaller muscles, such as those around the eye, have much smaller motor units.

The type of motor unit chosen, fast- or slow-twitch, depends on the requirements of the muscle contraction. You use fast-twitch fibers for lifting heavy weights or sprinting because they are more powerful. Slow-twitch fibers are chosen for prolonged standing or slow walking because they are more resistant to fatigue.

The body exerts force by calling on one or more motor units to contract. This process of calling on motor units to contract is called motor unit recruitment. When you want to pick up a small weight, for example, you use few motor units to do the task. However, when you want to pick up a large weight, you will use many motor units. When a motor unit calls on its fibers to contract, all the fibers contract to their maximum capacity.

Motor units are activated by size: smaller motor units are used for light loads; large, powerful motor units are activated only when the body is required to exert maximum force. The muscle fibers in large, high-threshold motor units can increase in size more than smaller motor units. These fibers are not trained to any extent unless you push them. It is necessary to include heavy reps in your program if you expect to recruit these hard-to-train motor units. Failure to do so will limit muscle size.

Increased Strength Through Improved Motor Unit Recruitment. Training with weights improves the nervous system's ability to coordinate the recruitment of muscle fibers. It involves "muscle learning" and is a principal way of increasing strength. Neurological adaptations cause most of the changes in strength during the first weeks of weight training.

Most people concentrate on muscle tissue size when trying to increase strength. They try to increase muscle bulk with elaborate diets and ergogenic aids, such as anabolic steroids and growth hormone, and training cycles are usually aimed at increasing muscle size. However, strength depends on not only the size of muscles but also the ability of the nervous system to activate them. Strength training causes the nervous system to more fully "turn on" the muscles required in specific movements and to better coordinate their actions. These neural changes make you stronger.

Muscles increase force by activating more motor units. When you're going for a maximum lift, the ideal situation is to recruit as many motor units as possible. The more motor units you can recruit, the more strength you have.

Neural adaptations to strength training include increased electrical activity of the muscle, increased rate of motor unit activation, the ability to turn on motor units when the muscle is suddenly stretched, improved coordination of antagonistic muscle groups (the muscles that make the joint go in the opposite direction), cross-training effects (training one limb results in training effect in the complementary limb on the other side of the body), enhanced motor unit coordination, enhanced recruitment of high-threshold motor units, and increased time that high-threshold motor units can be activated.

Increased electrical activity of the muscle occurs early in the strength-training process. The increases in strength achieved by the novice weight trainer during the first weeks of training are due mostly to improved neural activation rather than muscle growth. This early strength is a result of an increased ability to recruit motor units. In children and women, these neural changes are critical for maximum strength because muscle hypertrophy does not occur in women and children to the same extent as in men. As discussed, this is because men have higher testosterone levels.

Some motor units are harder to recruit than others. The high-threshold units are the hardest to activate, but they are also the strongest and most powerful. Two related neural adaptations—enhanced recruitment of high-threshold motor units and increased time during which high-threshold motor units can be activated—have direct implications for overall strength development. *A motor unit is trained in direct proportion to its recruitment.* What this means is that the high-threshold motor units (muscle fibers and their motor nerve) will not be trained unless they are recruited and used during training. Neural adaptations that result in activating high-threshold motor units must occur before these motor units can be trained. When trying to develop explosive power, you must concentrate on recruiting the high-threshold motor units and turning them on for as long as possible.

In summary, to achieve maximum strength, it is essential that you train the high-threshold motor units. These units are trained only if you activate them. To recruit these motor units, you must train intensely and concentrate on accelerating your reps.

Elastic Muscle Energy

Your muscles have untapped elastic energy that can increase strength and add to your training gains. Most great athletes are very effective at using elastic muscle energy. It makes their movements look smooth and explosive. Elastic muscle energy allows them to exert much more force than is possible during normal muscle contractions.

Elastic muscle energy is much like a rubber band. When you stretch the rubber band and let go of the ends, it rebounds back to its normal shape. Muscle works in a similar way. If you stretch a muscle suddenly, it tries to rebound to its resting state. The elastic energy is captured in the muscle as potential energy. Potential energy in muscle is stored energy that can be used later to help exert force.

When muscle stretch is immediately followed by a muscle contraction, the rebound from the stored elastic energy greatly increases the force of contraction. It is much like getting a push when you start to run or an

active assist during a weight lift. The stretched muscle rebounds back to its shorter length. When the muscle is contracting at the same time that it rebounds from the stretch, the combined forces of muscle contraction and elastic recoil produce more force than either factor by itself.

Stored elastic energy must be used immediately or it is lost as heat. The secret of using elastic energy effectively is to coordinate the nervous and muscle contraction systems with muscle stretch. After the stretch, the muscles must be turned on instantly to take advantage of the muscles' elastic recoil. Scientists call this process the stretch-shortening cycle. An exercise method called plyometrics—described in Chapter 11—uses the stretch-shortening cycle to build muscle power for sports.

Elastic muscle energy enhances muscle-force development in the stretch-shortening cycle. During sudden movements like jumping or throwing, elastic structures are stretched. The stretch represents potential energy that can enhance the force produced by the contractile component. Immediately after the muscle is stretched, it contracts actively. The elastic recoil assists in force development.

Many types of human motion incorporate stretch-shortening cycles. When jumping in basketball or high jumping, the leg muscles are stretched immediately prior to the jump; the elastic loading of the leg enhances the force development during the jump. Hitting a baseball or golf ball also includes a stretch-shortening cycle: movement of the legs and hips leads movement of the upper body, which creates an elastic load on the torso (the core muscles) and a subsequent whip-like motion of the upper body. More power is generated than would have been possible using the upper-body muscles alone.

Strength-training programs must consider the contractile, neuro-muscular, and elastic components of muscle contraction and movement. Many athletes and coaches focus on contractile tissue adaptations when designing training programs. However, maximum strength, power, and muscle size requires a coordination of neural activation, storage and release of muscular elastic energy, and contraction of muscle.

Skill

Many people train with weights and do plyometrics to increase power for sports. They hope the exercises will make them hit tennis balls harder, hit golf balls farther, or jump higher. The best way to increase power in sports, though, is to improve skill.

Movement skills, such as hitting a forehand in tennis or driving a golf ball, are highly specific. They involve precise motor-unit recruitment patterns that are orchestrated by the nervous system. Franklin Henry, from the University of California, Berkeley, compared this process to that of a computer program that is stored on a disk. The program, imprinted on the brain, is played back as a motor reflex. Research on most high-power sports shows that athletes benefit more from improvements in skill than through improvements in strength. Weight training and plyometrics help sports performance best in people who are skilled in the sport. Skill development should never be sacrificed for strength and fitness training.

COORDINATING CELLULAR, NEURAL, ELASTIC, AND SKILL COMPONENTS OF STRENGTH

Maximizing force development requires coordination of the four components of strength. Some evidence suggests that muscle stiffness and elasticity can be altered slightly with training. However, elastic energy is most useful if it can be coordinated into movement skills. Neural changes occur early in the strength-training program. Muscle cell changes occur later and are probably the main limiting factor of strength. Improvements in skill can occur throughout life and can thus contribute to maximum force development.

SUMMARY

Strength development must consider muscle cells, neuromuscular activation, elastic energy, and skill. Muscle hypertrophy requires tension, anabolic hormones, nutrients, and rest. Muscles increase in size by adding myofibrils rather than new muscle cells. Neural activation of motor units is an important way to increase strength. The body increases force output by turning on more motor units. It regulates force through the number of units activated and the amount of time it activates specific units. Successful athletes must learn to use elastic energy. Activating muscle elastic recoil can greatly increase the muscle force output. Improving skill is the fastest and most efficient way to increase force output in sports. Never substitute conditioning for skill development. Both are important, and they complement each other.

3

Mold Your Body with Weight Training

*"Your opponent, in the end, is never really the player on the
other side of the net, or the swimmer in the next lane, or the team on
the other side of the field, or even the bar you must high-jump. Your
opponent is yourself, your negative internal voices,
your level of determination."*
—Grace Lichtenstein, author

Designing a weight-training program—
or any component of your exercise
program—requires a basic knowledge
of the effects of exercise on the body.
The basic principles of training are the
same for beginners and athletes. Both
groups use exercise stress to shape the
body and increase physical fitness. The
beginner's program might include one
set of 10 repetitions of 8 to 10 exercises and a brisk walk or bike ride three
times a week. The serious athlete
might vary the sets, repetitions, and
exercises, using sophisticated cycles
that change from week to week. Both
types of exercise stress the body and
improve fitness.

The processes of stress and adaptation are similar in world-class athletes,
working mothers trying to squeeze in a
workout, and college students taking
an exercise class. Fitness improves by
giving the body an unaccustomed
exercise stress, such as lifting a heavier
weight, walking instead of sitting, running faster or farther, or stretching a

muscle more than usual. The body
adapts to the stress by improving its
function.

In the late 1940s, Dr. Hans Selye,
from Canada, formulated the theory of
stress adaptation. This theory has had
a profound effect on medicine and has
tremendous implications in conditioning for physical activity and sports. He
called the process of stress adaptation
the "general adaptation syndrome"
(GAS). Selye described three stages of
stress reaction: alarm reaction, resistance development, and exhaustion.
The stress may include exercise, cold or
heat, bacteria, or emotional trauma—
anything that upsets the body balance.

The *alarm reaction* is the initial
response to stress. This process
involves the mobilization of the organ-
ism. During exercise you react to the
stress by breathing harder, sweating,
and increasing your heart rate. The
alarm reaction disturbs your
physiology and disrupts the body's
balance.

The *resistance development* stage is an adjustment phase that results in improved fitness, increased strength, or larger muscles. Your body improves its function so that the stressor is less disruptive to your physiology. For example, when you lift weights, your muscles get larger (hypertrophy), so that the load becomes less stressful. Resistance development (improved fitness) is the reason you lift weights, run, or stretch.

You adapt and improve physical fitness only if the stress is intense enough to disturb body balance. During exercise, if the stress is below a critical intensity, you don't improve fitness. On the other hand, you get injured if the stress is too intense and you can't tolerate the training load.

The amount and intensity of weight training necessary to improve fitness depends on current level of fitness, age, health, motivation, and a number of unknown factors. Bench-pressing 100 pounds for 10 repetitions might be exhausting or impossible for a sedentary, overweight 40-year-old but would cause essentially no adaptive response in a world-class discus thrower. Likewise, a weight-training workout that is easily performed one day may be completely inappropriate on a day following a prolonged illness. Environment also can alter performance. Extreme heat or cold, high altitude, or polluted air will decrease fitness and the capacity to exercise.

If the stress is too great, then you enter the third stage of GAS, *exhaustion*. This stage is an excessive stress that causes injury. The stress can be acute (applied all at once) or chronic (occurring over time). Examples of acute exhaustion include fractures, sprains, and strains. Chronic exhaustion is subtler and includes overtraining, stress fractures, and emotional stress.

PRINCIPLES OF TRAINING

Fitness development from weight training or any other kind of exercise depends on the degree of overload (how hard you push yourself), specificity of training (training the way you want your body to adapt), individual differences (genetics), progression (taking it one step at a time), and reversibility (use it or lose it).

The Overload Principle

Lifting more weight or doing more repetitions than before will improve strength and muscle size. The degree of overload depends on the load, number of repetitions, rest between sets, and frequency. Load refers to the weight used or intensity of the exercise. Repetition refers to the number of times a load is administered. Rest is the time interval between repetitions. Frequency is the number of training sessions per week. For example, in weight training, you might do three sets of eight different exercises using a weight you can barely lift for 10 repetitions (load and repetition), with one minute between each set (rest). You might do this workout three times per week (frequency).

The nature of overload in an exercise program is not an exact science. Start conservatively and build up. The overload is excessive if you are exceedingly sore, get injured, or don't recover easily from your weight-training workouts. Design a program that promotes strength, power, and muscle mass but does not cause injury or excessive soreness.

Specificity of Training

The body adapts specifically to the stress of exercise. For example, the adaptation to endurance exercise, such as distance running or swimming, differs from that of strength exercise, such as weight training, and from power exercises, such as sprinting. Any training program should reflect the desired adaptation. Train the way you want the body to change.

Doing the wrong type of training can impair certain types of fitness. For example, training for strength and endurance at the same time interferes with strength development. This is not a problem for a person who exercises for improved health and appearance, but it is a significant consideration for a person trying to develop maximum strength and power.

Many people ignore the principle of specificity when designing a weight-training program. Establish the reason you want to train with weights. If your goal is to build shapely, healthy-looking muscles and decrease body fat, you should do bodybuilding workouts that isolate specific muscles, as well as plenty of aerobics to help control body fat, and avoid explosive weight lifts. If you are a power athlete, such as a football or volleyball player, include large-muscle exercises that use several joints and many large muscle groups acting in unison. People interested in body-building commonly make the mistake of training like football players, while those interested in speed and power for sports often mistakenly train like bodybuilders.

Individual Differences

We are not all created equal physically. Anyone watching the Olympics, a professional football game, or a tennis match can see this immediately. Large individual differences exist in our ability to gain strength, power, and muscle size from weight training. Also, not everyone performs and learns sports skills at the same rate. Genetics can limit your capacity to benefit from a weight-training program. However, you can improve if you keep at it.

Genetics can also influence the degree to which you reap the health and wellness benefits of weight training. Some people are genetically healthier than others. People naturally lose bone and muscle mass with age. Weight training can prevent age-related deterioration, but it is more effective in some people than in others.

Progression

Adaptation to weight training works best when you increase resistance and training volume gradually. Increasing strength and muscle mass takes months and even years of training and involves progress in small stages. Superior fitness and physical performance represent a combination of many small gains in the weight room. You can't become fit overnight; it must be done gradually, one step at a time.

Reversibility

This basic principle of reversibility is "Use it or lose it." It is the opposite of the overload principle. Your body adapts to the stresses placed on it. If you exercise more intensely than usual, you improve fitness; if you do less, you lose fitness. A graphic example of reversibility is what occurs when you wear a cast for a broken bone. When the doctor removes the cast, your arm or leg is much smaller than before. This happens because the muscles atrophy (get smaller) as a result of inactivity.

DEVELOP YOUR BODY TO SUIT YOUR LIFESTYLE

The human body is extremely adaptable. Determine what you want from a weight-training program and then mold your body in that direction. If the goal is health promotion, choose 8 to 10 exercises and do one set of 10 repetitions of each. At least 35 research studies show that beginners get just as much benefit from doing one set of each exercise as they get from doing more than that.

Many people want to improve performance in recreational sports. If the sports you like require more endurance, concentrate on the oxidative energy system and endurance exercise. If you want to be a better tennis or volleyball player, you must not only develop skill but also work on muscle power and general endurance.

If you are mainly interested in improving your appearance, you must develop a healthy diet and exercise strategy that will help you lose fat and maintain or gain lean body mass. Weight training—and exercise in general—can be fun and rewarding, particularly if it helps you achieve your goals.

Muscles are highly adaptable. Overload them more than usual and they get bigger and stronger. Likewise, they lose strength and size when you stop exercising. You build strength by increasing the size of muscles, improving the way your nervous system transmits information to your muscles, and coordinating muscle elasticity with muscle contraction.

Get the most from your weight-training program by following the 17 Rules of Training. These rules are a guide to gradual, long-lasting, injury-free fitness development and will lead to improved performance with the smallest risk of injury.

Rules of Training

1. Train the way you want your body to change.
2. Eat a well-balanced, high-performance diet.
3. Establish realistic goals.
4. Have a workout plan.
5. Train year-round.
6. Get in shape gradually.
7. Don't train when you're ill or seriously injured.
8. Train first for volume (more repetitions) and only later for intensity (more weight or resistance).
9. Listen to your body.
10. Vary the volume and intensity of your workouts.
11. Work on your weaknesses.
12. Train systematically.
13. Warm up and cool down.
14. Train the mind.
15. Listen to "Coach Pain."
16. Learn all you can about exercise.
17. Have fun! Keep the weight-training program in perspective.

1. Train the way you want your body to change.

This means stress your body so that it changes the way you want. If you are primarily concerned with general fitness, choose a well-rounded program that concentrates on the major muscle groups. Besides the weight-training routine, the program should include endurance and flexibility exercises. If bodybuilding is your goal, isolate and build muscle and decrease body fat.

This is the most important training principle. The body adapts to a given stress in a specific way. For example, swimming will not improve endurance for running or cycling; if you lift weights, you will not become a better football player, discus thrower, skier, or swimmer unless you practice the sport. The best way to improve performance in a sport is to practice that sport and supplement the practice with exercises such as weight training and plyometrics (bounce exercises).

The support exercises for your sport, such as weight training, power exercises, and endurance training, will *eventually* help improve performance. However, improvement occurs only if you practice the skill and incorporate your new fitness (strength, power, flexibility, endurance) into it.

The principle of specificity should be the central consideration in any training program designed to improve skilled performance. Skill practice in activities such as tennis, skiing, golf, football, and softball should be a central part of the program. Support activities designed to improve physical capabilities, such as strength, power, and endurance, are secondary to skill development.

Physical support activities have to be consistent and long-term. Lifting weights for two months before tennis, football, or track season is practically worthless. The increased strength will not transfer that rapidly to your sports skills. A support program that develops high levels of fitness over a long period can be more effectively integrated into your sport. It will inject greater strength, power, endurance, and flexibility into your movement skills, and you will perform better.

Another critical factor regarding specificity of training is that weight training, plyometrics, and speed training transfer to motor skills in skilled athletes better than in novices. So, if you are a beginner and your goal is improved performance in sports, work on basic skill development before emphasizing strength and power. As your skill improves, add more conditioning exercise to boost sports power.

In summary, train the way you want your body to adapt. If increased sports performance is your goal, remember that support activities designed to improve power during sports movements create change slowly. You must develop strength, power, endurance, and flexibility slowly and consistently and integrate your new fitness into sports skills. Improving fitness without practicing the skill will have no effect on sports performance.

Work on your weaknesses—even if the exercises necessary to correct them are unpleasant. For example, if you are a skier, having strong, flexible lower-body muscles is more important than having strong arms and shoulders. Analyze your program. A well-designed program will be more effective and less time-consuming than a casual or unsystematic one.

2. Eat a well-balanced, high-performance diet.

During the past 20 years, sports scientists have shown that the right diet can improve performance and keep off unwanted pounds of fat. All the training in the world will not give you a great body if you eat too much. Eat a sensible, nutritious diet—one containing a balance of the basic food groups. The diet should supply enough calories to meet energy needs but still allow you to control your weight. If you want to lose weight, do so gradually— no more than two and a half pounds per week. If you are training hard, eat more complex carbohydrates and fewer saturated fats and trans-fatty acids. Your diet should be high in fruits, vegetables, fish, and whole grains. Foods containing monounsaturated fats, such as olive oil, nuts, and avocados, should also be included.

3. Establish realistic goals.

Your goals should reflect your capability and motivation. If you've never trained with weights, don't expect to look like a professional bodybuilder during your first year. Set achievable short-term goals, such as bench-pressing 10 more pounds. Get in the habit of achieving short-term goals and you will soon do things you never thought possible. Set a new goal after you achieve that one. The accumulation of small achievements adds up to incredible progress.

This method is appropriate for improving physical performance in sports. A beginning tennis player might set a goal of keeping a rally going for 10 strokes. A beginning golfer might set a short-term goal of putting the ball in two strokes on 25 percent of the holes. A beginning runner might set a goal of completing a six-mile fun run. A more accomplished athlete might set more difficult goals ranging from running a six-minute mile to making the Olympic team. The principle is the same for everyone: set goals you can achieve. After you achieve them, reevaluate your program and set new goals. Your new goal might be to maintain your present level, or it could be to achieve a higher level of performance.

A personal trainer can help you set and achieve goals. More important, he or she will help you internalize goal-setting behavior that is critical for long-term success in weight training. A good trainer will help you with program design, teach you proper exercise techniques, and help motivate you to stay with the program.

4. Have a workout plan.

Write down your goals and your plan for achieving them. If you are overweight, do more than just wish to look good in your bathing suit next summer. For example, if you want to lose 20 pounds of body fat and increase muscle mass, set up a realistic program for achieving this goal. A sensible approach might be to lose one pound per week and strive to go to the gym three times per week. You might achieve your goal by cutting down on desserts and junk food in your diet and devoting 60 to 90 minutes a day to aerobic exercise and weight training.

Contrast this method with a more casual approach. It's January and you're tired of looking bad in your swimsuit during the summer. You want to lose 20 pounds of fat but have no plan. You exercise and diet from time to time but make no progress because

you're inconsistent. Soon, it's May and you look the same as you did in the wintertime. So, you go on a crash weight-loss program and exercise regime. In spite of great pain and suffering, you fail to meet your goal and end up wearing a baggy T-shirt to the beach.

In setting up a good workout plan, analyze the elements necessary for achieving your goal. For example, if you want to be a better skier, you must practice skiing and develop good endurance, strength, power, and flexibility. During the off-season, systematically improve your physical fitness through weight training and aerobic exercise. Once the ski season comes around, shift emphasis to skill development and try to maintain fitness.

A football player should follow a similar procedure. After the football season, begin a program designed to gain muscle mass and improve power-output capacity. Do a weight-training program designed to stress the major muscles of the body. Do flexibility and endurance exercises to improve overall fitness. In the spring, integrate more power training into the program, such as plyometrics and speed exercises. During the summer, shift the training emphasis to maintaining strength and maximizing power, speed, and skill.

Contrast this systematic approach with the more common crash weight-training program started two months before the football season. The athlete might gain strength, but there is little improvement in power, speed, or football skills. The athlete wasted the two critical months before the season doing exercises that should have been done during the winter.

Keeping a training diary is the best way of ensuring a systematic program. Write down your program for the next four to six weeks and jot down your progress in the diary. The diary doesn't have to be anything fancy; go to the stationery store and buy a small spiral notebook. Put it in your gym bag and carry it with you to all your workouts. Record such things as weight, how you feel each day, your exercises (sets, reps, etc.), morning heart rate, and performances (for example, how long you ran on the treadmill or how much weight you lifted). Write down tentative workouts for the next six weeks in the training diary. Also, write down a rough workout plan for the next year. Writing down the plan in the training diary will help you get where you want to be next month and next year.

The training diary is integral to maintaining consistency in weight-training workouts. Training diaries are essential to anyone who is serious about fitness—actual athletes as well as people who just want to get into good shape. Start using a training diary today!

5. Train year-round.

Take too much time off from your exercise program and you will lose the gains you have made. You will get injured more easily if you try to get back in shape too rapidly. Establish a year-round program; have specific goals and procedures for each period of the year—and stick to them.

Have alternative training plans for when you don't have access to your usual training facility. For example, if you are on a trip, you can substitute calisthenics exercises—such as push-ups and knee bends—for your regular weight-training routine.

People who miss workouts don't improve fitness and even lose the gains they made. Plan regular times for weight training and stick to them. Don't let things interfere with your workout. All of us have many responsibilities that compete for our time. If fitness and performance are important, then make your workouts a priority. Workouts are your time, and don't let people take this important time away from you.

6. Get in shape gradually.

Achieving fitness is a gradual process of adaptation. Try to increase fitness too fast and you will get injured or overtrained. You cannot push the process too fast. High levels of fitness represent many small adaptations. If you introduce the stresses of exercise gradually, you will eventually become more fit at a lower risk of injury.

Many sports, such as football, employ crash exercise programs known by names such as "hell week" and "double days." Research studies are unanimous in showing that these programs are ineffective, cause unnecessary fatigue, and lead to injury. You cannot "force" your body to get fit overnight. Attempts at doing so almost always backfire and lead to injury and depressed immune function (overtraining makes it difficult for your body to fight disease). Instead of reaching high levels of fitness, you end up trying to exercise with a cold or flu and muscles so sore that you have trouble moving effectively.

Contrast this with a yearlong program that gradually develops fitness. By following this program, you will be capable of high levels of injury-free performance because you have conditioned gradually. *Successful athletes are built during the off-season.* By the same token, it takes months of training and preparation if your goal is to look better on the beach or ski better in the winter.

Training is a stress that the body must overcome, so give your body time to adapt to the stress of exercise. Muscles are more susceptible to injury during the early phases of conditioning. Overzealous training, or intense conditioning when you aren't prepared for it, will lead to injury and delay progress.

Staying in good shape all year long is much easier than trying to achieve fitness in a few months. It's much more practical to apply a little pressure instead of trying to go for a crash conditioning program.

7. Don't train when you're ill or seriously injured.

The body has problems trying to fight more than one stressor simultaneously. Training when you are sick or injured may seriously hinder your progress or even be dangerous. It is particularly important not to train when you have a fever. After an injury, return to intense workouts only if you can answer "yes" to these questions:

- Can you move the injured area (joint, muscle, etc.) normally?
- Do you have normal strength and power?
- Have normal movement patterns been restored (more than 90 percent recovered)?
- Are you relatively pain-free?

If the answer to any of these questions is no, then you should let the injury heal (through a combination of rehabilitation and rest) or modify the program before resuming the normal workout. Many people end up abandoning their favorite sports because they have many injuries that were not allowed to heal properly. Dealing effectively with injuries is just as important as having a well-designed training program.

8. Train first for volume (more repetitions) and only later for intensity (more weight or resistance).

Low-intensity, repetitive exercise prepares your body to withstand more intensive training with less risk of injury. High-intensity training designed to develop muscle mass or power and speed pushes the body to its limit. If you first develop a "fitness base" and increase the intensity of training gradually, you will develop muscle fitness with less risk of strains, sprains, and cramps.

Soft tissues, such as muscle, tendons, and ligaments, take a long time to adjust to the rigors of training. If your goal is to get as strong as possible, begin the program by doing more repetitions, not adding weight. This will prevent injury, strengthen your body gradually, and prepare it for heavy training.

During later training sessions, when you are in shape, you can use more weight and fewer repetitions to increase strength at a faster rate. If the goal is to have good muscle tone and muscular endurance, you do more repetitions instead of emphasizing using more weight.

9. Listen to your body.

Do not stick to the planned program too stubbornly if it doesn't feel right. Sometimes the body needs rest more than it needs exercise. Typically, an overtrained person has not recovered enough to train at an optimal intensity; so, a few days of rest is sometimes necessary to provide enough recovery to allow for training that is more intense. Overtraining is usually accompanied by fatigue, decreased performance, irritability, and sometimes depression.

Overtraining is an imbalance between training and recovery. Many active people live by the motto "No pain, no gain." While you have to work hard to achieve high levels of fitness, too much or too intense training is counterproductive.

Effective training occurs only if the body adapts to the stress of exercise. This adaptation occurs *after exercise*. If you don't give your body a chance to adapt, you will not improve fitness. Rather, progress comes to a halt and you get injured or sick.

Proper rest is just as important as intense training for improving fitness. When you work out, you are trying to get your body to adapt and improve its function. Before every workout, ask yourself, "What is the purpose of this exercise session and how will it cause my body to adapt?" If you are exhausted or have the flu, the workout may cause you to lose ground. You are better off resting for a day or two. When you come back, you will be ready for an intense workout that will improve your fitness. Improved fitness requires a balance of training and rest.

Exercise training is not an exact science. Sometimes you feel great and can train more intensely than planned. Other times, you feel tired and sluggish. Training intensely in this condition will actually impede progress. On the other hand, do not use this principle as an excuse to skip workouts. If you listen to your body and it always tells you to rest, you will never improve fitness. Follow a systematic program, but be flexible enough to change it slightly according to how you feel. Train consistently, work hard to improve fitness, and try to maintain a structured workout program.

10. Vary the volume and intensity of your workouts.

Fitness components, such as strength and power, improve best with intense training. However, it is difficult to recover from too many of these intense workouts. Balance rest and moderate-intensity workouts with high-intensity exercise sessions.

If you design the program properly, you can actually plan for effective intense workout sessions. This process requires a lot of trial and error. For example, you might balance an intense weight-training session with a day of rest followed by a more moderate workout. When you schedule the next intense training session, you will be recovered enough to train at 100 percent.

Don't exercise at maximum intensity every time you go into the gym. Most people can't do maximum large-muscle exercises, such as squats, cleans, and bench presses, at every workout. Emphasize one or two exercises at each training session. One time, train intensely on the squat; next time, emphasize the bench press or clean.

You don't need to do the same exercises at every workout. For developing maximum strength and power, do shoulder press exercises, such as the bench press, and pulling exercises, such as cleans and snatches, two times per week. Do squats three times in two weeks. Alternate between intense and moderate workouts for each exercise. This method will ensure the proper balance between intense and moderate workouts and rest.

This technique of varying the volume and intensity of workouts is sometimes called periodization or cycle training. It allows the body to recover more fully and to train hard when hard training is called for. The principle is simple: you do a particular exercise more intensely in one workout than in another rather than training at maximum intensity for every exercise during every weight-training session.

Although sophisticated workout cycles are most suitable to athletes, ordinary people like them because they allow the body to adapt and become stronger more rapidly. If your goal is to improve muscle tone and body composition (the proportion of fat and fat-free weight), you can benefit from cycle training also. Try varying the exercises in your workouts. For example, instead of doing bench presses three days a week, substitute incline presses one day. Cycle training makes weight training more interesting and helps you to progress faster.

11. Work on your weaknesses.

The inscription etched in marble on the facades of many libraries in America (and the Temple of Apollo at the Oracle at Delphi) is "Know Thyself." They probably should put that inscription over the entrance of the local gym, too. Analyze your weaknesses and correct them systematically. You can do this only if you establish goals and then systematically assess your capability of achieving them.

You don't need a degree in exercise physiology to assess your fitness. Are you strong or flexible enough? A good way to assess your physical readiness for a sport is to compare yourself with people who are successful in the sport at the level you hope to achieve. To be a good recreational skier or tennis player, you should have the speed and stamina of people who play at that level. If you want to be a professional football player or an Olympic shot-putter, you should have the same strength and power as the athletes who have reached those heights or you probably aren't going to make it.

Do you have any injuries that have not healed? You can relieve chronic back, knee, and ankle pain with a systematic exercise program. Rather than making excuses, have a physician, physical therapist, or athletic trainer evaluate the injury and start a rehabilitation program that will set you on the road to recovery.

12. Train systematically.

Plan a proper workout schedule for the coming months, but don't be so rigid that you can't change the program to fit unforeseen circumstances. The key is that you have a plan, so you can comfortably and consistently improve fitness.

A coach, training partner, and training diary will help your workouts become more systematic. A good coach or instructor, who is knowledgeable and experienced, can keep you from making common mistakes and will help motivate you to meet your fitness goals. For people who need a little more motivation and have the money, a personal trainer—who works with you during your workout—may help to make rapid gains.

A training partner is important for motivation and safety. It is a lot easier to make it to your workout if you are accountable to someone. A training partner can encourage you and help spot you when you need help (a spotter assists you during the exercise). He or she will share the agony and ecstasy that accompany weight training.

13. Warm up and cool down.

Muscles work best when they're slightly warmer than at rest and have plenty of blood. Warming up before exercise increases muscle temperature, muscle and heart blood flow, tissue elasticity, and joint lubrication and provides additional practice before competing or beginning formal practice. Cooling down helps to gradually restore normal resting blood-flow levels to the inner organs.

14. Train the mind.

One of the most difficult skills to acquire—but critical for attaining high levels of physical fitness—is mind control. Training the mind is thoroughly interrelated with training the body; you can achieve almost anything if you set your mind to it. To become physically fit or to succeed in sports, you must believe in yourself and your potential, have goals, and know how to achieve these goals. It requires discipline and is an ongoing process. You must be able to put yourself in the proper frame of mind.

Consistent training is the key to developing fitness. This takes discipline. Many people today want instant results. Unfortunately, fitness comes only after countless small steps. Gains are balanced with temporary setbacks and periods of stagnation. You must develop the self-discipline to train consistently if you want to improve performance and fitness for sports and exercise.

Make training a priority. Develop enough mental toughness and discipline to go to the weight room regularly. Don't procrastinate. Do your workout and get it over with. Often, people put off going to the gym. Consequently, they end up wasting a lot of time. The time they devote to thinking about working out, finally going to the gym, and "lollygagging" around when they get there can add up to two or three hours. Instead, they could have just gone to the workout, finished it quickly, and then gone home in about an hour. Develop the mental strength and discipline to exercise regularly.

15. Listen to "Coach Pain."

You will have little joint or muscle pain if you perform weight-training exercises correctly. Back, shoulder, and elbow pain are usually due to improper biomechanics. Sports-related pain usually stems from defects in technique or the training program. Pain is a good indicator that something is wrong with the program or movement technique.

16. Learn all you can about exercise.

If you know why the various components of training are important, you are much more likely to plan an intelligent, effective program. You will be less liable to jump into every training fad that comes along, and you will always be in control of your training program. Being informed, you'll buy better and more economical sports equipment, manage many of your own athletic injuries, and have a more efficient training routine. Learn everything you can about training in order to get the most from your exercise program.

A recurring theme of this book is that exercise training is as much art as science. The more you learn about the art and science of training and movements skills, the sooner you will develop a program that works and helps you achieve your goals.

Read books and magazine articles about training and sport. Some of this information will be contradictory or poor quality. That's OK. With time, you will learn to extract useful information that will improve your training program.

17. Have fun! Keep the weight-training program in perspective.

An old saying among exercise critics is "Exercise doesn't make you live any longer; it just seems longer!" The program doesn't have to be a chore if you choose activities you enjoy. If you like sports but hate to jog, play tennis instead of running on a treadmill in the gym. If working out with friends helps motivate you, consider participating in aerobics classes at the local health club.

Too often, the exercise program gains unequal emphasis in a person's life. Some people think of themselves almost solely as football players, aerobic dancers, runners, triathletes, or swimmers, rather than as people who participate in those activities. While exercise is valuable, you must also have time for other aspects of your life. Leading a well-rounded life will not diminish your chances for success and will make your training program more enjoyable. Keep the activity fun. Even highly motivated and successful athletes need more than sports. Strive for success, but try to keep balance in your life.

4

Getting Started: The Basics

"To exercise at or near capacity is the best way I know of reaching a true introspective state. If you do it right, it can open all kinds of inner doors."
—Al Oerter, four-time Olympic gold medalist in discus

Muscle strength is a mandatory fitness component for almost everyone. People interested in fitness for health need strength to maintain healthy joints, strong bones, and metabolically active muscle tissue. Those interested in building attractive, healthy-looking bodies need strength to develop lean, shapely muscles. Athletes need strength to make their movements forceful and powerful.

Starting a new type of exercise program is a lot like moving to a new town; you feel awkward, and everything is new and strange. To begin weight training, you must first make some decisions: where to train, what clothes to wear, and which exercises to do. You can increase muscle resistance using your body weight, barbells and dumbbells, and weight machines. You can build strength in your home, in a gym, or by taking a weight-training class at the local high school or community college. Hire a personal trainer if you need someone to help motivate you or if you need basic instruction. Some personal trainers have their own equipment that they take to their clients.

When you know the basics, you'll feel more at ease, your program will be safer and more enjoyable, and you'll be on the path to becoming an informed fitness consumer.

MEDICAL CHECKUP

Before beginning a program, you should determine if weight training is suitable for you. Most people can exercise safely if they are in good health and follow basic training principles. However, exercise may pose a risk to health and well-being if there are preexisting medical conditions, such as coronary artery disease. People who die suddenly from heart attacks—some of them during exercise—usually have risk factors for coronary artery disease, such as high blood pressure or cigarette smoking, that predispose them to the disease. Medical screening can help identify people who should not exercise or who should exercise only on a modified program.

For most people, it is safer to exercise than to remain sedentary. To paraphrase the famous exercise scientist

Olaf Åstrand: If you don't want to exercise, you should see a physician to determine if you can withstand the physical deterioration that occurs with the sedentary lifestyle. Men 40 years and older, women 50 years and older, and any person with significant health problems should get a medical examination before beginning a vigorous exercise program. If you are not in one of those categories, there is nothing preventing you from entering a weight-training program. Health problems that need medical evaluation include high blood pressure, coronary artery disease, stroke, obesity, and musculo-skeletal disorders.

It is best to choose a physician who is knowledgeable about exercise. Ideally, he or she should have training in exercise physiology or sports medicine, which deals with the medical problems of athletes. Local health clubs, college exercise physiology departments, and medical societies are often good sources for referrals to physicians with knowledge of sports medicine.

If you are over 40 to 50 (depending on your gender) or have significant health problems, beware of health clubs or fitness classes that offer fitness screening without proper medical supervision. Fitness evaluations by nonphysicians are not substitutes for a pretraining medical examination, and it could be dangerous to rely on them. Organizations such as the American College of Sports Medicine and the American Heart Association have established guidelines for fitness testing of adults and children. Make sure your club follows these guidelines.

CHOOSING A HEALTH CLUB AND PERSONAL TRAINER

Good health clubs typically have specialized weight machines that help you get the most from your program. These machines help you safely isolate and develop specific muscle groups in the chest, arms, hips, buttocks, and legs. You don't have to worry about a mountain of weights falling on your head when you miss a repetition of an exercise. Instead, if a weight is too heavy or light, you simply move the weight pin from one place to another in the weight stack.

Some clubs cater to athletes, weight lifters, bodybuilders, or people interested in lifting free weights. Typically, these clubs have well-designed platforms for doing whole-body lifts (cleans, snatches, clean and jerks, etc.), extensive dumbbell racks, and high-quality barbells, benches, and racks. If you are interested in lifting free weights, join a gym that caters to your needs.

Joining a health club allows you to get in some aerobic exercise, saving you a trip to the track or pool. Most clubs have aerobics classes going almost constantly. It's easy to catch a class for 40 or 50 minutes and then go to the weight room and finish your workout. If aerobics classes aren't for you, you can ride a stationary bike or train on a stair-climbing machine. Well-equipped clubs often have a running track, a swimming pool, racquetball courts, or computerized rowing machines.

A club is also a great place to socialize. Many have juice bars, where you can meet new friends. Socializing helps to take the drudgery out of working out. You can also hook up with people who have similar interests and exercise together.

A club is also the best place to hire a personal trainer. Even professional athletes have personal trainers. Trainers can help you design your program, provide training and nutrition advice, teach you proper exercise techniques, and help motivate you. Trainers are expensive and often not qualified, so be careful whom you hire. Making the wrong choice about where to exercise and selecting a poor coach will lead to a frustrating and possibly very expensive experience. The following guidelines can help you choose the right club and personal trainer.

- **The club should have a well-trained staff—particularly the personal trainers.** A recent study from UCLA showed that less than 50 percent of 115 personal trainers could pass a basic test on knowledge of anatomy, exercise physiology, nutrition, exercise prescription, and the prevention and care of athletic injuries. A university degree in exercise physiology or sports science or certification by a leading organization was shown to be the best predictor of competence. Many universities offer degrees in exercise physiology that call for extensive study in chemistry, physiology, anatomy, nutrition, exercise physiology, sports injuries, kinesiology (study of movement), mathematics, and psychology. The best health clubs have staff members with this training. National groups, such as the National Strength and Conditioning Association and the American College of Sports Medicine, certify exercise leaders after they have shown adequate training and knowledge.

  It is no longer acceptable for health clubs to rely solely on poorly trained ex-athletes or former bodybuilders for their personal trainers and exercise leaders. A professional personal trainer should have a dossier that outlines his or her education, certification, and experience. Look for clubs that employ people with practical experience and a solid educational background. Don't join a club with a poorly trained staff!

- **Get value for your money.** Be wary of signing up for a health club that does not yet exist. There have been many instances of clubs collecting money from potential members while the facilities are under construction; then the club never opens or delays opening for many months. Research the company thoroughly before signing a "preopening" contract.

- **Don't get cheated by unscrupulous owners.** Although most club owners are honest, it's also true that fly-by-night operators plague the industry. Check with your local Better Business Bureau or consumer affairs office if you think you are being treated unfairly or the deal sounds too good to be true.

- **Initiation fees and monthly dues are often negotiable.** Talk to club members to get an idea of the range of possible financial arrangements. Often, initiation fees are transferable; ask about people who might want to sell their membership, or check the classified section in the local newspaper for this information.

- **Try the club for a few months before signing a long-term contract.** Health clubs make their money from people who don't use the facilities. Be particularly wary of "lifetime" memberships. The club may go out of business long before you die! Join a club you can afford. Many clubs charge a "prestige" fee. A club that is more modest and less expensive than the $200-a-month "Health Club of the Rich and Famous" may provide you with the equipment and activities you need. Shop around!

- **Don't be pressured into signing a contract on your first visit.** Go home and think about the offer. Return only after all your questions have been answered and you are sure the deal is right for you. Make sure the contract extends your membership if you have a prolonged illness or go on vacation. The same goes for signing up with a personal trainer. Get to know the trainer first before signing up for a long-term commitment.

- **The club should be convenient.** You probably will not attend a club very often if it is in an inconvenient location. Find a place that is close to your home or work. Determine if it has adequate parking or is close to public transportation.

  Beware of memberships that offer reduced dues if you train during "nonprime-time hours." If you can train only at 6 A.M., then a discounted early-morning membership may be advantageous. If you want to train immediately after work or school at 5 P.M., then pay the extra money for an unrestricted membership. Check out the club during the time you want to train. Verify that you have easy access to the equipment and exercise classes.

- **The club should consider your medical history before putting you on a program.** This is important, especially if you are over 40 to 50 (depending on your gender) or have any health problems. Make sure the staff can accommodate you if you have any health problems or physical disabilities.

- **Beware of clubs that do exercise-tolerance tests without adequate medical supervision.** Organizations such as the American Heart Association and the American College of Sports Medicine have strict guidelines regarding exercise stress tests. A physician should supervise the test if you are over 40 or have significant health problems. Some clubs try to get around these regulations by doing submaximal tests. If your fitness is low, however, it is easy for

such a test to stress you maximally. Don't let clubs cut corners with your health.

- **The club should have established emergency procedures.** Accidents can happen, and you should be particularly wary if your family will exercise at the club. Professional clubs have formal emergency plans that can save precious minutes in the event of a heart attack or serious injury to muscles or joints.

- **Choose a club that puts its members on systematic programs.** Many different weight-training programs will improve strength and fitness if practiced systematically. The club should have some way of monitoring your program. Some modern health clubs are so technologically advanced that a central computer keeps track of your workout as you move from one machine to another. The next time you work out, the computer remembers what you did the time before. Although such a high-tech approach is not necessary for most people, you should make some effort to chart your progress.

- **The club should offer amenities besides weight training.** If you have children, ask if the club offers reliable and reasonable child care. Some clubs offer fitness activities for children. Is there a chance to develop other types of fitness besides strength and power? Well-equipped clubs have equipment such as stationary bikes, rowing machines, and stair machines, and facilities such as swimming pools; racquetball, volleyball, basketball, and tennis courts; and rooms for aerobics classes.

- **Determine if you are socially compatible with the membership.** Different clubs attract different types of people. If you are down-to-earth, you may be better off avoiding a posh, pretentious health club. Some clubs cater to hard-core body-builders, who can sometimes seem overbearing to the more casual weight trainer. The best way to determine the social environment is to observe the club on several occasions and talk to the members. Find a club where you will fit in.

- **Consider other features of the club.** Many clubs have a restaurant or snack bar that sells smoothies or healthy lunches. Others have shops that sell exercise clothing, weight-training accessories, and club logo merchandise. Although the products may be overpriced, health club shops are convenient and could be a selling point for the facility.

WHAT TO WEAR

Weight-training clothing and equipment are relatively inexpensive, unless you want to dress like a fashion model. In most cases, spending more than $300 to $400 is difficult, even if you buy weight-lifting shoes, a bench-press shirt, a lifting belt, gloves, and wraps. In most cases, all you need are workout shoes, shorts, a shirt, and—if you're a woman—a sports bra.

Clothing
Sports clothing has come a long way since the old high-school gym suit. Modern exercise clothing is attractive, comfortable, and functional. Shorts made of elastic material, such as spandex, hug and support the body. If you prefer, you can wear running shorts and a T-shirt. The main requirement for workout clothes is that they let you move easily. Clothing should not be so loose that it gets caught in the exercise racks or machines. Don't wear street clothes in a weight room because sweat, oil, and dirt can ruin

them. Also, belt buckles and buttons can tear the exercise equipment.

Shoes
Wear shoes that provide good lateral support, such as tennis shoes, aerobics shoes, or cross-training shoes. It is important that you wear shoes at all times to protect your feet against falling weights and people stepping on them.

If competitive weight lifting interests you, consider buying a pair of weight-lifting shoes. They provide excellent lateral support and raise your heels slightly so that you have better balance during your lifts. These shoes are available through weight-lifting and fitness magazines, such as *Power-lifting USA*, *Muscular Development*, and *Fitness Rx*, or from leading sports shoe companies, such as Adidas, Nike, and Puma. Hiking boots, which have a low heel, are a good substitute.

Weight-Lifting Belt
Many experts urge weight trainers to wear a weight-lifting belt when doing whole-body exercises, such as squats, dead lifts, Olympic lifts, and bench presses. They believe that the belts prevent injuries by stabilizing the spine. However, most studies show that back belts do not prevent on-the-job injuries in people doing manual labor. Some researchers think that back braces give people a sense of invincibility, so they lift beyond their capacity and get injured.

Belts will enable you to lift more weight during squats, cleans, snatches, and bench presses, but you won't condition the stabilizing muscles of the trunk. Don't use a belt when training. Do your lifts strictly, and lift within your capacity. Use a belt only when you are attempting maximum lifts and want to achieve maximum performance. Belts come in a variety of

Caution: Don't rely on a belt to protect your back. Good lifting technique and strong, flexible muscles are critical for preventing back injury.

colors that complement exercise clothing and look fashionable and attractive. You can buy them through exercise equipment stores or fitness magazines.

Lifting Shirts and Suits

Serious power lifters often use special clothing, such as bench shirts or stiff lifting suits, to help them lift more weight. This clothing is made of stiff material that provides a "rebound effect" while you are doing bench presses or squats. While lifting shirts and suits are effective, they should not be used consistently during workouts. They may decondition stabilizing muscles that would normally be trained if you weren't wearing the special clothing.

Wraps

Wraps are used to support injured joints or just provide extra support. They can be made of elastic bandage, athletic tape, leather, or neoprene. Although many advanced weight trainers use wraps to support their knees, wrists, or elbows, wraps are unnecessary for the recreational weight trainer.

Some people use wraps to counteract knee pain during and after weight-training sessions. Knee pain has many causes, such as the kneecap putting too much pressure on the bone underneath. Knee wraps may increase this pressure and make the pain worse. One solution is to buy a knee wrap that has a hole built in for the kneecap. The wrap provides support while the hole reduces pressure on the kneecap.

Grip wraps are strips of cotton webbing (such as the webbing used in karate belts) wrapped around the wrist and the weight bar; they take stress from the forearm muscles during lifts such as cleans and lat pulls. The grip is often the limiting factor in these lifts. Grip wraps allow you to use more

weight during workouts so you can make faster progress.

Breast Support for Women

Although breast support is not as important in weight training as in running or volleyball, it is wise for women to wear a good sports bra when exercising. The breasts can be injured if barbells press too firmly against them or if they aren't properly supported when you run. If weight training is combined with aerobics, a good sports bra is essential.

A sports bra should support the breasts in all directions, contain little elastic material, absorb moisture freely, and be easily laundered. Seams, hooks, and catches should not be irritating. Consider buying a bra with an under-wire for added support and a pocket in which to insert padding if you do exercises that could cause injury.

Gloves

Gloves are not recommended for weight trainers. It's best to condition the hands for the activity by training without gloves. However, weight training can severely roughen your hands if you don't protect them. Barbells, dumbbells, and some weight machines are knurled with small ridges to aid in gripping, and the knurls are abrasive. Gloves may prevent your hands from getting rough and calloused. Buy gloves that fit snugly and follow the contours of the hands enough so that you don't lose too much of your sense of touch. Using hand lotion after a weight workout protects the hands from roughening.

RESISTIVE EXERCISE EQUIPMENT AND TECHNIQUES

Muscles get stronger if you make them work against resistance. Use of free weights is the most common form of resistive exercise. Other forms of resistive exercise employ weight machines, rubber tubing, water, immovable objects (isometrics), or gravity (calisthenics that use your body weight). It is beyond the scope of this book to present exercises for all of these. You can do isometrics and calisthenics almost anywhere. They are a good way to develop strength when you don't have access to equipment. They are, however, less effective than free weights and weight machines for gaining strength.

Free Weights

Most serious strength trainers prefer free weights because they are inexpensive, readily available, and easily adaptable to almost any movement or muscle action. As opposed to machines, which stabilize the body, free weights demand that you stabilize the body with your muscles. Whole-body dynamic exercises, such as the clean and snatch, are impossible using weight machines. These advanced exercises are popular with serious power athletes.

Free weights include barbells and dumbbells. Barbells are usually five to seven feet long, with weights placed at both ends, secured by collars. The two most common types of barbells are standard and Olympic. Specialized barbells are available for doing curls, squats, and rotator-cuff exercises.

Standard barbells vary in length and weight. To determine the total weight you're lifting, you must know the weight of the bar as well as that of the weight plates at the ends. In general, standard barbells weigh 15 to 30 pounds (without plates).

Olympic barbells are seven feet long, weigh 45 pounds (20 kilograms), and have a rotating sleeve at each end. The finest bars are made of spring steel; these bars bend and recoil during heavy lifts but remain straight after the lift. Poor-quality bars are often permanently bent when loaded with a lot of weight.

The holes in Olympic weight plates are larger than those in standard plates, so Olympic plates can be used only with Olympic barbells. The most common weight-plate denominations are 20, 15, 10, 5, and 2.5 kilograms per plate (45, 35, 25, 10, 5, 2½, and 1¼ pounds if the set is calibrated in English measurements). Heavier or lighter plates are available for weight-lifting contests or leg-press machines. Olympic weight lifters use rubberized plates called "bumper plates" to protect the floor during training or competition. Some new plates contain built-in handles that make the weights easier to manipulate.

Olympic bars have special markings to help you get an even grip. The middle of the bar is typically smooth, but most of the bar is knurled to provide a good grip. Markers toward the end of the bar help you get an even handhold for wide-grip exercises, such as the snatch (an Olympic lift).

Collars are used to prevent the weights from falling off the bar. Collars weigh 2.5 kilograms apiece. A relatively new innovation is the clip collar, which secures the weights tightly and slides easily onto and off the bar.

Dumbbells are much shorter than barbells and are generally held in each hand. They are constructed from various combinations of weight plates or are molded into a particular weight. Most well-equipped gyms have large racks of dumbbells, ranging in weight from 2½ pounds per dumbbell to well in excess of 100 pounds.

Weight Machines

The weight room has gone high tech. It is amazing to go to a commercial fitness show and see the array of computerized exercise machines, rowing machines that allow you to compete against a computerized rower, and machines that "remember" and automatically provide the right resistance for you. Are these technological marvels going to make you twice as strong, in half the time, with less work? No!

Weight machines come in a variety of designs that can be overwhelming to even an experienced weight trainer. Some incorporate variable resistance so that the resistance increases progressively throughout the range of motion of the exercise. Machines can provide resistance by using weight stacks, weight plates, air, rubber bands, and hydraulic fluid. Some provide resistance only during the active phase of the lift (concentric), while others provide resistance during both the active and recovery (eccentric) phases of the exercise. Among the latest innovations are machines that provide resistance while the lifter is in a standing position. These machines, made by companies such as Life Fitness, not only work the target muscles but also force other muscle groups to stabilize the rest of the body to complete the exercise. You can increase strength on almost any weight machine if you exercise on it regularly and consistently.

Exercise machines are the preferred method of weight training for many nonathletes because they are safe, convenient, and technologically advanced. All you need to do is to set the resistance (usually done by placing a pin in the weight stack), sit down on the machine, and start exercising. You don't have to bother anyone for a spot (assistance) or worry about a weight crashing down on you. Many people can work out in a small area. Also, free weights tend to twist in your hands when you try to balance them, which can cause blisters and calluses, whereas

weight machines require little or no balancing, so beginners find the machines easier to use.

Some weight machines vary the resistance during the exercise—the weight is heavier as the exercise progresses. The theory behind this feature is that the stress on the muscle is more uniform as it contracts through its range of motion. It is not known whether this is superior to the resistance supplied by free weights for gaining strength and muscle size.

Few skilled strength-speed athletes train on machines. Their programs center on three main exercises: presses (bench press, incline press, etc.), pulls (cleans, snatches, etc.), and squats. Explosive lifts, such as pulls, are difficult or impossible to mimic on machines. Machines restrict you to a few movements, whereas many exercises are possible with free weights. Free-weight exercises, such as cleans, squats, and standing presses, require coordinated use of many joints and muscles. Many coaches believe that increased power for sports movements is better achieved by doing large-muscle, multi-joint free-weight exercises rather than machine exercises that isolate specific muscles.

Popular weight machines are expensive to buy and maintain. You can buy an elementary free-weight set at a small fraction of the cost. However, to equip a gym with a full array of free-weight equipment, including Olympic weights, dumbbells, and racks, is also expensive. So, don't base the choice between weight machines and free weights on cost alone.

Free Weights or Machines?

Many coaches and athletes feel that free-weight exercises are essential to developing explosive strength for sports. Because free weights are not on a controlled track the way machine weights are, you must control them, which probably helps to increase strength. Free weights help to overcome asymmetrical strength and let you do a greater variety of exercises. Free-weight exercises often involve many joints at once and better simulate muscle actions used in sports.

So, which is better? Your choice depends on your goals and motivation. If you want a good, quick workout in a safe, attractive environment—join a health club that caters to the average person. If your interests lie in bodybuilding, weight lifting, or power lifting, join a gym that specifically caters to those interests. Power athletes, such as football, tennis, or baseball players, should join gyms that have lifting platforms and equipment for plyometrics and speed exercises. Table 4.1 summarizes the advantages of free weights and exercise machines.

OTHER FORMS OF RESISTIVE EXERCISE

You don't need expensive weight machines or even free weights to achieve a good weight workout. Anything that provides resistance to your muscles can help you increase strength.

Isometrics

Isometrics, which reached popularity during the 1950s, involve muscle contraction without movement. You can perform these exercises by contracting specific muscles or pushing against immovable objects. Unfortunately, you increase strength only in the joint positions you work during the exercise. There are several effective isometric exercises for areas such as the abdominal and neck muscles that you can incorporate easily into your program.

Table 4.1 A COMPARISON OF FREE WEIGHTS AND EXERCISE MACHINES

EXERCISE MACHINES

Advantages	Disadvantages
Safe	Expensive to buy
Convenient	Expensive to maintain
Don't require spotters	Inappropriate for performing dynamic movements
Provide variable resistance	Offer only limited number of exercises
Have high-tech appeal	
Require less skill	
Make it easy to move from one exercise to the next	

FREE WEIGHTS

Advantages	Disadvantages
Allow whole-body dynamic movements	Not as safe
Develop control of weight	Require spotters
Help overcome strength differences between the two sides of the body	Require more skill
Allow greater variety of exercises	Can cause equipment clutter
Less expensive to buy and maintain	Cause more blisters and calluses

Rubber (Surgical) Tubing

Rubber tubing is an excellent and inexpensive source of resistance. You can simulate the movements of many popular free-weight and weight-machine exercises using a few dollars' worth of surgical tubing. If you need more resistance, use thicker tubing.

Water

Water has become a popular resistance medium because the risk of injury is low and this type of exercise is less threatening to beginning exercisers. Water is much more viscous than air, so almost any movement becomes more difficult. Using fins on the hands and feet increases the resistance and thus the intensity of the exercise.

Gravity (Calisthenics)

Calisthenics are resistive exercises that use body weight as the resistance. People should learn to handle their own body weight. Exercises such as pull-ups, step-ups, and push-ups—which use body weight as resistance—are excellent for beginners. They are also excellent for people who want to develop muscle strength but are unwilling to join a health club or devote much time to the activity. Nevertheless, if you are serious about increasing your strength, you should join a gym or health club. These facilities typically offer equipment beyond the scope of a home gym. Also, they give beginning athletes the opportunity to mingle with advanced athletes. Beginners gain the value of seeing what is possible in a training program and what they need to shoot for.

Other Devices

Weight-equipment manufacturers show considerable ingenuity in designing resistive-exercise devices. These devices range in complexity from friction placed on a rope that is wrapped around a cylinder to complicated instruments that use variable-speed motors. The point to remember is that almost any equipment or technique that provides resistance to muscle contraction will increase strength—if you train systematically with it.

5

Designing Your Program

> "Far better it is to dare mighty things, to win glorious triumphs, even though checkered by failure, than to take rank with those poor spirits who neither enjoy much nor suffer much, because they live in the gray twilight that knows not victory nor defeat."
> —*Theodore Roosevelt*

Increasing strength is quite simple: overload the muscles by making them work against increased resistance. You can even control the rate at which you gain strength. Train intensely three or four times a week for one to two hours per workout and you will increase muscle strength and size rapidly. Train two times a week for 30 minutes and you will make gains but progress more slowly.

STRUCTURING THE PROGRAM: THE FITT PRINCIPLE

Program design for weight training is as much art as science. Structure the program for the desired results. A bodybuilder's program will be different from a tennis or football player's program. A program to prevent back pain is structured differently from one designed to help lose weight.

A good way to remember the components of overload is to use the acronym FITT—frequency, intensity, time (duration), and type (mode of exercise). Some experts like the

acronym FITTE—the *E* stands for enjoyment. A chief consideration is that your current level of fitness determines FITT. As you become more conditioned, you can exercise longer, harder, and more often. Fitness will also allow you to engage in physical activities, such as running or downhill skiing, that are difficult or impossible for sedentary people.

Choosing the Exercises

Choose weight-training exercises that develop the major muscle groups of the body. Most people should select exercises that develop the shoulders, chest, upper back, arms, abdomen, lower back, thighs and butt, and calves.

People interested in power sports (e.g., football, basketball, most track-and-field events, baseball and softball, soccer) should concentrate on three primary types of lifts: presses, pulls, and squats. Examples of presses include the bench press, incline press, flat or incline press using dumbbells, standing press (military press), and seated press. Pulls include the power clean and snatch, squat or split clean and snatch, dead lift, and snatch and clean high pull. Squat exercises include the squat, leg press, lunge, and step-up. People interested in developing power for sports should do these central exercises before doing auxiliary exercises, such as biceps curls and curl-ups. Power athletes should build core strength (abdominal and back strength) and avoid doing too many bodybuilding exercises. Bodybuilders should concentrate on building muscle size and definition and minimizing surface fat.

Warm-Up

Most experts agree that warming up is essential before exercise, and empirical evidence suggests that warming up improves performance and prevents injury. Warming up raises body temperature so that the muscles respond better. It increases tissue blood flow and elasticity, making tissues less prone to injury. Warming up also promotes joint lubrication. Intense exercise without a warm-up may place the heart at risk. Warming up also helps reinforce motor patterns within the brain, which helps you do the exercise more efficiently.

The warm-up can be either general or specific. General warm-up involves the whole body with large-muscle exercises such as jumping jacks, running in place, or stationary cycling. Specific warm-up involves doing the same lift you intend to do to begin your program, but using a lighter weight. For example, a person who plans to do three sets of 10 repetitions of 160-pound bench presses might do one set of 10 repetitions with 90 pounds as a warm-up. (A repetition is one execution of the exercise, and a set is a group of repetitions followed by rest.) Do similar warm-up exercises for each major lift that forms your program.

Do not do static stretching (stretch and hold) as part of your warm-up. Stretching a muscle decreases its

strength for 15 minutes or more, which could decrease the intensity of your workout. Flexibility is important; stretch after exercise when your muscles are warm and decreased muscle strength is no longer a factor.

Cooldown

Cooling down returns muscle temperatures and metabolic rate to normal levels. Cooling down after weight training usually consists of relaxing in a comfortable environment. In contrast, after endurance exercise, it is important to gradually wind down the tempo of activity.

Weight training is not a continuous activity, so winding down is unnecessary unless you drastically increase your heart rate during the workout (such as in circuit training). In that case, do an active cooldown during recovery, such as riding a stationary bicycle at a slow cadence and with no friction on the flywheel.

Some experts recommend stretching after a workout to help prevent muscle soreness. This is also a particularly good time to work on flexibility because the muscles and joints are warmed up.

Don't take a shower or whirlpool bath immediately after a vigorous weight-training workout. During intense training, blood is shunted to the skin and muscles, and hormones mobilize to help you exercise. Taking a hot shower immediately after exercise places stress on the heart that some people may not be able to tolerate. Give yourself at least 5 to 10 minutes to relax first.

Order of Exercises and Development of Antagonistic Muscle Groups

If your primary goal is to gain strength, do large-muscle exercises, such as presses, pulls, and squats, before doing exercises for smaller muscle groups, such as wrist curls and

---

Caution: Always warm up before exercise. Adequate warm-up may enhance performance and prevent injury.

Caution: Cool down after a workout before taking a hot shower or whirlpool bath. Exercise redirects blood to the skin for cooling and to the muscles for exercise metabolism. The combination of inadequate cooldown and exposure to a hot shower or whirlpool after exercise could result in fainting or other problems.

calf raises. During weight training, smaller muscle groups fatigue more easily than larger ones. Therefore, do exercises that use more than one joint at a time (for example, bench presses, squats, or power cleans) before those using only one joint (for example, biceps curls, leg extensions, and wrist curls).

Most experienced weight trainers work one body part at a time. For example, they do all the leg exercises before doing upper-body exercises. Some even work lower-body and upper-body muscle groups on separate days. Intensity (i.e., the amount of weight used during the exercise and the tension developed in the muscles) is the most important factor in increasing strength. If you mix exercises for large- and small-muscle groups and those for the upper and lower parts of your body, you decrease the amount of weight you can use— and slow your progress.

Circuit training—performing a number of exercises rapidly in series— often purposely mixes exercises. This type of training is effective for developing muscular endurance but is less effective for gaining strength. Include in your program exercises for antagonistic muscle groups.

Muscles work a lot like a seesaw: an antagonistic muscle group opposes each movement initiated by a muscle group. For example, the quadriceps muscles cause the knee to extend (straighten), while its antagonistic muscles—the hamstrings—cause it to flex (bend). If you develop the quadriceps muscles without working on the hamstrings, you create a muscular imbalance that can lead to injury and faulty movement patterns.

Number of Training Sessions per Week

You increase strength by making the muscles work against increased resistance. This stress is called overload. It is best to overload specific muscles two or three days per week. Most people choose 6 to 10 exercises and do them three times per week. Others train four days per week (called a split routine), alternating between exercises for the upper and lower body. In split routines, you might exercise the chest, arms, shoulders, back, and abdominal muscles two days per week (e.g., Monday and Thursday) and your butt, thigh, and calf muscles the other two days (e.g., Tuesday and Friday). Split routines are excessive for most beginning weight trainers.

Balance hard work in the gym with rest. Muscles increase strength and size after the workout is over. You won't make significant gains if you don't allow your muscles to rest adequately between workouts. Sometimes rest is just as important as hard work for improving fitness.

Choosing the Correct Weight

Don't use too much weight when you begin your program. For the first set, choose a weight you can move easily for 10 repetitions. If you aren't sure about a good starting weight, use only the barbell or the lowest starting weight on the exercise machine. You can always add weight later.

Do only one set of each exercise during the first workout. The exercises may feel easy to do, but you must be careful not to overexert yourself. As discussed in Chapter 2, tissue damage causes muscle soreness one or two days after a workout. Some delayed-onset muscle soreness is common, and perhaps it's necessary for improved strength, but excessive soreness suggests that you trained too hard.

Devote the first weeks of weight training to learning the exercises. Not only do you have to understand how to do the exercises, but also your nervous system has to learn to communicate with the muscles so you can

Caution: Training too many days per week can lead to overtraining and injury. The body needs time to adapt. Sometimes it is better to train less often but more intensely. Most experts recommend training three or four days per week.

exert the necessary force. This takes time. Gradually add sets to your program. By the end of the second week of training, you should be doing a complete workout.

During later training sessions, gradually add weight until you are bearing a significant load and the 10-repetition set becomes difficult. The time to add weight is when you can finish each set with relative ease. If you feel as though you can do 11 or 12 repetitions with a particular weight, it's time to add more resistance. If, after adding weight, you can do only 8 or 9 repetitions, stay with the weight until you can again complete the 10 repetitions per set. If, after adding weight, you can do only 4 to 6 repetitions, then you have added too much weight and must remove some.

Experienced weight trainers should avoid using too much weight after a layoff because they may get sore or injured. Getting in shape gradually is a basic principle of training. Excessive training loads do not encourage the body to adapt faster; they only cause injury and delay progress.

Repetitions, Sets, and Rest

Weight-training programs are subdivided into repetitions, sets, and rest between sets. Each time you complete the exercise movement, you do a repetition. In theory, you could do almost any number of repetitions (one to thousands). However, in practice, most people do 5 to 10 repetitions of each exercise.

Each group of repetitions is called a set. Weight trainers generally do three to five sets of each exercise. For example, if you were doing three sets of 10 repetitions of the bench press exercise, you would perform 10 repetitions of the exercise, rest for one to two minutes, and then perform the same process two more times, for a total of three sets.

Caution: Don't use too much weight after coming off a layoff from training because you may get sore or injured.

The American College of Sports Medicine (ACSM), the premier professional organization for sports scientists, recommends that beginners practice only one set of each exercise. The organization cites studies that doing one set increases strength just as much as doing two or more sets. If you practice only one set, make sure that it is high intensity. The advantage of one-set training is that you can work out quickly and have time for other types of exercise you enjoy. Practice more sets if you want to make faster progress or reach higher levels of strength. Many strength experts vehemently disagree with the ACSM's recommendation, saying that training intensely for two or more sets per exercise produces much better results than performing only one set.

The amount of time you should rest between sets depends on your fitness goal. If you are trying to develop a combination of strength and endurance through resistive exercise, rest one to two minutes between sets. However, if your goal is to develop maximum strength, you may rest up to five minutes or more in between sets. Here, your goal is to exert maximum force during the exercise. This will be impossible if you haven't recovered adequately from the last exercise.

Your goals determine the ideal number of repetitions, sets, and rest. Generally, if you want increased endurance, do more repetitions (10 or more) and more sets (three or more), and rest for a short time (one minute or less between sets). If increased strength is your primary goal, do fewer repetitions, use more weight, and rest until you are recovered. Doing four to six repetitions per set for one to five sets is typical for building strength. People interested in doing single maximum lifts must occasionally do one- to three-repetition sets so they can adjust to the heavier weights. Experienced weight trainers use a variety of combinations of sets and repetitions. (The next section, on cycling techniques, discusses some of these programs.)

Beginners should start off with more repetitions and lighter weights, which gives the tissues a chance to adjust to increased muscular loading and minimizes the chances of injury. Start with one set of 8 to 10 repetitions of about 8 to 10 exercises. Practice this program, gradually increasing the weight, for at least one to two months before decreasing repetitions in each set. If you want to progress more rapidly, try increasing the number of sets per exercise to two or three. If rapid increases in strength are not a major goal, stay with 10 repetitions per set. An example of a beginning weight-training program appears in Table 5.1. You can do these exercises with free weights or weight machines.

Several training systems use a technique called pyramiding, which contains a built-in warm-up. In pyramiding, you practice an exercise for three or more sets, increasing the weight during each set. T. L. Delorme introduced this technique in the 1950s. Delorme recommended three sets of 10 repetitions of each exercise. The resistance should progressively increase from 50 percent of maximum capacity to 75 percent to 100 percent. Pyramid training routines are variations of the original Delorme method.

Other systems for regulating loads include the constant set method, failure method, circuit training, super sets, giant sets, and drop sets. Some of these techniques reduce the weight during later sets after the maximum weight is reached. Any technique you choose should allow you to warm up before significantly loading your muscles.

Basic Cycling Techniques

Many elite athletes use cycle training, or periodization of training—a powerful technique that allows the body to increase strength rapidly without overtraining and prepares it to accept and benefit from intense workouts.

In cycle training, you vary the type, volume, and intensity of training throughout the year. In athletics, the year is divided into off-season, pre-season, early season, and peak season. The weight-training program is different during each part of the year.

During the off-season, athletes do general conditioning exercises. The program maintains fitness and provides mental and physical rest from the rigors of training. A tennis or field

Table 5.1 EXAMPLE OF A BEGINNING WEIGHT-TRAINING PROGRAM

Exercise	Sets	Repetitions
Bench press	1–3	10
Lat pull	1–3	10
Lateral raise	1–3	10
Biceps curl	1–3	10
Triceps extension	1–3	10
Abdominal curl	1–3	10
Back hyperextension	1–3	10
Leg press	1–3	10
Calf raise	1–3	10

SELECTED WEIGHT-SET-REPETITION METHODS

Circuit Training

Uses 6 to 20 exercise stations set up in a circuit (i.e., in series). The person progresses from one station to the next, either performing a given number of repetitions or doing as many repetitions as possible during a given period (e.g., 20 seconds) at each station.

Constant Set Method

Uses the same weight and number of sets and repetitions for each exercise. Example: bench-press five sets of five repetitions at 80 pounds.

Pyramid Method

Uses multiple progressive sets, either ascending or ascending-descending, for each exercise. Variations: increase weight while decreasing repetitions or decrease weight while increasing repetitions.

Ascending Pyramid

Set 1	5 repetitions	75 pounds
Set 2	5 repetitions	100 pounds
Set 3	5 repetitions	120 pounds

Ascending-Descending Pyramid

Set 1	5 repetitions	75 pounds
Set 2	5 repetitions	100 pounds
Set 3	5 repetitions	120 pounds
Set 4	5 repetitions	100 pounds
Set 5	5 repetitions	75 pounds

Delorme Method

Uses three sets of 10 repetitions at 50, 75, and 100 percent of maximum. Example for a person who can do 10 repetitions at 100 pounds:

Set 1	10 repetitions	50 pounds (50%)
Set 2	10 repetitions	75 pounds (75%)
Set 3	10 repetitions	100 pounds (100%)

Super Sets

Usually uses two exercises, typically with opposing muscle groups, in rapid succession.

Set 1	10 repetitions	30-pound knee extensions
Set 1	10 repetitions	75-pound knee flexions
Rest		
Set 2	10 repetitions	30-pound knee extensions
Set 2	10 repetitions	75-pound knee flexions
Rest		
Repeat		

Giant Sets

Uses multiple exercises in succession for the same muscle group.

Set 1	10 repetitions	75-pound bench presses
Set 1	10 repetitions	5-pound dumbbell flies
Rest		
Set 2	10 repetitions	75-pound bench presses
Set 2	10 repetitions	5-pound dumbbell flies
Rest		
Repeat		

Drop Sets

The drop set technique is terrific for pushing your muscles to their absolute max. Use this technique during the last set of an exercise. Do as many reps as you can. Then, immediately drop the weight by 10 to 15 percent and try to squeeze out a few more reps. Continue to use even less weight, and do as many reps as you can. Keep going until you can't do any more repetitions. This technique is difficult but a great way to overload muscles.

A similar high-tension training method is called "training down the rack." Use this technique with any dumbbell exercise, such as curls or inclines. Choose dumbbells heavy enough so that you can complete only five reps of the exercise. Take a 30-second rest and then move to the next-lightest set of dumbbells and do as many reps as you can. Rest 30 seconds and move to the next set of dumbbells. Continue down the rack until you can't complete any more repetitions or you run out of dumbbells.

hockey player might benefit from running, playing volleyball, swimming, and performing some kind of circuit training. Light training in the sport helps to maintain skill.

During the preseason and early season (sometimes called the "load phase"), if the goal is to develop maximum power for a strength-speed sport, such as track and field, the program develops base fitness—strength that serves as the basis for maximum lifts later in the season. The weight-training program involves much volume (five sets of five to eight repetitions for the major exercises, at moderately high intensities). This phase typically is exhausting.

The peak phase (competitive phase) helps you achieve peak performance. The weight-training program involves high-intensity workouts with much less volume than in the preseason and early season. The athlete gets plenty of rest between intense workouts, a technique that allows peak performance, or "peaking." If you time workouts and rest correctly, you can predict and achieve top performances.

Each major cycle contains microcycles in which volume, intensity, and rest vary from workout to workout or from week to week. The purpose of microcycles is to allow muscle systems adequate recovery time. According to several studies, intensity—muscle tension—is the chief factor in enhancing fitness. In traditional training programs, athletes train hard every session, which may lead to over-training. Microcycles prepare people for intense training days by giving them time to recover.

In this way, cycle training encourages your body to increase strength steadily with a minimum risk of injury. You make small, consistent gains over a long time. The system improves fitness, and peak performance happens at a predetermined time in the season. One basis for this method is that people increase strength better in response to changing stimuli than to a constant program because learning is fastest when a new activity is introduced and because change is psychologically stimulating.

Considerable muscle and connective tissue damage happens during and after intense endurance or strength training. Although scientists don't completely understand the relationship between tissue healing rate and the structure of the training program, common sense tells us there is such a

relationship. Muscle fibers need to heal to some extent before you can safely stress them again.

Cycle techniques are ideal for people doing general conditioning programs. It is unnecessary to do the same exercises every session using the same weights. Vary your program. Do some exercises intensely during one workout and other exercises intensely during the next. A basic three-day-per-week conditioning program using the cycle-training technique appears in Table 5.2.

Making Progress

Initially, gains seem to come easily, but eventually you will reach a plateau where progress comes more slowly. Because the body increases strength rapidly at first, many gains are due as much to learning new exercises as to actual changes in the muscles. The best thing to do when you're no longer improving is to examine your program. The cause is usually either too much work, not enough work, or a bad program.

If you're working hard every session and never miss a workout but are still not making any progress, then maybe you're doing too much. Try cycling your workouts, or take a week or two off. Rest can do amazing things; often you can expect to return to personal records in the weight room if you just take a brief rest.

Sometimes you may not work hard enough. Are you only going through the motions when you train, not putting much effort into the exercises? Try adding more weight for at least one set of each exercise, even if that makes you do fewer repetitions. Make sure you complete each workout: cutting a few exercises out of the program each session can amount to a lot of work not accomplished after a few weeks.

Table 5.2 EXAMPLE OF A CYCLE-TRAINING PROGRAM FOR GENERAL CONDITIONING

MONDAY

Exercise	Sets	Repetitions	Weight (pounds)
Bench press	4	10	60
Lat pull	3	10	30
Squat	4	10	80
Abdominal curl	3	20	–
Back extension	3	15	–
Arm curl	3	10	25
Triceps extension	3	10	15

WEDNESDAY

Exercise	Sets	Repetitions	Weight (pounds)
Incline press	3	10	40
Modified pull-up	5	5	–
Pull-over	3	10	20
Leg press	3	10	150 (machine)
Calf raise	4	20	150 (machine)
Abdominal curl	3	40	–
Good morning	3	10	15

FRIDAY

Exercise	Sets	Repetitions	Weight (pounds)
Bench press	4	10	50
Lat pull	3	10	40
Squat	4	10	70
Abdominal curl	3	20	–
Back extension	3	15	–
Arm curl	3	10	30
Triceps extension	3	10	20

Many people get enough rest and complete their workouts but still don't make progress. In cases such as this, you can often begin to make progress again by changing your program. Do exercises that are slightly different from the ones you usually do. For example, if you do bench presses on a machine or with barbells, try switching your program to include the incline press. Changing the way you do a lift sometimes helps you make progress. Having a spotter assist you so you can use more weight may also help get you over the hump. If you are doing normal-grip bench presses, do the exercise with a narrower or wider grip.

Another effective technique is to add exercises that strengthen muscles needed for the primary exercises. For example, doing bar dips is effective in improving the bench press. If you have trouble doing dips, have a spotter put his or her hands around your waist and help you with the movement, or use a dip-assist machine. Knee exten-

SAFETY RULES FOR WEIGHT TRAINING

Weight training can be dangerous if safety guidelines are not followed. These are basic principles for preventing injuries in the weight room:

- Lift weights from a stabilized body position.
- Be aware of what is going on around you.
- Stay away from other people when they are doing exercises. Bumping into them could result in injury.
- Always use collars on barbells and dumbbells.
- Remain clear of the weight stack when someone else is using a weight machine.
- Don't use defective equipment. Report malfunctions immediately.
- Protect your back by maintaining control of your spine (protect your spine from dangerous positions). Observe proper lifting techniques, and use a weight-lifting belt for heavy single or double lifts.
- Don't hold your breath. Avoid the Valsalva maneuver (forcefully attempting expiration while holding your breath), which results in greatly reduced blood flow from the heart and could cause fainting.
- Always warm up before training.
- Don't exercise if you're ill.

---

sions will improve the squat. Change the exercise, and your body will again adapt more quickly.

COMBINING WEIGHT TRAINING WITH OTHER SPORTS AND EXERCISES

Intense weight training is exhausting, which interferes with performance in other activities. After a vigorous weight-training session, you may be more susceptible to injury if you immediately do another sport. If possible, get plenty of rest after an intense workout before doing a sport in which you might get injured. If most of your program consists of general conditioning exercises, schedule strength and endurance workouts on different days. At least schedule intense weight training on light endurance-training days. If you weight-train and have an aerobics class on the same day, go to the class first.

Weight-training exercises improve power in sports skills best when the exercise uses the same muscles and resembles the movements required for the skill. If you want to transfer power to motor skills (e.g., jumping), large-muscle leg exercises, such as squats or power cleans, are better than those that develop isolated muscle groups, such as knee extensions or leg curls. Exercises done on many popular exercise machines usually develop isolated muscle groups, while free-weight exercises, such as squats, cleans, and snatches, more closely resemble movements used in many sports.

PREVENTING ACCIDENTS

Accidents and injuries do happen in weight training. Maximum physical effort, elaborate machinery, rapid movements, and heavy weights can combine to make the weight room a dangerous place if you don't take proper precautions.

Spotting

Spotters help the lifter during a failed repetition, help move the weight into position to begin a lift, and actively help with the lift.

Helping with the weight after a failed repetition is the critical job of the spotter, who must be quick to go

Caution: Use spotters whenever you might be in danger of missing a lift and being caught under the fallen weight.

SKILLS AND RESPONSIBILITIES OF THE SPOTTER

- Be strong enough to assist with the weight being lifted.
- Know the proper form of the exercise and the spot.

- Know the number of repetitions being attempted.
- Establish signals for beginning and ending the exercise with the lifter.
- Pay constant attention during the lift, but don't interfere unnecessarily unless requested.

- Pay particular attention to collars or weight plates that are sliding and when the weight trainer is using asymmetrical lifting techniques (i.e., moving one arm at a different speed than the other). These situations may require immediate intervention.

Caution: Spotters must be wary of injuring themselves. Use proper lifting techniques when spotting someone.

to the lifter's aid if necessary. You will need one or two spotters. During a bench press or an incline press, one spotter is sometimes preferable because it is easier to coordinate between one spotter and a lifter than between two spotters and a lifter. During a squat, you will need two spotters, one to stand on each side of the weight and help if the lift cannot be finished.

The lifter must indicate when he or she wants the weight removed. A spotter who removes the weight too soon may deprive the lifter of the chance to make a maximum effort and complete the lift. If there is too much delay in removing the weight, the lifter may get injured. Spotters must position themselves so as to be ready to help the lifter if needed, and they must use proper lifting techniques themselves: bend the knees, maintain a straight back, and keep the weight close to the body. During the lift, spotters should be attentive but should not disrupt the lifter's concentration.

When spotters are used to help move a weight into position to begin an exercise, coordination between the spotters and the lifter must be ensured. Work out signals before the lift so that everyone understands when to raise the weight from the rack. For example, the lifter may count "one, two, three," with the weight being lifted into position on "three." It's best to work with

the same spotters regularly because you'll learn what to expect from each other after a while.

You will sometimes want a spotter to actively help with the exercise when you're using either free weights or weight machines. When you're doing negative exercises (eccentrics), the spotter may do most of the work for you during the active phase of the lift. The spotter can also provide the extra amount of force needed to finish an

Proper lifting technique

exercise. Lifters sometimes call this "the magic fingers" because the spotter may be able to help complete the lift by lifting with just a couple of fingers.

Collars

Collars secure weights to a barbell or dumbbell. Lifting weights without collars is dangerous. It is easy to lose your balance or to raise one side of the weight faster than the other. Without collars, the weights on one side of the bar will slip off, resulting in the weights on the opposite side crashing to the floor. This can knock you off balance and lead to injury. Clip collars, which weigh very little, are a good safety compromise for lifters who don't like to use standard collars.

Preventing Accidents on Weight Machines

One of the attractions of weight machines is their safety. But weight machines are not totally harmless, so be cautious around them. Keep away from moving weight stacks. It's easy for someone to jump onto the machine ahead of you and begin an exercise while your fingers are close to the weight stack. Be particularly attentive when changing weights.

Don't do exercises near moving parts and weight plates. Also, don't walk near a machine when someone else is on it—you may break the person's concentration or collide with the moving machine.

Many weight machines can be adjusted to accommodate people of different sizes. Make sure the machine is properly adjusted and locked in place before you begin an exercise; it can be dangerous to begin an exercise only to have the machine move suddenly.

Beware of broken machines. Broken bolts, frayed cables, broken chains, and loose cushions can give way and cause serious injury. If you notice that a machine is broken or damaged, tell an instructor or weight room attendant immediately.

Make sure the machines are clean. Equipment upholstery should be cleaned daily. Dirty vinyl is a breeding ground for germs that can cause skin diseases. A good practice is to carry a towel around with you and place it on the machine where you will sit or lie down. If you're sweating a lot, wipe down the upholstery with a towel after you finish the exercise.

Weight Room Etiquette

Weight trainers should always have the utmost respect for the equipment because misuse can lead to a serious injury. Lack of focus in the weight room can cause injury. Be attentive to what's happening around you.

Be courteous to others. When you are doing more than one set and other people are waiting to use the machine, let them do a set of the exercise while you are resting. Likewise, don't use exercise machines as resting stations. This disturbs other people's workouts and slows the flow in the gym.

Sign up for equipment that requires reservations, and get off the machine when your time is up. People tend to feel uncomfortable asking someone to get off a machine they have reserved. The next person's workout is probably just as important to him or her as your workout is to you.

Medical Concerns

Report any obvious injury to muscles or joints to the health club instructor or a physician. Don't keep working out in the hope that the injury will go away. Training with an injured joint or muscle usually leads to more-serious injury. Be careful not to overdo. It's easy to strain or cramp a muscle by doing too many sets or repetitions. If you injure yourself, either work on another body part or take the rest of

Caution: Always use collars when lifting weights, and be sure that they are secured properly.

the day off. Make sure you get the necessary first aid. Even minor injuries heal faster if you follow the "RICE" principle of treating injuries: rest, ice, compression, and elevation.

Weight training tends to increase blood pressure, which in some people can cause serious medical problems. In people with coronary artery disease, weight training can cause symptoms such as arm or chest pain. Weight training can be deadly in people who have arterial weaknesses called aneurysms. Consult a physician if you are having any unusual symptoms during exercise or if you are not sure that weight training is a proper activity for you.

Don't overtrain. Even experienced professional athletes often forget the primary purpose of exercise training: stimulating the body to improve its function. You will not improve if you overtrain or do the exercises improperly. Worse, you may get injured or become ill.

Proper Mechanics of Exercise

Each exercise has a proper technique. These techniques are discussed in Chapters 6 through 11. Several principles, however, are common to all exercises. These principles will help you prevent injury and derive the maximum benefit from your weight-training program. Do all of the exercises strictly and properly. Your back is extremely vulnerable to poor lifting technique. Observe the following principles when lifting weights:

- During squats or exercises from the floor (i.e., dead lifts), lift the weight with your legs rather than your back. The muscles in your legs and butt are the strongest in your body. The muscles surrounding your spine are small and vulnerable.

- Keep the weight close to your body when lifting. This helps you lift the weight with your legs and hips rather than your back.
- Keep your back straight and head level when picking up a weight from the floor.
- Lift the weight smoothly from the floor.
- Don't twist your torso when lifting a weight. This puts abnormal pressure on spinal muscles and disks.
- Don't lift if you are so tired that you can't use proper lifting technique. Lift within your capacity.
- When using weight machines, make sure they are adjusted correctly to your body. Sit properly so that the machine supports your spine.

Breathing

Breathing is important when you're doing weight-training exercise. Never hold your breath when lifting. Holding your breath and straining (the Valsalva maneuver) will increase your blood pressure and cut off blood flow to the brain and may cause you to faint. In general, exhale during the active phase of the lift and inhale when returning to the starting position. For example, in the bench press, inhale when lowering the weight to your chest and exhale when pushing the weight.

Exercise Movements

Exercises should be done smoothly and in good form. With practice, you will "groove" your lift so that the weight is moved in the same general way every time you do the exercise.

Generally, move the weight into position for the active phase of the exercise slowly and with control. Lift or push the weight forcefully during the active phase of the lift. Obviously, if you are using enough resistance, these powered movements will be slow—but you should still try to do

Caution: Report any headaches; chest, neck, or arm pains; dizziness; labored breathing; numbness; or visual disturbances to the health club staff immediately. If you're training alone at home, see your physician immediately because these may be signs of a serious health problem.

the movements explosively. Remember the old weight-lifting saying, "Go down slowly and up fast."

Do not "bounce" the weight against your body during the exercise. Bouncing means that you make an explosive transition between the pushing and recovery phases of the lift. Advanced weight trainers sometimes do this so that they can practice an exercise using heavier weight. This practice is not recommended, however, because it can cause serious injury.

Do all lifts through the full range of motion. Limiting the range of motion increases strength only in the part of the range you are exercising. Practiced correctly, weight training improves flexibility. "Muscle-boundness"—a decrease in flexibility developed from weight training—happens only when exercises aren't done through a full range of motion.

Grips

Use the correct grip for each lift. There are three basic types of grip: pronated (palms away from you), supinated (palms toward you), and dead-lift (one palm toward you, one away). The pronated grip is used in most presses, pulls, and squats. The supinated grip is used in exercises such as biceps curls and chin-ups. The dead-lift grip is used in the dead-lift exercise to increase grip strength during the lift.

The thumbless grip and thumblock grip are not recommended. The thumbless grip, as the name implies, involves placing the thumb in the same plane as the fingers. This grip places the thumb under less stress, but it is dangerous. For example, in a bench press, you could easily lose control of the weight, and it could fall on you. The thumblock grip, in which the thumb is wedged between the index and middle fingers, places the thumb at increased risk of injury.

OVERLOAD TECHNIQUES FOR BODYBUILDING

Tension builds muscle size—the more, the better. The only way you will get cannonball arms, boa constrictor back muscles, washboard abs, or tree trunk legs is if you push your muscles to the max and then push them some more. Choose exercises that isolate and stress your muscles, and then turn on the juice.

Tension causes small-muscle injuries that the body repairs by laying down new proteins. Also, tension draws amino acids—the chemicals that make new protein—into the muscles and makes them grow. High-intensity workouts also turn on anabolic hormones—such as growth hormone, insulin, and testosterone—to go into overdrive and trigger muscles to make new protein. You will be amazed at how fast your muscles grow when you combine high-tension workouts with plenty of protein, calories, rest, and muscle-building supplements.

Your Goal: Lift One More Pound or Do One More Rep

Muscles grow when you overload them because they don't like stress. When you work them hard during a bodybuilding workout, they lay down new proteins because larger muscles are harder to stress.

Muscles get used to stress quickly. If you do the same old workout every time you go to the gym, your muscles grow but have no further need to make new muscle tissue. They will continue to get bigger only if you continually stress them more and more.

Increasing muscle strength and size takes time. You can't expect to go from a novice to a bodybuilding champion overnight. Rather, it takes a series of adaptations: you stress the muscles and they get larger; you stress them more,

Caution: Never bounce a weight against the body.

and they get even larger; and so on. Your goals should be to make a series of small gains. Every workout, try to lift just one more pound or do one more rep than you did before. If you continually try to do just a little more than before, you will make gains. You won't be able to do this in all your lifts. However, if you make progress in just a few exercises each workout, you will soon be bigger and stronger than you thought possible. Consistency is the key.

Bodybuilders have six proven overload methods for making muscles grow: assisted reps, negatives, drop sets, super sets, unilateral training, and isolated movements on the power rack. Use them and you will get super muscle mass and definition.

Assisted Reps: "The Magic Fingers"

Having a spotter help you with those last few, difficult reps is one of the easiest ways to get a high-tension workout. You can use this technique with any exercise. As the exercise gets difficult, have the spotter give you just enough assistance to finish the set. Don't give up during a difficult set. If you continue to push hard, you will need surprisingly little help from your spotter. That's why they call it the magic fingers: the weight goes up with minimal assistance from the spotter; often, only a finger on the bar will make it move. Assisted reps help you produce maximum muscle tension and get the most from your workout.

Negatives (Plyometrics)

Negatives, or eccentric muscle contractions, create more muscle tension than any other form of exercise. During conventional weight lifts, such as a bench press or squat, you can lower more weight than you can push during the lift. You create more muscle tension by contracting the muscles eccentrically (lowering the weight) than contracting them concentrically (pushing the weight). Bodybuilders call eccentric exercises negatives.

You can do negatives for almost any exercise. There are two basic ways to use this technique: (1) Use more weight than you normally use. Lower the weight under control, and then have a spotter help you raise the weight to the starting position. (2) Use a normal weight, but lower the weight slowly into the pushing position. For example, when doing dumbbell bench negatives, lower the dumbbells to your chest slowly, and then push them back to the starting position quickly.

Use experienced spotters when doing negatives. You sometimes use heavy weights when doing negatives, particularly during squats or bench presses. There is almost nothing worse than getting a weight stuck on your chest because you chose an inexperienced spotter. If you don't have your usual training partner, look for someone with obvious experience. A clumsy spotter can ruin your workout or cause serious injury.

Drop Sets

Do as many reps of an exercise as you can. Then, immediately drop the weight by 10 to 15 percent and try to squeeze out a few more reps. After that, use even less weight and do as many reps as you can. Keep going until you can't do any reps. This technique is a killer but a tremendous muscle builder.

"Training down the rack" is a similar high-tension training method. Choose dumbbells heavy enough so that you can only complete five reps of the exercise. Take a 30-second rest, and then move to the next-lightest set of dumbbells and do as many reps as you can. Rest 30 seconds and move to the next set of dumbbells. Continue down the rack until you can't complete any more reps or you run out of dumbbells.

Super Sets

This technique involves decreasing the resting time between sets. Many bodybuilders combine two or more exercises, doing either complementary exercises—such as dumbbell bench presses and flies—or antagonistic exercises—such as knee extensions and leg curls. Your rest intervals between exercises should not exceed 30 seconds.

Some experts have criticized this technique because it cuts down on the amount of weight you can use during each set. However, others say that it increases the overall muscle tension, which promotes growth.

Unilateral Training

Unilateral training—working out one side of the body at a time—is an effective overload method for building muscle mass and strength. Unilateral training takes more time than training both sides of the body at once, but it has some advantages that will make it a worthwhile alternate training method:

- Unilateral training helps isolate muscles better than training both sides of the body at once. San Diego State researchers found that doing one-leg squats overloaded the glutes better than doing two-leg squats. This type of training shocks your muscles, which makes them adapt faster.
- Unilateral training increases muscle blood flow better than bilateral training does. Muscle blood flow can be at least 50 to 100 percent greater during unilateral training than during bilateral training. The greater the blood flow, the more muscle-building amino acids you deliver to the working muscle.

- Unilateral training improves muscle symmetry. Use this technique to correct strength or mass differences between limbs. If you have an injury, unilateral training will help bring the injured side back to speed so that you train to your potential.
- Unilateral training creates more muscle involvement because of bilateral deficit. This means that the total weight you can lift with each limb working independently is greater than with two limbs working together. An example is the leg press. The sum of the weight you can lift with each leg will often be greater than the total weight you can lift with both legs. Because the weight you lift with both legs is less than with each leg lifting a weight independently, you have a strength deficit. You have also overloaded your muscles more than you could have using both legs at the same time. You can correct bilateral deficit by practicing unilateral training.
- Unilateral training increases the strength of the inactive side. This is a little-known fact of neurophysiology. For example, if you do knee extensions with your right leg, your left leg gets a small training effect—without doing anything. Granted, the gains are minimal, but they exist.

Isolated Movements on the Power Rack

The power rack is great for overloading your muscles and helping you overcome sticking points in your lifts. It can often get you over the hump when gains are difficult and allow you to use more weight than is possible during unassisted exercises.

Use the rack during isolated parts of lifts; you can often handle more weight than during the regular exercise. For example, do power-rack bench presses with the bar set close to the lockout position. Do your lifts to failure on the rack. You will use much more weight than you ever could doing the entire lift. Doing partial power-rack lifts will create more muscle tension and build larger muscles. The power rack is effective for creating muscle-building tension during bench presses, inclines, squats, dead lifts, high pulls, and curls. You can do many of these same power-rack exercises on a Smith machine. This machine includes a bar attached to a track that allows isolated or full-range-of-motion exercises.

Hanging Weight from a Belt

Chaining weights from your weight belt or using a special waist harness is excellent for creating more muscle tension during exercises, such as pull-ups or dips. Progress in these lifts is usually limited by your body weight. Pull-ups are one of the best exercises for developing the latissimus dorsi muscles, and dips are excellent triceps and bench-press builders. Adding weight to your belt while doing these exercises creates more muscle tension than using your body weight alone, which will make your muscles grow. For behind-the-neck pull-ups, suspend weights from your lifting belt using a chain. Grasp the bar with a wide grip and pull up until the back of your neck reaches the bar. Lower yourself slowly until you reach a full hang. Repeat the exercise for reps.

How Often Should You Use High-Tension Training Techniques?

Each of these techniques pushes your muscles to the max. These training methods help you create as much tension in your muscles as you can for as long as you can. Tension is the most important trigger that makes your muscles grow.

Unfortunately, you can overdo high-tension training. Your tolerance will depend on your body, diet, and use of supplements. If you use anabolic steroids or growth hormone—or even food supplements like creatine—you will be able to train to failure more often. See Chapter 14 to learn more about how steroids work and the health risks that can be associated with them. Many world-class bodybuilders train to failure in almost every workout. However, these athletes are superbly conditioned and often take anabolic steroids to promote muscle growth. In addition, they eat plenty of calories and protein. A bodybuilder who doesn't use steroids or supplements should train to failure only about once a week. That said, each person is different. If you can train harder and recover adequately—go for it!

6

Developing the Chest and Shoulders

"Let us run the risk of wearing out rather than rusting out."
—Theodore Roosevelt

Chest and shoulder exercises are by far the most popular with people who train with weights. For women, these exercises improve the form of the chest and shoulders. For men, chest and shoulder exercises give them the T-shaped look of a dynamo. Many sports require a strong upper body. Strong shoulder and chest muscles are an advantage when you're serving a tennis ball, for example, or rock climbing, or windsurfing. Chest and shoulder exercises build strength and power that help men and women excel in the activities they enjoy.

The chest and shoulders are more difficult to develop in women than in men because women carry less muscle mass in that part of the body. Also, there is no exercise that will increase the size of women's breasts. Breast tissue is made largely of fat. If the size of the chest muscles is increased, the breasts may look a little larger. But because women have a limited ability to increase muscle size through weight training, the increase in breast size can be only minimal.

The major muscles of the chest and shoulders are multipennate muscles,

which means the muscle fibers are aligned in several directions. Because of this, you should do several exercises to develop the muscles. For example, the pectoralis major muscle (the principal muscle of the chest) can be divided into upper, middle, and lower parts according to how the fibers are aligned. To completely train and develop this muscle, you must do exercises that build each of the muscle's three segments. Likewise, the deltoid (the principal muscle of the shoulder) is a three-part muscle that requires three or more exercises to develop fully.

It is difficult to present exercises that functionally isolate specific muscle groups. For example, exercises for the chest, such as the bench press, also train the muscles of the arms, back, abdomen, and, to a limited extent, the legs (the legs stabilize the upper body in some chest and shoulder exercises). Therefore, throughout Chapters 6 through 10, exercises are grouped according to the body part they work the best.

Also, it would be difficult and cumbersome to list exercises for every

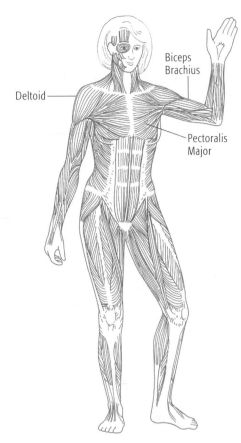

FIGURE 6.1 Major muscles of the chest, shoulders, and upper arm (anterior)

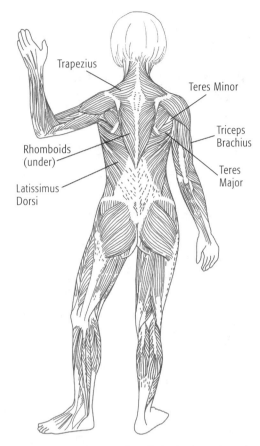

FIGURE 6.2 Major muscles of the back, neck, and upper arm (posterior)

type of machine. So, the book presents exercises that can be done using free weights and on many types of weight machines. See the table "Weight-Training Exercises for Machines from Selected Manufacturers" in the Appendix. Follow the basic guidelines for the machine exercises described in the text. They usually will be appropriate for most machines you will encounter in different gyms and clubs.

THE CHEST MUSCLES AND HOW TO TRAIN THEM

Building a powerful, round-looking chest is an ideal of many bodybuilders. Follow the principles outlined in this chapter and you will be well on your way to developing strong, shapely chest muscles. If you haven't been training, it will take about six weeks to see noticeable improvements in the size, shape, and strength of your muscles.

The pectoralis major and the pectoralis minor make up the chest muscles. The pectoralis major is a large, fan-shaped muscle that originates on the collarbone and breastbone and attaches to the upper arm. The pectoralis minor lies beneath the pectoralis major and assists it in moving the shoulder. The chest muscles move the arms across the chest and lower from overhead to waist level. They are particularly important in any pushing movement such as blocking in football or doing a chest pass in basketball. You use them when hitting a forehand in tennis or racquetball, throwing a ball or discus, or doing the freestyle stroke in swimming.

Muscles work by shortening and pulling on the bone to which they're attached. The pectoralis major is divided into upper, middle, and lower parts that you can build with specific exercises. Work the upper chest muscles with incline presses or incline flies. Do dumbbell or barbell bench presses to work the middle chest, and decline presses to work the lower chest. Emphasize the upper chest if you want to develop a full, round chest.

Muscles grow best when you load them: the heavier the stress, the more they grow. You can load and build the chest muscles better when you do multiple-joint exercises, such as bench presses and incline presses. These exercises allow you to use heavy weights and overload the chest muscles to the max. They also build accessory muscles, such as the triceps and deltoids, that allow you to work the chest muscles harder. Finish off your chest-building program by doing exercises that isolate the chest muscles, such as incline dumbbell flies and pec deck flies.

EXERCISES FOR THE CHEST MUSCLES

You will build the chest muscles best by training them twice a week. Do more than that and you will develop sore shoulders and overtrain. Train less than that and you won't progress very fast. Good chest-building exercises include the following:

- Bench presses
- Barbell inclines
- Dumbbell inclines
- Push-ups and modified push-ups
- Dumbbell incline flies
- Pec decks (fly machines)
- Cable crossovers
- Pull-overs

Bench Presses

The bench press is a mainstay for developing the pecs, deltoids, and triceps. It enables you to overload the pecs and develop upper-body strength better than almost any other exercise.

Bench press (a)

Bench press (b)

The technique: Lie on the bench with your feet flat on the floor. Grasp the bar, with your hands slightly more than shoulder-width apart. Have the spotter help you move the bar from the rack to a point over your chest. Lower the bar in a straight line slightly below your nipples (end of the breastbone). Then push the weight straight up to the starting position. Most equipment manufacturers make chest- or bench-press machines. The instructions are similar to those for free-weight bench presses.

Most people use poor technique when doing the bench press. Use the major muscles in your body to assist with this lift: tighten the muscles in your legs, abs, and back and squeeze your shoulder blades together. When lowering the bar to your chest, inhale and expand your chest and belly; this will help you generate more power during the lift. Keep your elbows in so that your upper arms are at 45-degree angles to the sides of your body. Bench-pressing with your elbows out places too much strain on your shoulders and reduces power. As you push the bar upward, contract your glutes and press your feet into the floor, and drive the bar upward explosively, exhaling as you perform the lift.

It is best to use a bench with a built-in rack constructed so that the weight can be put on and taken off with little danger of pinching your hands. The rack and bench should be sturdy enough so that large weights can be supported safely. The bench should allow your arms and shoulders to travel freely during the exercise.

Emphasize different muscle groups by varying the width of your grip. Narrow your grip to increase the stress on the triceps muscle (the muscle on the back of your upper arm); use a wider grip to stress the pectoralis major muscle (chest).

Barbell Incline Presses

These are excellent exercises for developing mass in the upper chest. Do them on an incline bench with a built-in rack. Use a spotter even when lifting a light weight because when setting up for the exercise, you grasp the bar with your shoulders externally rotated, which is a vulnerable position. The spotter will help protect your shoulders from injury.

The technique: Lie or sit on the incline bench and grasp the bar, with your hands placed slightly more than shoulder-width apart. Have the spotter help you to move the bar directly over your upper chest. Lower the bar to your upper chest, and then press the bar to the starting position. Use the same techniques described for the bench press for increasing power during the lift.

Caution: During the motion, be careful not to arch your neck or back because this could injure the spinal disks. Never bounce the weight off your chest because this could injure the ribs, sternum (breastbone), or internal organs.

Seated bench press (a)

Caution: Pushing the weight too far in front of you will make the exercise more difficult to perform and may result in a back, shoulder, or elbow injury.

Seated bench press (b)

Barbell incline press (a)

Barbell incline press (b)

Dumbbell Incline Presses

These exercises are excellent for isolating and balancing the muscles of the upper chest.

    The technique: Grasp the dumbbells and sit or lie on the incline bench. Place the right-hand dumbbell on your lower quad and boost it to chest level using your thigh. Do the same with the left-hand dumbbell. Keeping the dumbbells high on the chest, press them overhead simultane-

Dumbbell incline press (a)

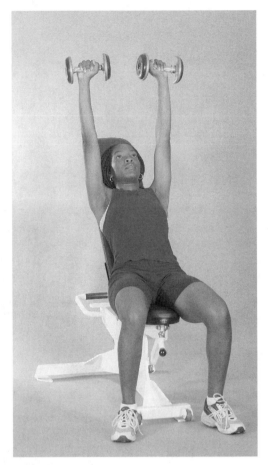

Dumbbell incline press (b)

ously and then return them to the starting position. Try this exercise on an exercise ball to build chest and shoulder strength and core (abdomen and back) strength at the same time.

Push-Ups and Modified Push-Ups

Push-ups build the chest, shoulder, and arm muscles. Many people lack sufficient strength to perform even a single push-up when using standard push-up technique. The modified push-up, in which you support yourself with your knees, is less difficult than the standard technique. Use the modified technique if you can't do more than eight standard push-ups. When you can do more than 30 modified push-ups, revert to the standard push-up technique.

1. Starting position
   - Standard push-ups: Start in the push-up position, with your body supported by your hands and feet.
   - Modified push-ups: Start in the modified push-up position, with your body supported by your hands and knees.
2. Lower your chest to the floor with your back straight, and then return to the starting position.

Dumbbell Incline Flies and Machine Flies

These exercises are good for isolating the upper chest.

The technique: Lie on the incline bench, holding the dumbbells together

Push-up and modified push-up (a)

Push-up and modified push-up (b)

at arm's length with elbows bent slightly and palms facing each other. Lower the dumbbells to the side of your chest and in line with your ears. Return to the starting position using the same path. Keep your chest high and your head on the bench.

You can also do this exercise on a flat bench or on machines, such as the pec deck, that simulate dumbbell flies. If you use a fly machine, sit on the machine with your back flat against the seat. Adjust the wings at 90 degrees. Place your forearms on the pads and draw the wings toward the middle until they touch. Return to the starting position.

Cable Crossovers

Cable crossovers are good exercises for building the upper-body muscles. Also, you build the core muscles—the abs,

Caution: Don't use too much weight when you first start doing incline flies because there is a possibility of injuring your elbows. For the same reason, don't do straight-arm flies.

Dumbbell incline fly (a)

Dumbbell incline fly (b)

Fly on a pec deck (a)

back, and side muscles—which must stabilize your spine when doing the exercise.

The technique: Grasp the handles of the upper pulleys and extend your arms upward in a V with palms facing downward. Bend your arms slightly and bend at the waist. Pull the handles downward until your hands touch each other at about waist level; return slowly to the starting position.

Barbell Pull-Overs

Pull-overs are good for developing the pectoralis major, rib muscles, and latis-

Fly on a pec deck (b)

simi dorsi (lats—large muscles of the back). Pull-overs can be done with either weights or machines.

The technique: Lie on your back on a bench; your head should lie at the end of the bench. Grasp a barbell, with the hands about eight inches apart.

Barbell pull-over (a)

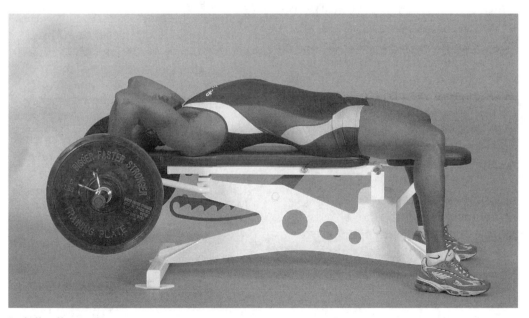

Barbell pull-over (b)

With arms bent slightly, lower the bar behind your head and reach toward the floor. Return to the starting position. As a variation to bent-arm pull-overs, you can work with straight arms, but you should use less weight to prevent elbow injury. You can also do these exercises on the low pulley station of the crossover pulley machine. The exercises are identical to those described for free weights, except they are done on the floor. A single dumbbell can be used in place of the barbell. Generally, this exercise is accomplished with the bench placed perpendicular to the weight trainer. Dumbbell pull-overs are described in Chapter 9.

Machine Pull-Overs

The technique: Adjust the seat so that your shoulders are aligned with the cams. Push down on the footpads with your feet so you can place your elbows on the pads. Rest your hands lightly on the bar. To get into the starting position, let your arms go backward as far as possible. Then pull your elbows forward until the bar almost touches your abdomen.

Other Exercises for the Chest

Many other exercises develop the chest muscles to some extent, including decline presses, lat pulls, catching and throwing medicine balls, and standing chest presses. Standing chest presses require a special machine that forces you to stabilize the body with your legs and core muscles (abs and back), which has excellent strength carryover to sports.

Tips on Building the Chest Muscles

Get plenty of rest and don't overtrain. Muscles grow during recovery. Exercising before muscles have fully recovered interrupts muscle growth processes. Work hard, but give your muscles a chance to recover.

Make sure to work the upper-back muscles, including your traps, lats, rhomboids, and posterior deltoids. Many people do plenty of chest exercises but neglect the back muscles. This creates muscle imbalances and increases the risk of overuse injuries to the shoulder and upper back.

Finally, chest muscles—like any other muscle group—look best when they are not covered by excess fat. Work hard, but don't neglect your diet and aerobic exercise. You need adequate calories for muscle growth, but don't use your intense exercise program as an excuse to overeat. Manage body fat and work hard, and you will soon develop shapely, fit-looking chest muscles.

EXERCISES TO DEVELOP THE SHOULDERS

The shoulder is one of the most complex joints of the body. It is composed of four specific joints and more than 12 different muscles. The rest of this chapter focuses on the principal exercises that develop the shoulder's major muscle groups.

The Deltoid and Rotator Cuff Muscles

The deltoid consists of the anterior (front), middle, and posterior (rear) deltoids. It is a large muscle that works on several planes on the shoulder, so it has several—sometimes opposing—actions. The deltoid elevates the arm. The anterior deltoid raises the arm in front of the trunk (shoulder flexion) and across the chest (horizontal flexion); the middle deltoid raises the arm to the side (abduction); and the rear deltoid hyperextends the shoulder (moves the arm to the rear) and horizontally extends the shoulder. The posterior deltoid is the main muscle that hyperextends the shoulder because the pecs and lats don't operate anymore once the arms are extended to the side. You build the posterior deltoids when you do backward raises and rowing exercises.

The rotator-cuff group demands attention because it is often injured by swimmers; baseball, volleyball, softball, and tennis players; carpenters; and artists. Rotator cuff exercises are described at the end of the chapter. Although all the exercises described in the previous section on how to build the chest muscles train the shoulder muscles as well, the following exercises are generally recognized as the best for developing the major muscles of the shoulder:

- Overhead presses (shoulder or military presses)
- Behind-the-neck presses

- Raises
- Incline reverse dumbbell laterals and pec deck reverse laterals
- Incline reverse dumbbell rows
- Upright rows

Overhead and Shoulder Presses

The overhead press, also called the "military press," can be done standing or seated and with barbells or dumbbells. Many equipment manufacturers make shoulder-press machines, and most health clubs have at least one. This exercise develops the deltoids (the large triangular muscles covering the shoulder joints), upper chest, and back of the arms.

The overhead press with a barbell begins with the weight at your chest, preferably on racks. If you are a more advanced weight trainer, you can "clean" the weight to your chest, but attempt this only after instruction from a knowledgeable coach. This is one of the best exercises for transferring strength from the weight room to sports because you must use your legs and core muscles to stabilize your upper body to do the lift.

1. **The clean:** To perform the clean, place the bar on the floor in front of you. Keep your feet approximately one to two feet apart. Grasp the bar, palms down, with your hands at slightly more than shoulder width, and squat down, keeping your arms straight, your back at a 30-degree angle, and your head up. Pull the weight up

Caution: When standing, be careful not to arch your back excessively, or you may injure the spinal muscles, vertebrae (bones of the spine), or disks. Also, this exercise may increase the severity of rotator cuff injuries.

Overhead (military) press (a)

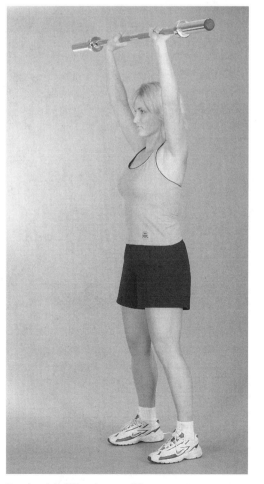

Overhead (military) press (b)

past your knees to your chest while throwing your hips forward and shoulders back. Much of the power for the clean should come from your hips and legs. Ask your weight-training instructor or coach to help you learn this lift because doing it improperly can lead to injury. If you are not an experienced weight trainer, use a rack to place the weights in the starting position.

2. **The overhead press:** Push the weight overhead until your arms are extended, and then return to the standing position (weight at chest). Again, be careful not to arch your back excessively.

Overhead-Press Machines. Most equipment manufacturers make overhead-

press machines. The machines usually require that you do the exercise from a seated position with your back supported and feet firmly on the floor. The pressing movement will be either in front of or behind the neck. Beware of behind-the-neck press machines if you have shoulder problems because the movement could make your injury worse.

Behind-the-Neck Presses
A variation of the standing press is the behind-the-neck press. This exercise develops the shoulders, back of the arms, and upper-back muscles. Again, don't do this exercise if you have rotator cuff problems.

This exercise can be done standing or seated and requires the use of a barbell. Use a rack to place the weight

Behind-the-neck push-press (a)

Behind-the-neck push-press (b)

in the starting position. With a fairly wide grip, place the weight behind your head and rest it on your shoulders. Push the weight above your head until your elbows are extended, and then return to the starting position.

The behind-the-neck push-press is a variation of this lift and is an excellent whole-body exercise because you also push with your legs to help complete the repetition. Do this exercise on a lifting platform using rubber bumper plates so you can let the weight hit the floor if you can't complete the repetition. Also, consider wrapping the bar with a pad to protect your upper back. The behind-the-neck push-press is an advanced lift that should not be attempted by beginners.

Shoulder Raises

Shoulder raises develop the deltoid muscle, the three-part, round muscle making up the most prominent part of the shoulder. This exercise must be done to the front, side, and rear in order to develop the deltoid fully. Raises are usually done with dumbbells, although they also can be done with wall pulleys or on specialized exercise machines.

Lateral raises: From a standing position, with a dumbbell in each hand and arms straight, lift the weights on both sides until they reach shoulder level, and then return to the starting position. Bend your arms slightly if your elbows hurt. Some people continue the exercise until the weights meet overhead, but this is inadvisable, as it may injure the shoulders. Lateral raises develop the middle section of the deltoid muscle.

Front raises: In a standing position, using dumbbells or a barbell, and with arms straight, lift the bar in front of you to shoulder level, and then return to the starting position. This exercise develops the front part of the deltoid muscle.

Dumbbell lateral raise

Dumbbell front raise

Rear raises: This exercise requires dumbbells. In a standing or seated position, with knees bent slightly, bend at the waist. Lift the weights to the side until they reach shoulder level; return to the starting position. Bent-over lateral raises develop the back portion of the deltoids.

Dumbbell rear raise

Incline reverse dumbbell lateral (a)

Incline Reverse Dumbbell Laterals

Lie facedown on a standing incline bench set at 45 degrees and grasp a dumbbell in each hand with palms facing down. Stay high with your head down. Keeping your elbows straight, hyperextend your shoulders and move the weights as high as you can. You can do this exercise unilaterally—one arm at a time—for better effect. Also, some pec deck machines allow you to reverse directions and do reverse laterals.

Incline Reverse Dumbbell Rows

Lie facedown on a standing incline bench set at 45 degrees. Grasp a dumb-bell in each hand and let them hang in front of you. Keeping your head down and the dumbbells high, pull the dumbbells toward your chest in a rowing motion. As with reverse dumb-bell laterals, you can do this exercise unilaterally—one arm at a time—for better effect.

Upright Rowing

Upright rowing develops the shoulders, the front of the arms, the neck, and the upper back. Because if affects so many large-muscle groups at the same time, it is an excellent upper-body

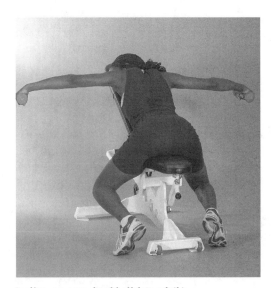

Incline reverse dumbbell lateral (b)

exercise. Rowing exercises (upright and front) help strengthen and balance the muscles of the shoulder joint. They are good complements to the bench press, shoulder press, and deltoid raise.

The technique: Using a pronated grip (palms toward the body), grasp a barbell with hands close together, and stand with the weight at waist level. Pull the weight to the upper part of

Incline reverse dumbbell row (a)

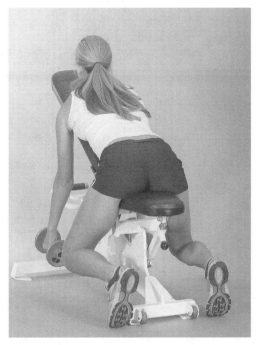

Incline reverse dumbbell row (b)

Upright row (a)

Upright row (b)

your chest; then return to the starting position.

ROTATOR CUFF EXERCISES

The rotator cuff is a group of four muscles that helps to lift your shoulder up over your head and also rotate it toward and away from your body. The muscles of the rotator cuff are the supraspinatus, teres minor, infraspinatus, and subscapularis. The muscle group is often injured in activities that require the arm to go above the shoulder level, such as swimming, tennis, and throwing. The best way to prevent injuries is to make the muscles strong and flexible. Exercises to strengthen this muscle group include

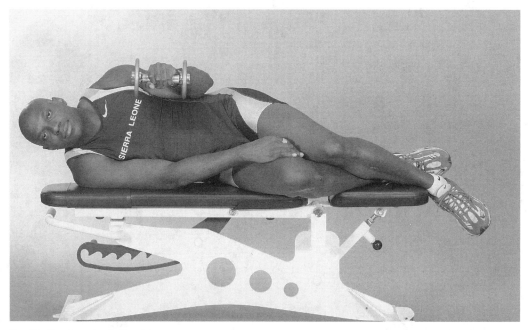

Dumbbell external rotation (a)

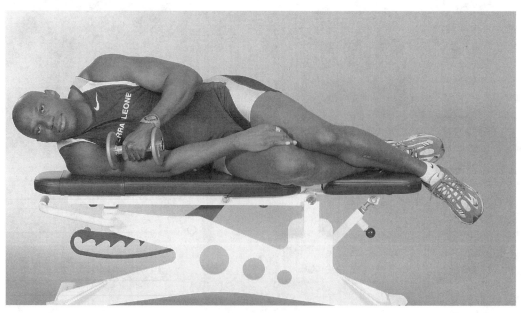

Dumbbell external rotation (b)

the dumbbell external rotation, dumbbell internal rotation, and empty-can exercise.

Dumbbell External Rotation

This exercise strengthens muscles that cause the arm to rotate outward—the infraspinatus and teres minor.

The technique: Grasp the dumbbell and lie on your side on a table, resting on one elbow. Bend your other elbow halfway (90 degrees), keeping the elbow tight to the rib cage. Slowly lower the weight, and then lift it back to the starting position.

Dumbbell Internal Rotation

This exercise develops the muscles that cause the shoulder to rotate inward—the subscapularis.

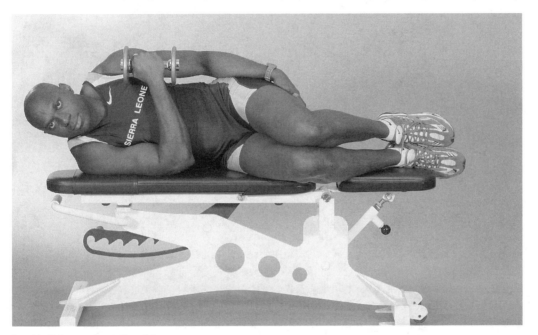

Dumbbell internal rotation (a)

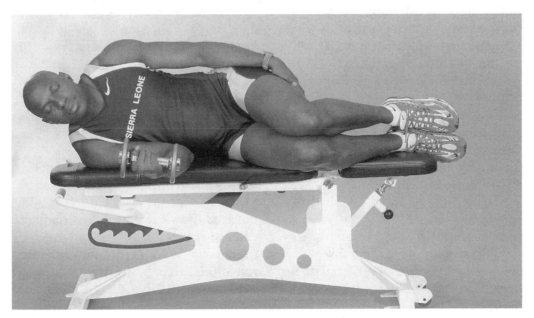

Dumbbell internal rotation (b)

Empty-can exercise (a)

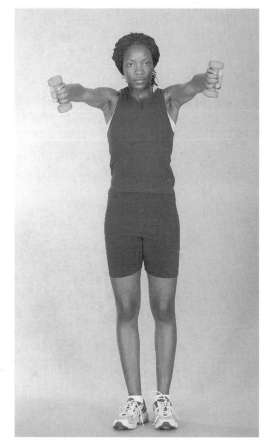

Empty-can exercise (b)

The technique: Grasp the dumbbell and lie on your side on a table with your elbow bent halfway (90 degrees) and held tightly against your side and with your hand extended over your chest. Slowly lower the weight to your side, and then slowly lift it back to the starting position.

Empty-Can Exercise

This is an important rotator cuff exercise because it strengthens the supraspinatus muscle, the muscle of the rotator-cuff group that is most often injured in sports.

The technique: Stand upright and hold a dumbbell in each hand. Keeping your arms straight, raise your arms to shoulder height, move them horizontally about 30 degrees, and rotate them inwardly as much as possible so that the palms are facing the floor. Slowly lower and raise the weights through a 45-degree arc. It should look as if you are emptying liquid from two cans— that's how the exercise got its name.

Preventing Rotator Cuff Injuries

The shoulder is an extremely complex joint that can easily become unbalanced if you work some muscles around the joint more than others. Build the shoulder muscles by exercising muscles in all the joint's motions. For example, balance a bench press with a rowing exercise; do raises to strengthen the shoulder flexors and do lat pulls to strengthen the shoulder extensors. Poor technique and overtraining are more significant causes of rotator cuff injury than muscle weakness.

7

Developing the Arms

"My 90 percent athlete going 100 percent will beat your 100 percent athlete going 90 percent every time."
–Bear Bryant

We use our arms for almost every activity in work and play. It helps to have strong arms for a wide variety of tasks—gardening, opening jars, throwing a ball, or playing tennis. Strong, attractive arms are within reach of anyone who will devote a little time to developing them. This chapter presents basic arm and forearm exercises as well as specialized arm exercises for preventing tennis elbow and increasing grip strength. The exercises are divided into three categories: the front of the arm, the back of the arm, and the forearm. The table titled "Weight-Training Exercises for Machines from Selected Manufacturers" in the Appendix lists some other examples.

EXERCISES FOR THE FRONT OF THE ARM

Curls are the best exercises for developing the muscles of the front of the arm. The principal muscles of this area include the biceps brachius and the brachialis. Curls can be done using a barbell, dumbbells, special curl bars, or

curl machines. Curl bars are useful because they reduce stress on the forearm muscles. They allow you to use more weight and prevent injury to your forearms. Among the many variations of curl exercises are the following:

- Standing barbell curls
- Dumbbell curls
- Preacher curls
- Reverse curls
- Curls, exercise machines
- Pole curls with a partner
- Double-arm curls, low pulley

Standing Barbell Curls
This is the old standby for developing biceps strength. Be sure not to bend your back when doing this exercise, or you may hurt yourself. If your forearms get sore after a few weeks, you probably are straining the muscles; switch from a straight bar to a curl bar.

The technique: From a standing position, grasp the bar with your palms upward and your hands shoulder-width apart. Keeping your upper body rigid, bend (flex) your elbows until the bar reaches a level

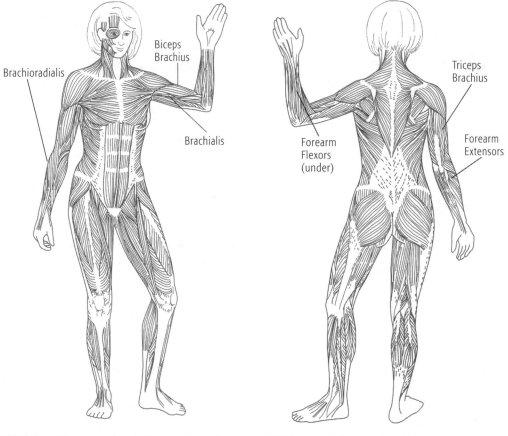

FIGURE 7.1 Major muscles of the arms (anterior)

FIGURE 7.2 Major muscles of the arms (posterior)

Standing barbell curl (a)

Standing barbell curl (b)

slightly below the collarbone. Return the bar to the starting position.

Dumbbell Curls

There are many ways of doing dumbbell curls. You may be standing or seated on a flat bench or on an incline bench, alternate between arms, do both arms at the same time, or do all the repetitions with one arm before doing them with the other arm. Although there is little difference among these lifts, each lift stresses the arm in a slightly different way. You can change your routine with these variations to add interest to your program.

Standing curls: Stand with your feet shoulder-width apart. Grasp the dumbbells using a supine grip (palms up). Begin with the arms extended, bend one arm at a time until the weight approaches your shoulders, return to the starting position, and repeat with the other arm.

Seated curls: While seated on a flat or incline bench, grasp the dumbbells using a supine grip (palms up). Begin with the arms extended, bend the arms until the weights approach your shoulders, and then return to the starting position. Swinging the weights or bending your back while doing dumbbell curls will make the exercise less effective.

Preacher Curls

Preacher curls effectively isolate the biceps, the muscles of the front of the arm. This lift is so effective because it is difficult to cheat while doing it. The exercise requires a special apparatus called a preacher stand or seated preacher bench, so named because it resembles a pulpit. If a preacher stand is not available, an incline bench can be substituted.

The technique: This lift can be done using a barbell, dumbbells, or a curl bar. Use a supinated grip (palms up) to hold the weight, place your elbows on the preacher stand, and fully extend your elbows. Bend your

Dumbbell curl (a)   **Dumbbell curl (b)**

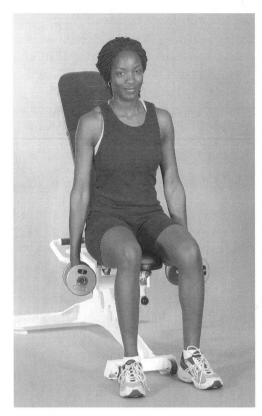

Incline dumbbell curl (a)

Incline dumbbell curl (b)

Preacher curl with barbell (a)

Preacher curl with barbell (b)

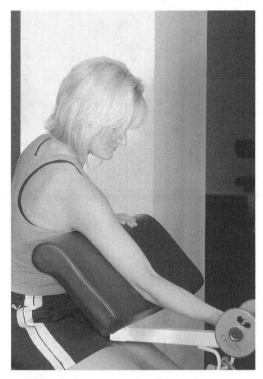

Preacher curl with one-arm dumbbell (a)

Preacher curl with one-arm dumbbell (b)

arms ("curl" the weight) until they almost reach your collarbone; then return to the starting position. With dumbbells, this exercise can be done one arm at a time.

Reverse Curls

Reverse curls have an effect similar to that of preacher curls, except they place a different stress on the forearm muscles. You can do this exercise with a barbell, dumbbells, or a curl bar, and in a seated or standing position.

The technique: Stand holding the weight at your waist, using a pronated grip (palms down, the opposite of barbell curls). Lift the weight by bending your elbows until the bar almost reaches your collarbone; then return to the starting position.

Curls, Exercise Machines

These machines resemble the preacher-curl exercise with free weights because they stabilize the upper arms and isolate the biceps.

The technique: Adjust the seat so that your upper arms are almost parallel to the supporting pad. You should be able to comfortably bend your arms through their full range of motion. Grasp the handles and extend your lower arms (starting position). Flex your arms as much as possible while keeping your elbows on the supporting pad; then return to the starting position.

Pole Curls with a Partner

You can do an entire resistive exercise routine using a pole, softball bat, or strong broom handle.

The technique: With your hands shoulder-width apart, grasp the pole or bar in a palms-up grip (supinated grip). Begin with your arms extended and the bar below your waist. Curl the bar to your upper chest while your partner resists the motion. This exercise produces functional strength for you and your partner because you must stabilize the muscles of your back,

Reverse curl (a)

Reverse curl (b)

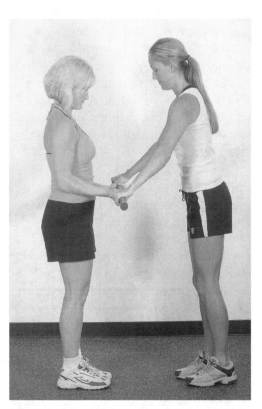

Pole curl with a partner

abdomen, and legs to complete the movement.

Double-Arm Curls, Low Pulley

The same basic technique used with free weights is used for curls on the crossover pulley machine.

The technique: Adjust the chain of the low pulley station so that the weights you're using go above the weight stack when you stand with the bar at your abdomen. With hands at waist level, grasp the bar with a supinated grip (starting position). Keeping your elbows close to your sides, curl your elbows until the weight touches your upper chest; then return to the starting position.

Other Exercises for the Front of the Arm

Any exercise that adds stress to the arm muscles as you bend your elbow will work this part of your body. Exercises that work the biceps, as well as other muscles, include pull-ups, chin-ups, lat pulls, and rowing exercises. You also work the biceps eccentrically (tension as the muscle lengthens) during upper-body lifts such as the bench, incline, and military press.

EXERCISES FOR THE BACK OF THE ARM

The triceps is the major muscle of the back of the arm, and it is trained during all exercises that involve pressing. Exercises that are particularly good for building the triceps include the following:

- French curls
- Bench triceps extensions
- Parallel-bar dips
- Chair dips
- Triceps extensions on the lat machine
- Triceps extensions, exercise machines

French Curls

This exercise appears to be similar to the behind-the-neck press, which develops the shoulders (see Chapter 6), but it is particularly effective in isolating the triceps when done properly. The basic difference between the two exercises is that the behind-the-neck press involves movement of both the shoulder and elbow joints, whereas in French curls the shoulders are fixed and the movement occurs in the elbows. Use a spotter for this exercise.

The technique: Grasp a barbell behind your head, using a pronated grip with your hands approximately 6 to 12 inches apart. Your palms will face upward toward the ceiling when you're doing this exercise. Keeping your elbows up and stationary, extend your

French curl (a)

French curl (b)

arms until the weight is overhead; then return to the starting position. Although somewhat awkward, this exercise can also be done using one handle on the seated-press station of several brands of weight machines.

Bench Triceps Extensions

This exercise is similar in many ways to French curls. Use a spotter if you are not familiar with the exercise or you are using a heavy weight.

The technique: Lie on a bench, grasping a barbell with a pronated grip, hands 6 to 12 inches apart. Push

the weight above your chest until your arms are extended (starting position). Keeping your elbows in a fixed position, carefully lower the weight until it touches your forehead, and then push the weight back to the starting position. Use a spotter for this exercise.

Parallel-Bar Dips

This exercise is excellent for helping you improve your bench press as well as building your triceps. Several equipment manufacturers make parallel-bar-dip machines that actively assist you with the movement.

Caution: Be careful not to use too much weight; if you lose control of the bar during the exercise, you could seriously injure yourself.

Bench triceps extension (a)

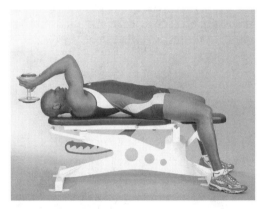

Bench triceps extension (b)

Parallel-bar dip (a)

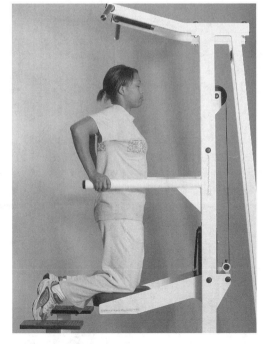

Parallel-bar dip (b)

The technique: Adjust the weight on the machine according to how much help you need to complete the set. Support yourself between the parallel bars on your fully extended elbows. Lower yourself by slowly bending your elbows until your chest is almost even with the bars. Then push up until you reach the starting position. A good way to improve if you can't do any repetitions initially is to have someone hold your waist and assist you during the motion.

Chair Dips

This exercise is similar to parallel-bar dips, and you can do it at home using a couple of chairs.

The technique: Support yourself between two sturdy chairs placed slightly more than shoulder width apart. Face toward the ceiling with your elbows and legs fully extended. Lower yourself by slowly bending your elbows. Then push up until you reach the starting position.

Triceps Extensions on the Lat Machine

The triceps extension on the lat machine is an excellent exercise for isolating the triceps muscles. If you develop elbow pain as a result of doing

Triceps extensions on the lat machine (a)

Chair dip (a)

Chair dip (b)

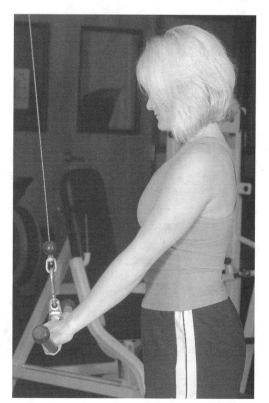
Triceps extensions on the lat machine (b)

this exercise, try another of the triceps exercises listed in this section.

The technique: Using a narrow, pronated grip, grasp the bar of the lat machine and fully extend your arms with your elbows held closely at your side. From this starting position, with elbows locked at your side, allow your hands to be pulled up to your chest; then firmly push the weight back to the starting position. If your elbows move during this exercise, you are cheating.

Triceps Extensions, Exercise Machines

Triceps machines are excellent for isolating the triceps muscle. The technique may vary slightly on different machines.

The technique: Adjust the seat so that when you sit down, your elbows are slightly lower than your shoulders. Place your elbows on the support cushion and your forearms on bar pads (starting position). Extend your elbows as much as possible; then return to the starting position.

EXERCISES FOR THE FOREARM

The forearm muscles are essential to any activity requiring a rapid wrist movement (snap), such as in golf, tennis, badminton, and throwing a ball. Weakness or overuse of the forearm muscles results in tennis elbow (also called carpenter's elbow)—inflammation of the soft tissue around the elbow, caused by overuse. The forearm muscles are also largely responsible for grip strength. There are two particularly good exercises for the forearms: pole twists and wrist curls.

Pole Twists

This exercise requires a partner and a rubberized pole or softball bat. One partner twists the bar using the forearm muscles while the other resists.

Pole twist

The technique: Grasp one end of the bar in both hands while your partner holds the other end of the bar. Twist the bar by turning your wrist—first inward and then outward.

Wrist Curls

Wrist curls are done using either a supinated or a pronated grip. Supinated wrist curls build the forearm flexors and are important accessory exercises to biceps curls. Pronated, or reverse, wrist curls build the wrist extensors, the muscles injured in tennis elbow.

The technique: You can do this exercise with either a barbell or dumbbells. In a seated position, with forearms resting on your thighs and hands extending over your knees, use a supinated grip to hold the weight and lower it as far as possible; then lift your hands upward ("curl" your wrists) by bending at the wrists as much as you can. Repeat this exercise using a pronated grip.

You can do wrist curls on the low pulley of the crossover machine with either the handles or the small bar. A variation of this exercise is the lateral wrist curl. It requires the use of a small bar with the weight affixed at one end. Do the exercise in the same manner as for wrist curls, except bend your wrist to the side.

Other Exercises for the Forearm and Grip

Grip strength is vital in certain sports—tennis, softball, and rock climbing, for example. People often don't have very good grips because they don't work to develop them. Serious weight-trained athletes have strong forearms and grips. Yet, few of them do wrist rollers or wrist curls because Olympic barbell exercises develop the grip better. Large-muscle weight lifts, such as cleans, snatches, and dead lifts, place considerable stress on the forearms and hands. If you do these kinds of lifts, you will develop a good grip and strong forearms—especially if you do them without using lifting straps. If you don't want to do these exercises, carry around a small rubber ball and squeeze it every time you think of it. This isometric exercise is effective for developing grip and forearm strength.

8

Developing the Abdominal Muscles

"The quality of people's lives is in direct proportion to their commitment to excellence, regardless of their chosen field of endeavor."
—Vince Lombardi

When are you going to lose that gut? How do I know you've got one? That's a no-brainer: two-thirds of Americans are overweight, so probability is on my side. Maybe you had tight stomach muscles 5, 10, or 15 years ago, but those days are a fading memory. Career, school, family, lack of exercise, fast-food restaurants, aging, stress, lagging hormones, and yo-yo dieting make it difficult to be the lean hard-body you were in high school. Now you have a one-pack instead of a six-pack. Your favorite pants don't fit anymore, and you're embarrassed to sit on the beach in a swimsuit.

Women's fashions are hard on those with less-than-perfect tummies. It is difficult to find women's pants or shorts that don't hug the hips or to find tops that don't show a bit of midsection. The hip-hugging short-shirt look made popular by rock singers says to the world: "Eat your heart out; don't you wish you had abs like these?"

If you look like a bodybuilder or fitness model, then you exercise intensely, watch what you eat, and have good genes that blessed you with a nice body. Most men and women aren't so lucky. Don't envy hard-bodied people with nice abs—join them. Stop procrastinating and do something about it. Follow the program described in this chapter and you will have a firmer, leaner midsection. If you already possess a fit physique, this program will put the finishing touches on your abs.

ABDOMINAL FAT: THE BAD AND THE UGLY

You already know that a bulging midsection is unattractive, but it's also bad for you. Everyone wants a firm, cut stomach, but usually for the wrong reasons. One fat cell looks like another under a microscope, but all fat cells are not created equal. Too much abdominal fat can kill you! Men tend to store fat in the abdomen, giving them an apple shape. Women store it in their legs, hips, and butt, which gives them a pear shape. The male "beer gut" is more damaging to health than the female "fat butt" because it is linked to a group of health problems that scientists call the metabolic syndrome—high blood pressure, insulin resistance, type 2 diabetes, high cholesterol, and blood-clotting abnormalities. Unfortunately, these days, even young women are storing more fat in their abdomens.

Abdominal fat consists of cavity fat—fat surrounding the internal organs—and subcutaneous fat—fat lying just under the skin that hangs over your belt. Ab cavity fat is dangerous because it is easily mobilized and can flood the liver and blood. Cutting ab fat helps fight the metabolic syndrome; reduces the risk of heart attack, cancer, and stroke; and boosts energy levels and sexual performance.

While men usually have more abdominal fat than women, genetics and age are also involved. Large midsections may run in your family, but you do not have to be a slave to your genes. You can lose abdominal fat if you are willing to change your diet and exercise. Men and women increase abdominal fat as they age. After people reach age 20, fat weight increases by an average of 17 percent per decade and waist size increases by 2 percent per decade. However, creeping waistlines are not inevitable—fight them with a lifelong program of exercise, counting calories, and reducing intake of saturated fat and simple sugar.

Falling levels of growth hormone, testosterone, thyroid hormones, and IGF-1 also contribute to abdominal fat. Exercise, healthy diet, stress management, and not smoking can help prevent hormone deterioration—to a point. Many aging people successfully use growth hormone and men use testosterone supplements to compensate for falling hormone levels and to lose body fat. This can be extremely expensive and is not recommended by many health experts. Nevertheless, prescriptions for supplementary hormone replacement increased by 300 percent in the past five years.

For men, the risk of heart disease and stroke is higher when the waist is more than 40 inches, and it increases substantially above 45 inches. For women, health risks increase as waist circumference exceeds 35 inches. Scientists also use waist-to-hip ratio as an indicator of excessive abdominal fat, but it is less useful than waist circumference. Most people want to have waists well below the danger point so they can be healthy and look good.

THE ABDOMINAL MUSCLES

The abdomen, unlike the arms and legs, depends largely on muscles rather than bones for support. Also, many people store fat around their middles, which makes it difficult to show off well-toned muscles. You will not have that six-pack look if abdominal muscles are covered in fat—no matter how fit and "cut" your abs. If your muscles are strong and conditioned, you will have a better-looking midsection even if you have some abdominal fat. Your stronger muscles will act as a girdle to hold in your midsection.

Four muscles make up the abs: the rectus abdominis, internal obliques (two muscles; one on each side), external obliques (two muscles), and transversus abdominis (also called transversalis). These muscles allow you to bend forward at the waist, rotate the trunk, and bend to the side. All of the abdominal muscles help stabilize the spine, which helps prevent back pain.

The Rectus Abdominis
The rectus is the muscle that everyone sees. It runs down the length of the abdomen, from the lower part of your chest to the top of your pelvis. The

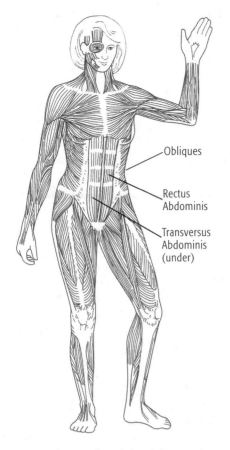

FIGURE 8.1 Major muscles of the abdomen

want. When activated, the entire muscle contracts, so it is extremely difficult to work only its upper or lower part.

The Internal and External Obliques

You use the obliques to rotate and flex the trunk and bend to the side. These muscles are critical for weight-transfer movements, such as hitting a baseball or tennis ball; throwing a discus, javelin, or softball; or punching a heavy bag.

The internal and external obliques form the sides of the abdomen and help twist and bend the trunk. They are critical in most sports and help give your body a T shape. Develop the obliques by twisting during crunches and doing twists and side-bending exercises.

The quadratus lumborum is a deep muscle (one on each side) that works with the obliques to help stabilize the spine and bend the trunk to the side. Building this muscle—through exercises such as the side bridge—is critical to the overall strength of the abdominal (core) muscles because it provides lateral stability to the spine.

The Transversus Abdominis

This muscle stabilizes the trunk and compresses your internal organs when you stand, lift, sneeze, cough, or laugh. It is an underappreciated muscle. Anytime you lift a weight or do any whole-body movement, the transversus abdominis steps in to stabilize your midsection. You develop this muscle anytime you do large-muscle lifts, such as squats, dead lifts, and bench presses. You can also work this muscle by tensing your abdominal muscles isometrically.

SIT-UPS FOR SHAPELY ABS?

The quest for perfect abs has become a multibillion-dollar industry. People

rectus flexes the trunk. This movement causes the spine to bend forward. The rectus also tilts the pelvis backward, making it important in maintaining a normal low-back curve and preventing back pain. You use it when you do crunches or pelvic tilts.

The shape of the rectus abdominis is a source of confusion for many people trying to develop it. While the six-pack shape of the muscle suggests a series of muscles that can be developed separately, it is actually one large muscle. Four strips of connective tissue called tendinous incriptions divide it. These structures help reinforce the muscle and protect it from rupture during vigorous movements. The linea alba is another connective-tissue structure that runs down the center of the muscle. It also helps protect the muscle and gives it that six-pack shape we all flock to buy expensive abdominal exercise machines, exercise tapes and books, and weight-reducing drugs. When these approaches fail to get results, people sometimes go to their local plastic surgeons for liposuction and tummy tucks.

Sit-ups have been the mainstay of abdominal exercise for more than a hundred years. Anyone who wants great-looking abs probably does sit-ups—hundreds of them. Is this the best ab exercise? And more important, are they safe?

The sit-up test is a rite of passage for virtually anyone enrolled in junior or senior high school physical education classes. Also, many people do sit-ups religiously to achieve the optimal fit-looking body with firm abs. Conventional wisdom suggests that sit-ups will build firm-looking abdominal muscles and develop core strength for doing everything better from waxing the car to hitting a tennis ball.

It's not that simple. Dr. Stuart McGill and colleagues from the University of Waterloo, in Canada—in a series of elegant studies on the abdominal muscles and spine—found that sit-ups put so much stress on the spine that we shouldn't do them at all. Their work also suggests that the sit-up test is dangerous and is not a good measure of fitness.

You can develop beautiful, shapely abdominal muscles and have a healthy back at the same time. Good ab-muscle strength contributes to good back health—if you do the correct exercises. Doing abdominal exercises improperly can cause back injuries that will never heal. Chronic back pain is a big price to pay—particularly since you could develop fit-looking abs doing other exercises. As for developing abdominal strength for sports, there are also better ways than sit-ups to generate more powerful movements when playing golf, tennis, or volleyball.

The Canadian National Institute of Occupational Safety and Health (NIOSH) sets limits for body stresses in the workplace. Dr. McGill's research shows that stressing the back repeatedly, lowers its tolerance to injury. NIOSH set an upper limit of back compression at 3,300 newtons (N). A newton is a measure of force. One bent-knee sit-up creates an average of 3,350 N, while straight-leg sit-ups create a whopping 3,506 N—both greater than the maximum level set by NIOSH for predicting back injuries. Curl-ups, on the other hand, create only 1,991 N of spinal compression, and side bridges (a great exercise for your obliques, the muscles on the sides of your abs) create 2,585 N. Curl-ups develop the ab muscles without overloading the spine.

Part of people's preoccupation with sit-ups comes from a misunderstanding of the role of the abdominal muscles in movement. The torso region needs stability to transmit forces between the upper and lower body. The main function of the rectus abdominis—the long, wide muscle on the front of the abdomen—is not to shorten, and flex the trunk. Rather, it is an important stabilizer and force transmitter. This is suggested by the structure of the muscle: tendons break the muscle into four portions, which give the well-developed rectus that six-pack appearance. The muscle is designed to transmit stresses around the spine, which increases the efficiency of the obliques—the muscles on the sides of the abdomen. The rectus abdominis functions more as a spinal stabilizer than as a major factor in trunk movement.

THE CORE AND KINETIC CHAIN

Most movements use several joints and many muscles—either as prime movers, assist muscles, stabilizers, or antagonistic muscles. The link and coordination between these joint movements is called the kinetic chain. The key to most linked movements is the core, or midsection—the abdominal muscles, deep lateral stabilizing muscles, and spinal extensor muscles. The core is critical to most sports movements because it transmits forces between the lower and upper body.

Build the core muscles by forcing the trunk muscles to stabilize the spine while standing, sitting, or lying down. Whole-body exercises—such as curl-ups on the exercise ball, side bridges, standing chest presses on a crossover pulley machine, squats, and medicine ball passes—that stress the upper- and lower-body muscles will also develop the core muscles.

SAFE, EFFECTIVE EXERCISES FOR THE ABDOMINAL MUSCLES

The goal of your ab program is to have fit, attractive, functional muscles that support the spine and help prevent back pain. It's true that doing sit-ups overloads the abs, but sit-ups also cause back injury. If you complete too many traditional sit-ups (straight-leg or bent-knee), you will most likely develop a back injury. The message from scientific studies is clear: *Don't do sit-ups!*

The recommendations for abdominal-muscle exercises in this chapter are based on the results of studies using electromyography (EMG)—a powerful technique that shows how muscles are activated during exercise. Do these exercises three or four days per week. The ab exercises include the following:

- Isometric abdominal stabilizers
- Crunches
- Crunches on the exercise ball
- Side bridges
- Reverse crunches on a bench
- Bicycle exercise

Isometric Abdominal Stabilizers
The abdominal muscles stabilize the midsection of the body and help transmit force from the lower to the upper body. As discussed, building endurance in the core muscles (abdomen, sides, and back) will prevent back pain and help you perform better in sports.

The technique: Do this exercise on a bench with back support or on the floor. When first doing this exercise, have a spotter hold your feet and hold your trunk in a 60-degree position

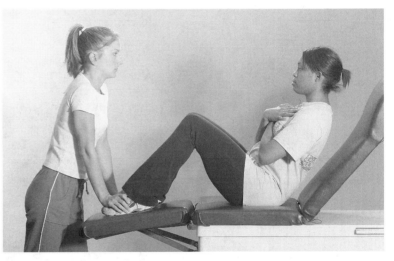

Isometric abdominal stabilizer (a)

Isometric abdominal stabilizer (b)

relative to horizontal (flat bench). Hold this position for 10 seconds, rest 30 seconds, and repeat 3 to 10 times. Gradually build up until you can hold the position for 30 to 60 seconds. Maintain a straight back during the exercise to prevent injury. Eventually, you should be able to do this exercise without assistance.

Crunches

Crunches are great for isolating the abdominal muscles.

The technique: Lie on the floor on your back; bend your knees and place your feet flat on the floor. Some experts say to bend only one knee and leave the other leg extended. Place your hands across your chest. Contract your front abdominal muscles, drawing your breastbone downward. Try not to lift your neck or shoulders; let the abs do the work.

Crunches on the Exercise Ball

EMG, which measures muscle activation during exercise, shows that crunches work the abs best on an exercise ball.

The technique: Lie on your back on the ball so that your thighs and torso are parallel with the floor. Cross your arms over your chest and contract your abdominal muscles, raising your torso to no more than 45 degrees. Increase the stress on your oblique muscles by

Crunch

Crunch on the exercise ball (a)

Crunch on the exercise ball (b)

moving your feet closer together and placing your hands on your ears.

Side Bridges

This is not a well-known exercise. However, EMG studies show that side bridges strengthen the obliques and help stabilize the spine. You can avoid back pain by doing this exercise at least twice a day.

The technique: Lie on your side and support your body between your forearm and knees. As you increase fitness, first move your nonsupport arm across your body as you hold the side bridge; later, support your weight between your forearm and feet. Do this exercise on your left and right sides and try to hold your spine straight—don't let it sag during the exercise.

Side bridge

Reverse Crunches on a Bench

Lie on your back on a bench and stabilize your body by grabbing the bench above your head. Lift your legs so your feet are pointed at the ceiling, and bend your knees slightly. Contract your lower abdominal muscles and lift your tailbone off the bench and push your feet toward the ceiling, pushing your lower back into the bench. Return to the starting position.

Reverse crunch on a bench (a)

Bicycle Exercise

Lie on the floor on your lower back, with your hands beside your head with elbows bent. Bring your knees toward your chest to about a 45-degree angle and make a bicycle-pedaling motion with your legs, touching your left elbow to your right knee and then your right elbow to your left knee.

HARNESS YOUR METABOLISM AND FIGHT ABDOMINAL FAT

Positive energy balance, or taking in more calories in the diet than you

Reverse crunch on a bench (b)

expend through metabolism and exercise, is the major cause of increased fat. Unfortunately, getting rid of fat is more complicated than cutting back on calories and exercising more. You have trouble losing abdominal fat because your metabolism won't let you.

The body tries to maintain a constant weight (called the weight set-point) by slowing metabolism as you lose weight. Most people who lose weight lose muscle mass as well as fat. Muscle burns a lot of calories: the more muscle you have, the higher your metabolism. As you lose muscle, you burn fewer calories. Also, as you lose weight, the body releases chemicals and sends signals from the nervous system that increase appetite and slow metabolism further.

Late-night television infomercials promise that doing exercises on abdominal machines reduces abdominal fat—a method called spot reducing. The classic way to get a flat, firm abdomen was to do hundreds of sit-ups. The idea of spot reducing made sense: if you have a fat gut, work the gut muscles to get rid of it. While doing abdominal exercises will do little to get rid of abdominal fat, burning plenty of calories through exercise will do much. Several recent studies showed that people who exercised intensely tended to lose most of the fat from the abdominal cavity and the fat

EXAMPLE OF A WORKOUT TO IMPROVE THE APPEARANCE OF YOUR ABS

Here is a sample program. There are countless variations to these workouts. The program is intense and is designed to produce measurable results within two to three months. Work hard and stay with the program, and you will be pleased with the results.

Monday
Weight training (2 or 3 sets of 10 reps for 8–10 exercises)
- Bench presses
- Bent-over rows
- Lat pulls
- Curls
- Triceps extensions on lat machine
- Squats
- Leg curls
- Calf raises

Abdominal exercises
- Isometric abdominal stabilizers (2 sets of 30 seconds)
- Crunches (2 sets of 10 reps)
- Bicycle exercise (2 sets of 20 reps)
- Reverse crunches (on a bench) (2 sets of 10 reps)
- Exercise ball crunches (2 sets of 20 reps)
- Side bridges (hold for 2 sets of 30 seconds on each side)

Aerobics (60–90 minutes)
- Running, cycling, health club aerobic machines

Tuesday
Interval training: Running track, 2 miles—sprint the straightaways, walk the turns

Aerobics (60–90 minutes)

Wednesday (see Monday)
Weight training

Abdominal exercises

Aerobics (60–90 minutes)

Thursday
Interval training: Running track, 2 miles—sprint the straightaways, walk the turns

Aerobics (60–90 minutes)

Friday (see Monday)
Weight training

Abdominal exercises

Aerobics (60–90 minutes)

Saturday
Aerobics (60–90 minutes)

Exercises

Sunday
Rest

covering the abdominal muscles (sub-cutaneous fat).

Lose abdominal fat and improve the appearance of your abdominal muscles by developing and toning the abdominal muscles, building muscle mass to increase metabolism, burning plenty of calories through exercise, and speeding up your 24-hour metabolic rate. As discussed, muscle is the most metabolically active tissue in the body. The more muscle you have, the higher your metabolic rate. Also, muscle pushes against the fat near your skin and makes it look smoother—improving the appearance of the fat. Exercise, particularly intense exercise, burns a lot of calories. Exercise for 60 to 90 minutes a day and you will lose fat faster than you ever thought possible. Finally, the combination of intense and endurance exercise will increase your metabolic rate so that you burn calories at a faster rate all day and all night long.

Weight Training

Weight training is a central part of your abdominal-fat-management program. The workout involves doing two or three sets of 10 reps of 8 to 10 general weight-training exercises three days per week. Train intensely: use as much weight as possible for each set. You will use less weight for the second set when you do more repetitions. Weight training will help you burn more calories during and after exercise.

A general program includes the following exercises:

- Bench presses
- Bent-over rows
- Lat pulls
- Curls
- Triceps extensions on lat machine
- Squats
- Leg curls
- Calf raises

Aerobics

Do aerobic exercises for 60 to 90 minutes, three to six times a week. Weight-bearing exercises such as running, power walking, treadmill running, stair-climber, and elliptical training are best for losing fat. Start with 5 to 10 minutes of exercise and build up until you can exercise continuously for 60 to 90 minutes without stopping. Also, increase the intensity until you can exercise at 70 percent of maximum effort or harder during your workout. You will burn at least 700 calories during each aerobic workout and help tip your metabolism toward fat loss.

Interval Training

Interval training includes intense exercises such as sprinting or cycling, interrupted by periods of rest or light exercise. Interval training will increase your metabolism so that you continue to burn calories at a higher level 24 to 48 hours after the workout is over. Long-term weight-control studies show that people who train intensely tend to lose more weight than those who exercise slowly. Run, ride a bike, or exercise on a gym aerobics machine (stair-climber, elliptical trainer, ski machine, etc.) for one minute at 90 percent to 100 percent of maximum, followed by two to three minutes of rest. Repeat 10 to 15 times.

Diet

Follow a sensible diet that includes plenty of fruits, vegetables, whole grains, lean meats (beef, chicken, and fish), olive oil, and nuts. Minimize high-sugar drinks, simple sugars, salt, desserts, and saturated and trans fats. Try to keep your caloric intake at less than 2,000 to 2,500 calories per day. Moderation is the key: keep portions small and avoid junk foods. You must exercise intensely, so avoid low-carbohydrate diets, such as the Atkins diet. Your body metabolizes mainly carbohydrates whenever you exercise more intensely than 65 percent of maximum effort.

YOU CAN IMPROVE THE APPEARANCE OF YOUR ABS

Improve the appearance of your abdomen by (1) burning plenty of calories during weight training, aerobics, and interval training, (2) increasing muscle mass, which speeds metabolic rate and smoothes the appearance of the abdominal muscles, (3) increasing 24-hour metabolism by boosting muscle temperature during high-intensity exercise, and (4) creating negative caloric balance by eating less than 1,500 to 2,500 calories per day (depending on your gender and body size; women usually need fewer calories than men, and smaller people need fewer calories than larger people). This program works. Stick with it, and you will cut down on abdominal fat and get the midsection you want.

9

Building the Perfect Back: Exercises for the Upper, Middle, and Lower Back

"Continuous effort—not strength or intelligence—is the key to unlocking our potential."
—Liane Cordes, author

Most serious weight trainers have good chest and abdominal muscles but fall short in other muscle groups, particularly in the back. The reason is simple: muscles on the front of the body are the first feature they notice when looking at themselves in the mirror. Most weight trainers—especially beginners and bodybuilders—spend more time working pecs and abs than any other upper-body muscles.

Overemphasizing chest and arm muscles gives you a freakish, unbalanced physique. You should work your back as much as you work the muscles on your front. Good back development gives your body symmetry and adds stability and balance to your shoulder joints, which helps prevent injury and overuse problems.

Slippery Rock University scientists—led by Dr. J. C. Barlow—found that most bodybuilders do not have balanced muscle development and are usually inflexible because they do only a few exercises and neglect the rest.

The bodybuilders showed muscle imbalances and restricted flexibility during a variety of shoulder and back movements, even though they were much stronger than the average person.

THE BACK MUSCLES

The back is subdivided into the upper, middle, and lower back. To build the back optimally, you should know the major muscles, their actions, and which exercises build muscles best. Fortunately, you don't have to guess. Scientific studies using sophisticated tools such as electromyography (EMG) and magnetic resonance imaging (MRI) show us how these muscles work and which exercises work best for building them.

The surface muscles of the upper back include the trapezius muscles (traps) and posterior deltoids. These muscles give height and breadth to

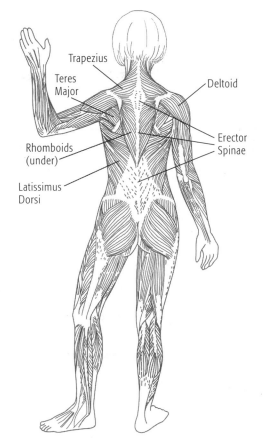

FIGURE 9.1 Major muscles of the back

back development and are discussed later in this chapter. The mid-back muscles include the latissimi dorsi (lats), rhomboids, and teres major. The low-back muscles are called collectively the erector spinae and include the longissimus, spinalis, and iliocostalis.

The lats are attached to the upper end of the arm bones (humeri) at one end and fan out down the length of the spine to the pelvis. The latissimus dorsi extends the shoulder, which means that it pulls the arm downward toward the hips. During pull-ups, the lats raise the body toward the arms when the arms are fixed. These muscles also stabilize the trunk during multiple-joint, large-muscle lifts, such as squats and bench presses. Good exercises for the lats include pull-ups, lat pulls, and pull-overs.

The rhomboids (major and minor) run from the spine to the scapulae (shoulder blades); the scapula is a large, flat bone that attaches to the upper-arm bone (humerus). When the rhomboids on both sides work together, the muscles squeeze the shoulder blades together. The rhomboids draw the scapulae toward the spinal column. The teres major muscle connects the scapula (shoulder blade) to the humerus. This muscle moves the humerus backward, meaning that it brings the arm toward the back. The rhomboids and teres major work together to move the arms backward during movements such as rowing. Exercises that build these muscles include rear deltoid raises, seated cable rows, wide-grip lat pulls, pull-ups, bent-over rows, and one-arm dumbbell rows.

The erector spinae muscles support and extend the spine. These muscles attach to the vertebrae, the ribs, and the pelvis. Good exercises for developing these muscles include back hyperextensions, bird dogs, dead lifts, and good mornings. Well-developed spinal muscles make you look as if you have two boa constrictors running up your back.

Strive to build all three parts of the back if you want to develop a superior physique and well-balanced muscles. Strong, symmetrical back muscles give balance to the shoulder joint by maintaining uniform tension on the front and back of the shoulder. This promotes joint health and prevents shoulder pain stemming from abnormal stresses on the joint.

EXERCISES FOR THE LATS (MIDDLE BACK)

The best exercises for the lats include the following:

BASIC BACK ROUTINE

Do this program two days per week.

Exercise	Sets and Reps
Pull-ups with a wide grip	3 × 10
Wide-grip pull-downs on lat machine	3 × 10
Dumbbell pull-overs	3 × 10
Seated reverse barbell rows	3 × 10
One-arm dumbbell rows	3 × 10
Seated cable rows	3 × 10
Bent-over barbell rows	3 × 10
T-bar rows	3 × 10
Back hyperextensions w/weight	3 × 10
Dead lifts on Smith machine	3 × 10

- Pull-ups
- Wide-grip pull-downs on the lat machine
- Dumbbell pull-overs
- Barbell pull-overs

Pull-Ups

Use a pull-up bar or assisted pull-up machine. Suspend weights from a weight belt when you want to increase strength faster or when you can do more than 10 repetitions.

The technique: Grasp the bar with a wide pronated grip (palms away from your body) and hang with elbows fully extended. Pull your body up until your collarbone reaches the bar. Return to the starting position and repeat. Use a spotter or assist machine if you can't do 10 reps.

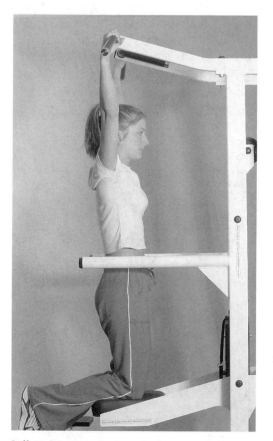

Pull-up (a)

Pull-up (b)

Wide-Grip Pull-Downs on the Lat Machine

Grasp the bar with a wide grip. Sit on the seat with your knees under the supports. Use a spotter if your lat machine does not have thigh supports. Start with arms and shoulders fully extended. Pull the bar steadily to your chest without jerking; then slowly return to the starting position.

Dumbbell Pull-Overs

Use a single dumbbell. Lie on your back on the bench with your feet flat on the floor and hips flexed slightly. Grasp the dumbbell around the nearest set of plates from behind and position it over your chest. Flex your elbows 15 to 30 degrees during the exercise. Lower the dumbbell over and beyond your head until your upper arms are

Wide-grip pull-down on the lat machine (a)

Wide-grip pull-down on the lat machine (b)

parallel to your head and torso. Return to the starting position and repeat.

Barbell Pull-Overs

Use a small barbell or curl bar to perform this exercise. Lie on your back on the bench with your feet flat on the floor and hips flexed slightly. Grasp the bar with a palms-away (supine) grip and position it over your chest. Flex your elbows 15 to 30 degrees during the exercise. Lower the bar over and beyond your head until your upper arms are parallel to your head and torso. Return to the starting position and repeat.

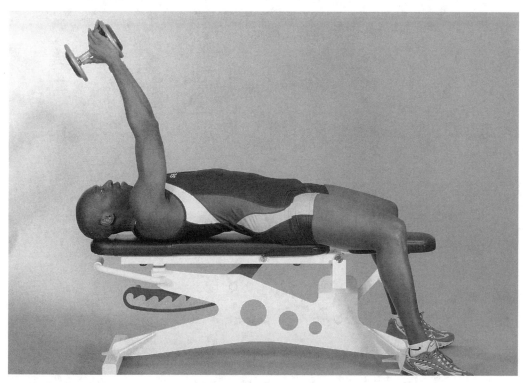

Dumbbell pull-over (a)

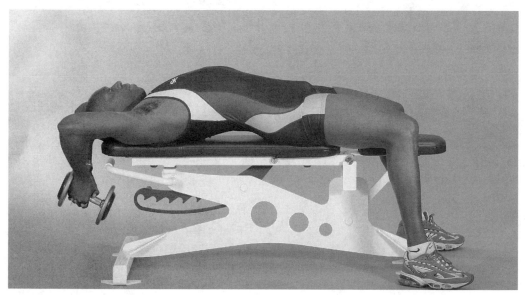

Dumbbell pull-over (b)

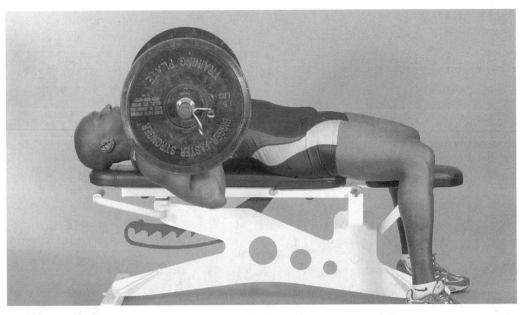

Barbell pull-over (a)

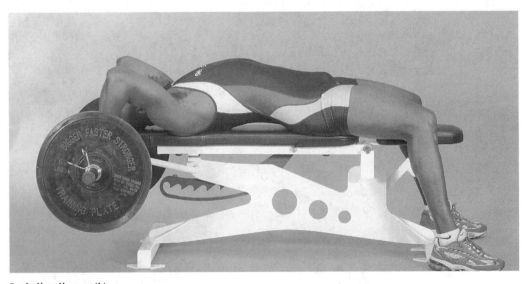

Barbell pull-over (b)

EXERCISES FOR THE RHOMBOIDS AND TERES MAJOR (MIDDLE BACK)

To give your back a full, muscular-looking appearance, use exercises that isolate and overload the rhomboids and teres major. These are among the best:

- One-arm dumbbell rows
- Incline rows
- Machine rows
- Seated cable rows

One-Arm Dumbbell Rows

Place your right knee and right arm on a bench, keeping your left foot on the floor. Your back should be flat. Grasp a dumbbell with your left hand using a palms-in grip (pronated) and extend your arm. Bring the arm toward your chest in a rowing motion; return to the starting position; repeat. You can also do this exercise with a barbell from a standing position (bent-over barbell rows). Bend at the waist with your arms extended and spine fixed.

One-arm dumbbell row (a)

One-arm dumbbell row (b)

Incline row (a)

Incline row (b)

Pull the barbell toward your chest in a rowing motion; return to the starting position; repeat.

Incline Dumbbell Rows and Reverse Flies

Lie facedown on a flat bench or on an incline board. With your palms facing inward (pronated grip), raise the dumbbells as high as you can to the side of your body. Hold at peak contraction; then lower to the starting position and repeat. Do this exercise either using both dumbbells at the same time or unilaterally—one arm at a time.

Some fly machines allow you to exercise the back muscles as well as those of the chest and shoulders—an exercise called reverse flies.

The technique: Put your chest on the pad and extend your arms to the front. Grasp and pull the bars backward, using the muscles of the upper back and shoulders (posterior deltoids and rhomboids).

Reverse fly (a)

Reverse fly (b)

Machine Rows

This exercise requires a row or T-bar machine. For the row machine, sit in the chair and grasp the bar in front of you at arm's length. Pull the bar toward you as you pull your shoulder blades together. For the T-bar machine, lie on your front side with your chest firmly on the pad and grasp the T-bar with your arms fully extended. Pull the bar toward your chest and then return it slowly to the starting position.

Seated Cable Rows

This exercise requires a cable rowing machine. Grasp the handles and place your feet on the rest in front of you. Extend your arms and legs fully; you should feel a stretch in your lats and rhomboids. Without jerking, pull the handles toward your chest, hold the contraction, and return to the starting position. Try to pinch your shoulder blades together during the exercise.

EXERCISES FOR THE LOW-BACK MUSCLES

More than 85 percent of Americans have back pain—active people included. Most scientists who study back pain and its causes think that people should emphasize muscle endurance and stabilization in the muscles of the back, abdomen, and sides of the abdomen. The three main exercises for developing a stable spine are crunches and side bridges, which were described in Chapter 8, and isometric spine extension (bird dog exercise). Exercises for the low back include these four:

- Isometric spine extensions
- Back extensions
- Superman on the exercise ball
- Dead lifts

Isometric Spine Extensions

The purpose of isometric extension is to strengthen the low-back muscles so that they are better able to maintain spinal stabilization and alignment. Most back experts feel that stabilizing the spine and building muscle endurance in the core muscles (abdomen, sides, and back) are the keys to a pain-free back.

The technique: Balance on your right hand and left knee. Lift your right leg and left arm. Extend your leg to the rear, and reach to the front with your arm. Hold this position for 10 to

Machine row (a)   Machine row (b)

Isometric spine extension

30 seconds. Repeat with the opposite arm and leg.

Back Extensions

Use a flat bench or back extension bench. Have a spotter hold your feet, or place your heels under the support (if using an extension bench), and hang over the support at waist level. Place your hands on your chest. Start with the body straight; bend at the waist, keeping your spine rigid. Return to the starting position and hold. Move slowly on this exercise. Emphasize endurance over strength. This exercise is also good for strengthening the hamstring muscles and will help you improve whole-body lifts, such as dead lifts and squats. Hold a weight plate close to your chest to increase the resistance.

You can also do this exercise on an exercise ball. Lie facedown on the ball at stomach level, with your legs fully

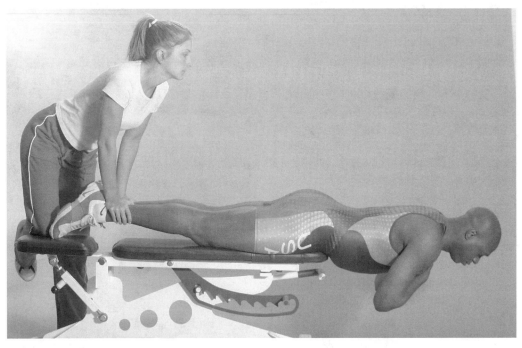

Back extension (a)

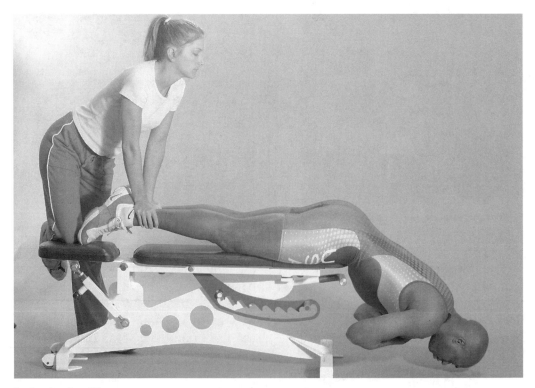

Back extension (b)

extended behind you, toes touching the ground, and hands touching each ear. Lift your head and chest off the ball slowly, using your low-back muscles. Return to the starting position.

Superman on the Exercise Ball

Lie on an exercise ball at chest level, with your legs extended to the rear. Extend your arms and place both hands in front of you as though you were flying like Superman. Hold the position for up to 30 seconds, rest, and repeat.

Dead Lifts

This is one of the best overall weight-lifting exercises for building the major muscles of the body and developing functional strength (strength that is useful during whole-body movements). It loads the quads, hamstrings, glutes, and spinal muscles. It also loads the shoulder and upper-back muscles. There are two dead-lift styles: traditional and sumo. While most power lifters use the sumo style, people interested in overall shaping and

conditioning should use the traditional style because it works the quads and glutes better.

The technique: Stand with your feet flat on the floor, shoulder-width apart and toes pointed slightly outward. Squat down and grasp the bar using either a dead-lift (right palm one way, left palm the other) or pronated (palms toward body) grip. Keep your back flat, chest up and out, arms straight, and eyes focused ahead. Lift the bar by extending your knees and hips. During the lift, maintain a flat back and straight arms, and keep the weight close to your body. Pull up the weight to a standing position. Slowly return the weight to the starting position, taking great care to keep your back straight.

You can also do dead lifts on a Smith machine. Put the weight on the lowest level of the machine. Perform the lift in the same manner just described.

Back Extensions, Exercise Machines

Weak back muscles are easily injured when you do squats and pulling exer-

Superman on the exercise ball

Dead lift (a)

Dead lift (b)

cises (e.g., cleans and snatches). So, if your weight-training program includes these exercises, it's a good idea to add low-back exercises. Back extensions help to stabilize the spine and prevent fatigue when you're standing and exercising in the upright posture.

The technique: The instructions vary with the machine. For most equipment, sit on the seat, place your upper legs under the large thigh-support pads and your back on the back roller pad, and plant your feet firmly on the platform (starting position). Placing your hands on your abdomen, extend backward until your back is straight; then return to the starting position. Try to keep your spine rigid during the exercise.

BUILDING THE TRAPEZIUS

You've learned the principles of building massive lats, rhomboids, and

low-back muscles. Now let's round off your back by building your trapezius—the major surface muscle of the upper back.

The traps make up much of the muscle mass of the upper body, yet most active people neglect to do exercises to develop them. Include these exercises as part of your back routine, and you will be amazed at how fast you gain and the positive changes that occur in your physique. A bonus is that you will balance the muscle development in your upper body and help keep your shoulder joints pain free.

The trapezius is one of the largest muscles in the upper body and—when well developed—sticks out prominently on the back of the neck and upper trunk. This large, diamond-shaped muscle attaches at the top of the neck and spreads to the shoulder attachment along the collarbone (clavicle) and down to the middle of your back, tying in your shoulder and lat. Like the lat, the trapezius has an irregular shape. Traps allow you to turn and tilt your head, raise and twist your arms, and shrug or fix your shoulders. Traps are also important posture muscles that support the upper spine. The muscles shrug, squeeze together, and depress the shoulder blades (scapulae).

The trapezius muscles are divided into three regions. The upper part allows you to shrug your shoulders. The middle and lower parts help move your shoulder blades during rowing movements. Building well-developed traps helps balance the muscles in the front of your upper body—the pecs and the deltoids. This helps to improve posture and reduce the risk of injury by preventing unbalanced stress on the shoulder joint. As discussed, if you work the front of the body such as the chest and front deltoids, do an equal amount of work on the back—the traps, lats, and posterior deltoids.

You use the trapezius when you lift a weight upward using your shoulders. Anytime your arms go below horizontal, as well, you get assistance from your traps. They also come into play as stabilizers during major lifts of the upper body, such as the bench press, overhead or military press, and incline press. In addition, the traps are important when you're doing back rows and posterior (backward) lateral raises. Electromyography studies show that shrugs and their variations are the best exercises for building the traps. As explained earlier, EMG is a measure of the electrical activity in muscle—the greater the electrical activity, the greater the muscle activation.

Recommended exercises for developing the trapezius include barbell shrugs and reverse barbell shrugs on the Smith machine.

Barbell Shrugs

While shrugs are the best way to develop the traps, you should never roll your shoulders when doing shrugs

Barbell shrug (a)

Barbell shrug (b)

because this can cause tendonitis of the rotator cuff muscles.

The technique: From a standing position with arms extended, hold a barbell with your palms toward the body (pronated grip). Shrug your shoulders toward your ears, hold the contraction, and return to the starting position.

Reverse Barbell Shrugs on the Smith Machine

Adjust the bar on the Smith machine so that you can grasp it with your arms bent slightly. Load the bar with an appropriate weight. Place the bar behind your back and grasp it at shoulder width. Unhook the bar from the machine and extend your arms fully. Holding the bar, shrug your shoulders toward your ears, hold the position for one to two seconds, return to the starting position, and repeat. When finished, hook the bar on the machine.

Other Exercises That Build the Traps

Large-muscle, whole-body exercises, such as cleans, snatches, and high pulls, are excellent techniques for building the trapezius. These exercises involve a dynamic shoulder shrug as part of the lift that overloads the traps.

"Olympic" lifts and their modifications should be part of the training programs of most power athletes. These exercises are described in Chapter 10.

EXERCISES FOR THE NECK

Most older weight-training books demonstrated exercises for the neck, while most recent books do not. Good neck strength is a demand for athletes in sports such as football, wrestling, and boxing. Unfortunately, many people who do neck exercises develop neck pain because they do the exercises incorrectly. As with the low-back muscles, neck endurance and stabilization take priority over strength for preventing neck pain and injury. Doing trapezius exercises as described in this chapter will help stabilize the neck without triggering neck injuries. Also, doing general range-of-motion exercises for the neck will help keep it pain free.

Several weight-machine manufacturers, such as Nautilus, make neck machines. Most health clubs no longer offer them. If you need a strong neck for sports, concentrate on repetitions before building strength. Take care to

---

BACK SUPER-SET ROUTINE

Do one set of each exercise, and then repeat the circuit within each group for a total of three sets for each exercise. For example, do one set of pull-ups, followed by a set of one-arm dumbbell rows, followed by back hyperextensions. Then do each exercise within the group two more times. Move to the next group of exercises and repeat.

Group	Exercise	Sets and Reps	Group	Exercise	Sets and Reps
1	Pull-ups with a wide grip	3 × 10 of each in sequence	3	Dumbbell pull-overs Bent over barbell rows	3 × 10 of each in sequence
	One-arm dumbbell rows				
	Back hyperextensions w/weight		4	Seated reverse barbell rows	3 × 10 of each in sequence
2	Wide-grip pull-downs on lat machine	3 × 10 of each in sequence		T-bar rows	
	Seated cable rows			One-arm dumbbell rows	
	Dead lifts on Smith machine				

do neck exercises slowly and strictly. Do not do exercises like neck bridges until you have very strong neck muscles. Bridges have the potential for causing serious neck injuries—particularly in young people with weak neck muscles.

Avoid doing neck circles. This exercise can cause excessive strain of the neck and may injure cervical disks. Rather, do range-of-motion exercises in single planes: flexion, extension (not hyperextensions), and lateral flexion to each side.

Neck range-of-motion exercise

10

Exercises for the Lower Body

"Run hard, be strong, think big!"
—Percy Cerutty, legendary track coach

The leg muscles are the largest and most powerful in the body. Powerful movements in most sports are initiated with the leg and hip muscles. Golfers, tennis players, pitchers, and shot-putters start with movement in their legs and finish the movement with their upper bodies. Those who fail to use the lower body effectively, relying instead on the weaker and more fragile upper-body muscles, perform inefficiently and are more prone to injury.

Most sports movements begin with the basic athletic position—bent legs and a low center of gravity, with hands in front.

This position allows easy movement in any direction and provides good stability. Movement is much easier and more effective if the lower-body muscles are strong and powerful.

This chapter discusses exercises for developing strength, power, and muscle shape in the lower body: multi-joint exercises, accessory leg-strengthening exercises, and advanced lifts. You will have stronger, more defined legs if you include some of these exercises in your program. See the table "Weight-Training Exercises

for Machines from Selected Manufacturers" in the Appendix for other exercises.

MULTI-JOINT LOWER-BODY EXERCISES

Multi-joint exercises involve movement in two or more joints. Squats and leg presses are multi-joint exercises that develop strength in the lower body, which can improve performance in most sports. They also increase strength, to a certain extent, in the back and abdominal muscles. The following exercises are featured in this section of the chapter:

- Squats
- Squats, Smith machine
- Front squats
- Hack squats
- Wall squats
- Leg presses, exercise machines
- Lunges

Squats
Many people avoid squats because of reports that deep knee bends

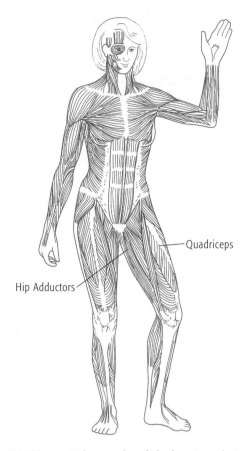

FIGURE 10.1 Major muscles of the legs (anterior)

Quadriceps

Hip Adductors

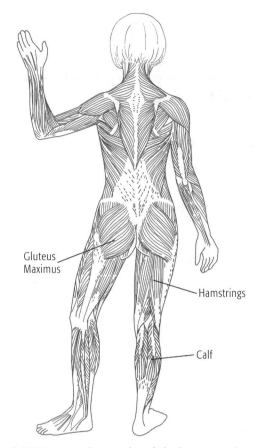

FIGURE 10.2 Major muscles of the legs (posterior)

Gluteus Maximus

Hamstrings

Calf

Basic athletic position

Caution: Never "bounce" at the bottom of the squat; this could injure the ligaments of your knee.

overstretch the knee ligaments. However, you can squat very low before the knee ligaments are stretched significantly. Good form is essential in this lift. Beginners often use too much weight; consequently, they bend their backs excessively during the lift and sometimes injure themselves.

Many experts recommend that people use a weight-lifting belt when doing squats with maximum weights. No belt is needed when warming up or doing lighter sets. Too many people rely on a belt to protect the back rather than concentrating on using good technique. You will not develop your back and trunk muscles if you always use a belt.

The technique: Begin the exercise standing with your feet shoulder-width apart and toes pointed slightly outward. Rest the bar on the back of your

Squat (a)

Squat (b)

shoulders, and hold it in that position with your hands. Keep your head up and lower back straight. Squat down (under control) until your thighs are approximately parallel with the floor and your butt is about one inch lower than your knees. Drive upward toward the standing position, keeping your back in a fixed position throughout the exercise. A general strategy for this lift is to go down slowly and up quickly.

Safety should be of primary concern. A good squat rack is a prerequisite. The rack should be sturdy and adjustable for people of different heights. Some racks have a safety bar at the bottom that can be used if the lift cannot be completed. Two spotters are also required—one standing on each side of the lifter, prepared to assist in case the person fails to complete the lift. For maximum lifts, use a third spotter—standing behind the lifter. Some people wrap their knees and use weight-lifting shoes to provide added support. You can do many variations of this exercise to increase squatting power, such as power-rack squats and bench squats. Due to the high risk of injury, I do not recommend bench squats.

Caution: Bench squats can be dangerous: You may unintentionally slam down on the bench during the exercise and injure your spine.

Squats, Smith Machine

The squat on the Smith machine is done in the same way as the squat described previously. The machine is excellent for doing squats because it helps keep your back in a good position. Perform squats on the Smith machine in the same way as with free weights. If you are experiencing back pain, step forward slightly so that you are leaning slightly into the bar. This will take pressure off your low back.

Front Squats

The front squat is a variation of the squat and is used mainly in the training programs of Olympic-style weight lifters. (Olympic-style weight lifting is a form of competitive weight lifting; power lifting is the other kind.) This lift is better for isolating the leg muscles than the regular squat, because the back cannot be used as much to assist in the movement; consequently, you cannot lift as much weight in this exercise.

The technique: Standing with your feet shoulder-width apart and toes pointed slightly outward, hold the bar on your chest and squat down until your gluteals are one inch lower than your knees. Do this exercise with good control because you can easily lose your balance. You can improve stability by wearing weight-lifting shoes.

Front squat

Hack Squats

Hack squats isolate the thigh muscles more than squats do because they force you to keep your back straighter—even more so than during front squats. This exercise is generally used as an auxiliary to squats rather than as the primary leg exercise.

The technique: In a standing position, hold a barbell behind you, with your arms fully extended down so that the weight rests on the backs of your

Hack squat (a)

Hack squat (b)

thighs. Slowly squat until the weight nearly reaches the ground; then push up to the starting position.

Wall Squats

The wall squat is an excellent exercise for your thigh muscles that requires no equipment. It is a particularly good exercise for ski conditioning.

The technique: Lean against a wall and bend your knees as though you were sitting in a chair. Support your weight with your legs. Begin by holding that position for 5 to 10 seconds. Build up to a minute or more.

Leg Presses, Exercise Machines

Leg presses are done on leg-press exercise machines and can be substituted for squats. They are safer and more convenient than squats because they don't involve handling weight, they place less stress on the back, and they don't require a spotter. Leg presses, however, are less effective than squats for developing strength in the quadriceps, gluteals, and hamstrings. Most manufacturers of weight-training equipment make leg-press machines.

Platform leg-press machine: Adjust the seat or lie on your back so that your knees are bent approximately 90 degrees when beginning the exercise (starting position). Push out forcefully

until your knees are fully extended; then return to the starting position.

Lunges

Lunges are a great exercise for the quadriceps (front of thigh), gluteus maximus (buttocks), and, to a lesser extent, the calf and lower-back muscles.

The technique: Stand with your feet shoulder-width apart. Hold a dumbbell in each hand, letting them hang by your side. Keep your arms parallel with your torso. Lunge forward with one leg, bending it until the thigh is parallel to the floor. The heel of the lead foot should stay on the ground. Do not shift your weight too far forward and let the knee move out past the toes. Repeat the exercise using the other leg. Keep your back and head as straight as possible and maintain control while performing the exercise.

AUXILIARY EXERCISES FOR THE LOWER BODY

Several accessory exercises for the lower body isolate distinct muscle groups, such as the quadriceps, hamstrings (back of thigh), and calf. Auxiliary exercises include the following:

Caution: Wall squats may cause pain under or around the kneecap. If you experience kneecap pain, particularly the day after doing the exercise, don't do this exercise, or decrease the time you stay in the squat position.

Leg press (a)   Leg press (b)

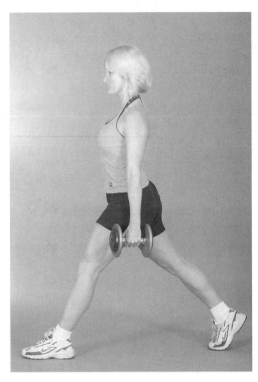

Lunge (a)

Lunge (b)

- Knee extensions (leg extensions)
- Knee flexions (leg curls)
- Heel raises
- Heel raises, leg-press machines

Knee Extensions (Leg Extensions)

Knee extensions are done on a knee-extension machine. Knee extensions are excellent for building the quadriceps muscle group and are good for supplementing squats or leg presses in the general program. Doing knee extensions with weighted boots is not recommended because it may strain the ligaments of the knee.

Doing knee extensions during the last 20 degrees of the range of motion (just before the knee is fully extended) builds up the muscle that tends to draw the kneecap toward the center of the joint. This exercise is often prescribed for people who have kneecap pain. Lumex, as part of its Eagle equipment line, makes a knee-extension machine that allows you to restrict the

motion done during the exercise. The Eagle knee-extension machine is available in many health clubs.

The technique: Sit on the knee-extension bench and place your shins on the knee-extension pads. Extend your knees until they are straight; then return to the starting position.

Knee Flexions (Leg Curls)

Knee flexions, more commonly known as leg curls, require the use of a leg-curl machine. This exercise is done in either a prone or standing position—depending on the machine. The upright leg-curl machines put the leg in a more functional position than the prone leg-curl machines do. Instructions for this exercise are similar for most leg-curl machines. This exercise develops the hamstrings, the muscles on the back of the thighs. Most sports build the quadriceps muscles, but few work on the hamstrings. Because injuries can be caused by imbalances

Caution: Knee extensions may cause kneecap pain. These exercises, particularly if done through a full range of motion, increase pressure on the kneecap and cause pain. If you have pain in your kneecaps either before or after doing this exercise, check with an orthopedic specialist before doing knee extensions.

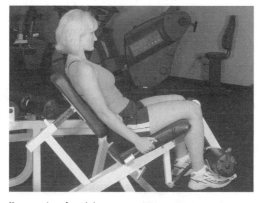

Knee extension (a)

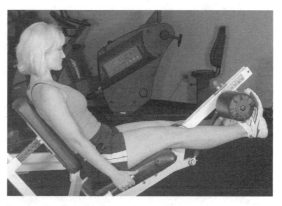

Knee extension (b)

Knee flexion (a)

Knee flexion (b)

between muscles, it is important to work on your hamstrings in addition to your quadriceps.

The technique: Lie on your stomach or stand, resting the pads of the machine just below your calf muscles. Flex your knees until they approach your buttocks; then return to the starting position (either one at a time or together, depending on the

machine). Because the hamstrings are weaker than the quadriceps, you will be unable to handle as much weight on this exercise as on the knee-extension machine.

Heel Raises

Heel raises strengthen the calf muscles—the soleus, gastrocnemius, and plantaris—and the Achilles ten-

Heel raise

don, which connects the calf muscles to the heel. These exercises can be done anywhere using a step or block of wood, or calf machine; they do not necessarily require weights.

The technique: Standing on the edge of a step or block of wood, with a barbell resting on your shoulders, slowly lower your heels as far as possible; then raise them until you are up on your toes. The calf muscles are strong and require much resistance to increase their size and strength. You can add calf exercises at the end of your squat or leg-press routine. Do some heel raises after your last repetition.

Most gyms have some kind of calf-exercise machine. Usually the machines are safer and easier to work with—you generally don't have to handle weights or worry about balance while carrying weights—and therefore

are more effective than doing heel raises. Calf-exercise machines may work the calf muscles from a standing or a seated position.

Heel Raises, Leg-Press Machines

For convenience, you can do heel raises on a leg-press machine immediately after doing leg presses.

The technique: Sit or lie in the leg-press machine and fully extend your legs (starting position). Press down with your toes and lift your heels; then return to the starting position. You can work different portions of the calf muscles by pointing your feet straight ahead, inward, and outward.

ADVANCED LIFTS AND FUNCTIONAL TRAINING TECHNIQUES

Popular with serious weight trainers, advanced lifts are complex exercises that take a considerable amount of time to learn. They are valuable because they develop strength from the basic athletic position and help improve strength and power for many sports. Advanced lifts include cleans, high pulls, and snatches.

Cleans and High Pulls

The clean is used to get the weight to the starting position for the overhead-press exercise (see "Overhead Press" in Chapter 6) or the jerk (part of the clean and jerk). It is an important exercise in the program of strength-speed athletes such as throwers, football players, multi-event athletes (e.g., decathletes and heptathletes), and volleyball and basketball players.

The technique: Place the bar on the floor in front of your shins. Keep your feet approximately 24 inches apart. Using a pronated grip, grasp the bar with your hands shoulder-width apart

Clean: starting position (a)

Clean: the pull (b)

Clean: the catch (c)

High pull

and squat, keeping your arms and back straight and your head up. Pull the weight up past your knees to your chest while your hips and shoulders move upward. After pulling the weight as high as you can, bend your knees suddenly and catch the bar on your chest at a level just above your collarbone. Stand up straight with the bar at chest level. Return the bar to the starting position.

The main power for this exercise should come from your hips and legs. Think of the middle phase of the lift as a vertical jump—this makes you drive up the weight with your legs rather than your arms.

Variations of this lift include the high pull, squat clean, and split clean.

The high pull is identical to the power clean except that you don't turn the bar over at the top of the lift and catch it at your chest. This procedure allows you to handle more weight and place less stress on your wrists and

forearms. The squat clean and split clean, which are beyond the scope of this book, are used in Olympic-style weight lifting.

Snatches

The snatch (an Olympic lift) is another pulling exercise that is fun and not that difficult for the novice to master.

The technique: Place the bar on the floor in front of your shins. Keep your feet approximately 24 inches apart. Using a pronated grip, grasp the bar with your hands as far apart as possible and squat, keeping your arms and back straight and your head up. Pull the weight up past your knees to your chest while your hips and shoulders move upward. After pulling the weight as high as you can, bend your knees suddenly and catch the bar overhead with your arms extended fully. Stand up straight with the bar overhead; return the bar to the floor under control.

Snatch: the starting position (a)

Snatch: the pull (b)

Snatch: the catch (c)

Functional Training Machines

Most modern weight machines isolate specific muscle groups, such as the chest, shoulder, upper back, or legs. While these machines are good for building muscle groups one at a time, they do little to build strength in several muscle groups at once—the way they are used in everyday movements and sports skills. Life Fitness's adjustable double-pulley machine requires that you do traditional exercises, such as chest presses and cable rowing, in a standing position. You must stabilize your legs, abdomen, and back to complete the lift. Functional training exercises develop strength and power you can use in sports and everyday activities.

Functional training machine (Life Fitness): standing chest press (a)

Functional training machine (Life Fitness): standing chest press (b)

Functional training machine (Life Fitness): standing row (a)

Functional training machine (Life Fitness): standing row (b)

11

Building Power and Speed

"The more I train, the more I realize I have more speed in me."
—Leroy Burrell, former world record holder of the 100m dash

Jumping and plyometric exercises rate high for building basic muscle strength, power, and speed. New research shows that they help build bone mass in girls and young women that will protect them against fractures as they age. These exercises are fun and challenging and make excellent additions to most people's programs.

Jumping exercises and plyometrics boost performance in sports because they increase leg power and train the nervous system to activate large-muscles groups quickly during movement. The exercises in this chapter enhance the capacity for single "explosive" movements, such as jumping, throwing a baseball or softball, and hitting a golf or tennis ball.

Plyometric exercises involve rapid stretching and then shortening of a muscle group during highly dynamic movements. The stretching causes a stretch reflex and elastic recoil in your muscles, which, combined with a vigorous muscle contraction, creates great force that overloads the muscles and increases strength and power.

Plyometrics range in difficulty from calf jumps off the ground to multiple one-leg jumps to and from boxes. Calf jumps are simple plyometric exercises

in which you jump in place repeatedly, using mainly your calf muscles. As you land after the first jump, you stretch your calf muscles as they help control your landing. The recoil from the stretch adds to the force of the muscle contraction used for the next jump.

The basic principle for all jumping and plyometric exercises is to absorb the shock with your arms or legs and then immediately contract your muscles. For example, if you're doing a series of squat jumps, as soon as you land after one jump, jump again as quickly as possible. The more quickly you jump, the more you overload your muscles. These exercises train your nervous system to react quickly.

In untrained people, the nervous system reacts slowly in turning on the muscles during repeated muscle contractions, such as occur during calf jumping. This is a protective reflex designed to prevent injury to the legs. With conditioning, you can train the nervous system to react more quickly and activate leg muscles rapidly. Stronger muscles and joints no longer need the protection of the reflex.

Jumping and plyometric exercises can cause great stress to your muscles, bones, and joints. All exercises in this chapter are considered moderate to high impact. It's essential to progress slowly. Don't do these exercises more than two or three days per week. If you feel pain in your muscles and joints for hours or days after a workout, modify your program or stop doing the exercises that give you trouble.

This chapter begins with simple, relatively low-impact exercises. More difficult exercises are presented in the later sections. Don't attempt advanced exercises until you are in good condition and can do the exercises without pain. Start off by doing one or two sets of about three or four exercises. As you become better conditioned, build up to three sets of 6 to 10 exercises. Do these exercises correctly and intensely. It is better to do only one set correctly than many sets incorrectly and at half speed.

Calf jump (a)

STATIONARY PLYOMETRICS

Start with these simple exercises before progressing to movements that place more stress on your muscles and joints. With these exercises, you jump to and from the same place on the ground or floor. More advanced exercises will progress to repeated distance jumps, and finally to box jumps.

Calf Jumps

This basic exercise helps develop jumping power in the calf muscles. This is an excellent beginning plyometric exercise.

The technique: Stand with your feet shoulder-width apart and hands on your hips. Bend your knees slightly. Using mainly your calf muscles, jump rapidly in place for 10 repetitions.

Advanced variations of this exercise include calf jump spins and one-leg calf jumps. With calf jump spins, attempt to spin as you jump, eventu-

Calf jump (b)

ally going 360 degrees between jumps. Do one-leg calf jumps the same way you do two-leg jumps, except lift one leg off the ground when doing the exercise.

Rope Skipping

Rope skipping is essentially the same as calf jumping, except that it is more vigorous. This is a recommended exercise for conditioning the nonoxidative energy system and developing jumping power, particularly in the calf muscles. Do this exercise using either the "boxer" or "playground" style. In boxer style, you use a short rope and jump by yourself. In playground style, two people swing the rope while you jump. For most people, boxer style is more practical.

Good jump ropes can be purchased at almost any sporting goods store. The best ones are made of leather with wooden handles and ball-bearing swivels. With these, the rope turns easily in the hands without tangling. Buy one that fits you: it shouldn't be so short that you can't turn the rope without hunching over during the exercise or so long that it's difficult to turn.

The technique: Hold one handle in each hand, with the rope behind you. Swing the rope over your head and jump over it when it reaches your feet. Continue swinging the rope and jumping over it. Speed up the tempo as your skill improves. Start off with 5 to 10 15-second segments and progress to 5 to 20 one-minute to three-minute segments.

As your skill improves, try some of the many rope-skipping variations. These include crossing your hands in front as you jump the rope and swinging the rope for two revolutions between jumps. You can also vary your foot movements so that they resemble running or dancing. Using a heavy rope or wearing a weighted vest increases the conditioning effect of rope skipping.

Squat Jumps

These are similar to calf jumps, except you bend your knees and squat in between jumps. This basic exercise is ideal for improving jumping power and is a fundamental part of any plyometric program.

The technique: Stand with your feet shoulder-width apart and bend your knees slightly. Jump up and drive your arms upward. As you land, retract your arms and squat down, and then jump back up again as quickly and explosively as possible. Do 5 to 10 repetitions per set.

Tuck Squat Jumps

Tuck squat jumps are similar to squat jumps but are more vigorous. You have to jump higher off the ground to perform the knee tuck and still achieve a balanced landing.

The technique: Stand with your feet shoulder-width apart and bend your knees slightly. Jump up and drive your arms upward. Tuck your knees underneath you as you reach the height of the jump. As you land, extend your legs and retract your arms and prepare to jump again. Do 5 to 10 repetitions, taking as little time as possible between jumps.

Mule-Kick Squat Jumps

This is another variation of squat jumps.

The technique: Stand with your feet shoulder-width apart and bend your knees slightly. Jump up and drive your arms upward. As you reach the height of the jump, kick your heels backward and touch the back of your thighs. As you land, extend your legs and retract your arms and prepare to jump again. Do 5 to 10 repetitions, taking as little time as possible between jumps.

Squat jump (a)

Squat jump (b)

Tuck squat jump

Mule-kick squat jump

360-Degree Squat Jumps

This exercise is another variation of squat jumps and is similar to the 360-degree calf jumps described earlier. It requires more fitness than most other squat jumps. Start with 45-degree to 90-degree turns and progress to 360-degree turns.

The technique: Stand with your feet shoulder-width apart and bend your knees slightly. Jump up and drive your arms upward, spinning in the air as much as possible. As you land, retract your arms and prepare to jump again. Start off by rotating in only one direction. As you become more advanced, rotate to the left on one repetition and to the right on the next. Do 5 to 10 repetitions, taking as little time as possible between jumps.

Advanced variations of this exercise include tuck 360s and mule-kick 360s.

360-degree squat jump (a)

360-degree squat jump (b)

360-degree squat jump (c)

One-Leg Squat Jumps

Don't do these until you have conditioned your legs with two-leg squat jumps. Progress slowly; if you feel ankle, knee, or hip pain after doing this exercise, cut down on the volume or eliminate it from your program.

The technique: Stand on one leg and bend your knee slightly. Jump up and drive your arms upward. As you land, retract your arms and immediately jump again. Do 5 to 10 repetitions, taking as little time as possible between jumps.

Advanced variations include one-leg tuck squat jumps, one-leg mule-kick squat jumps, and one-leg 360-degree squat jumps.

Ice-Skaters

This exercise is super for developing the thigh muscles for lateral movements and for stabilizing spinal muscles for dynamic movements. Make sure to use shoes that give good traction and choose an area that will give good footing.

The technique: Stand with your weight on the inside part of your feet. Using a speed-skating motion, drive off your left leg and swing both arms to the right, and then immediately drive with the right leg to the left. Move as quickly as possible when going from one leg to the other.

One variation is sand ice-skaters: do the ice-skater exercise in the sand. This is a good way to begin doing this exercise because it is less stressful to the knee, hip, and ankle joints. Another variation is to use angled boxes available from sporting goods companies. These wedge-shaped boxes allow better footing during the push-off phase and are popular with skaters and skiers. You can also do ice-skaters

Ice-skater (a)

One-leg squat jump

Ice-skater (b)

on a slide board. Slide boards are available commercially or can be manufactured cheaply using a piece of Formica and a wooden frame made from two-by-fours.

Lunge Jumps

The lunge or split jump builds your thigh, gluteal, and back muscles. It is a good exercise for developing striding power for sprinting and lower-body flexibility.

The technique: From a standing position, jump up, and land in a split position with your right leg bent and your left leg extended in back of you. After you land, immediately jump up again, and land in a split position with your legs reversed. One repetition occurs when each leg has been in the forward position. During this exercise, try to keep your body straight and jump as high as possible.

HORIZONTAL JUMPS AND HOPS

These more advanced exercises involve jumping and hopping horizontally.

They are excellent for developing basic leg power for jumping and running.

Standing Long Jumps

In addition to being excellent for increasing basic leg power, this is a good exercise for gauging your progress. Measure your standing long jump every few weeks. If you do speed and plyometric exercises regularly, you will be amazed at how rapidly you improve.

The technique: Stand with your feet shoulder-width apart and toes just behind the starting (scratch) line. Bend your knees and bring your hands below your waist; then jump as far as you can. Try to extend fully with your ankles, knees, hips, and arms to jump as far as possible.

Multiple Standing Long Jumps

This is similar to the last exercise, except that you take three jumps in succession.

The technique: Stand with your feet shoulder-width apart and toes just behind the starting (scratch) line. Bend your knees and bring your hands below your waist; then jump as far as

Lunge jump (a)

Lunge jump (b)

Standing long jump (a)

Standing long jump (b)

Standing long jump (c)

you can, extending fully with your ankles, knees, hips, and arms. As soon as you land, try to jump again as soon as possible. Repeat so that you have jumped three times.

Standing Triple Jumps

The triple jump is contested in track-and-field competitions. It used to be called the "hop, step, and jump," which describes its basic movements.

The technique: Stand with your feet shoulder-width apart and toes just behind the starting (scratch) line. Bend your knees and bring your hands below your waist; then hop as far as you can on one leg, extending fully with your ankles, knees, hips, and arms. Land on the same leg, and then step vigorously with the other leg. As you land, immediately jump with that leg and complete the exercise. A sequence might be to hop with the right leg, extend and land on the left leg (step), and then complete the jump with the left leg.

Skiers

Skiers are good for Alpine and cross-country skiers, skaters, and people who must change direction rapidly when running.

The technique: Stand with your feet together. Keeping your feet together, jump forward and to the left side; after you land, jump forward and to the right. You have done one repetition when you've jumped to the left and right sides. Jump as quickly as possible for 5 to 10 repetitions.

Four Squares

This exercise also helps build leg power for lateral movements. It is called four squares because you move forward, backward, and to the sides in box-like movements.

The technique: Keeping your feet together, jump in various patterns to the front, back, and sides. For example, jump front, back, left, and right; repeat. Many combinations are possible.

Cone Hops

This exercise is similar to the multiple standing long jumps, except you try to jump for height over the cones as well as for distance.

Space three to six two-foot cones (or similar objects) approximately

Skier (a)

Skier (b)

Four squares (a)

Four squares (b)

Cone hop (a)

Cone hop (b)

three feet apart. Stand in front of the first cone with your feet shoulder-width apart. Jump over the cones as quickly as possible.

Hurdle Hops

This is an advanced form of cone hops using hurdles. Don't attempt this exercise unless you are well conditioned and have good jumping ability and technique. If the hurdles have adjustable stabilization weights, make sure they are set so that the hurdle falls down easily if hit. You can construct small hurdles from PVC pipe. These are safer for the beginner.

The technique: Place three to five hurdles approximately three feet apart. Start with the hurdle at its lowest height (hurdles are adjustable). Keeping your feet shoulder-width apart, hop over the hurdles as quickly as possible using both legs.

Hurdle hop

UPPER-BODY POWER EXERCISES: BOUNCE PUSH-UPS

You can do bounce push-ups against a wall or steeplechase hurdle or on the floor. These exercises are excellent for developing pushing power in the upper body.

Wall Bounce Push-Ups

These are the simplest, least stressful push-ups. Start with these until your muscles and joints become accustomed to the stress of upper-body plyometric exercise.

The technique: Lean against a wall or steeplechase hurdle at a 45- to 60-degree angle. Push up forcefully; then allow yourself to go back against the wall and absorb your fall with your arms. Immediately push off again.

Floor Bounce Push-Ups

These are much more stressful and difficult than wall push-ups. Don't attempt these until you can do at least 10 to 15 push-ups. They can be done from a regular or modified push-up position. In the modified push-up position, you rest your weight on your knees instead of your toes.

The technique: From a standard or modified push-up position, push up forcefully, extending your elbows fully until your hands leave the floor. Bounce back to your hands; then repeat the exercise.

Clap Bounce Push-Ups

Do this exercise as described for floor bounce push-ups, adding a clap after your hands leave the floor. In this sequence, you push up and leave the floor, clap your hands, bounce back to the push-up position, and repeat.

One-Arm Push-Ups

This difficult exercise was popularized in the movie *Rocky*. Do it the same way as floor bounce push-ups, except use only one arm. Start off in a modified push-up position and graduate to the full push-up position when you gain the necessary strength and power to do the exercise.

Floor bounce push-up: starting position (a)

Floor bounce push-up: drive forcefully (b)

Clap bounce push-up

BOX JUMPING

Box jumping involves jumping to and from boxes, benches, or steps. Landing creates much more stress to the muscles and joints, so you should attempt these exercises only after doing exercises in which you jump to and from the ground or floor. Box height varies from approximately six inches to five feet. Start off with smaller boxes and progress slowly to higher ones. As with other plyometric exercises, the object is to attempt to jump as soon as possible after you land.

Step-Downs

Step-downs are the simplest, least stressful type of box jump. Begin with a low box, approximately one to two feet high. This exercise progresses from simply stepping down from the box and absorbing the shock with your legs and then vigorously jumping into the air. Finally, you progress to jumping

between a series of boxes as quickly as possible.

Phase 1—Step-down: Stand on a box or bench with your feet shoulder-width apart, knees bent, and spine erect. Step off and land with bent knees.

Phase 2—Step-down, jump-up: Stand on a box or bench with your feet shoulder-width apart, knees bent, and spine erect. Step off and land with bent knees, and then immediately jump up in the air using both legs and arms.

Phase 3—Repeat step-down, jump-up: Place three to six boxes or benches approximately three feet apart. Jump from the first box to the ground or floor, then up to the next box, then to the ground, and so forth. Jump as quickly as possible between boxes.

Standing Long Jumps from a Box

These are similar to the standing long jumps described earlier, except that they stress your legs much more when

Step-down (a)

Step-down (b)

Step-down, jump-up

you land. This exercise is sometimes called "depth jumping."

The technique: Stand on a box or bench with your feet shoulder-width apart. Jump as far as possible, fully extending your ankles, knees, hips, and arms and landing with bent knees. As your fitness improves you can increase the height of the box. A variation of this exercise is to land and then immediately perform a standing long jump.

Ski Box Jumps

This exercise is similar to the skiers described earlier, except that you jump to and from a box as you jump side-to-side.

The technique: Stand to the side of a box or bench. With your feet together, jump up vigorously onto the box, then immediately jump down on the other side, then jump back onto the box, then jump back to the starting position, and so on.

Step-down, jump-up with multiple boxes

Standing long jump from a box (a)

Standing long jump from a box (b)

Standing long jump from a box (c)

Single-Leg Jump-Ups

This exercise is excellent for isolating powerful thigh muscles and is great for developing jumping power in activities involving a single-leg takeoff (layup in basketball, jumping for a ball when running, etc.).

The technique: Stand to the side of a box or bench and place your foot on the top of it. Drive hard with your leg and extend fully with your ankle, knee, and hip and jump into the air; land on the box and return to the starting position, and then repeat immediately.

MEDICINE BALL EXERCISES

A medicine ball resembles a basketball in size but is heavier and softer. It is usually made of leather. However, newer ones are sometimes made of rubber, and some even have handles. Medicine balls weigh between 2 and 20 pounds. Because of their weight, they are excellent for plyometrics. When you catch a medicine ball, your muscles stretch and contract eccentrically as you attempt to slow down and control the ball. You can do medicine ball exercises by yourself or with a partner.

Play Catch with Yourself

Do this exercise with the ball starting from your chest, behind your neck, or at your waist. This is a good whole-body exercise because you must use your legs, arms, and trunk for proper execution.

The technique: Stand with your feet shoulder-width apart and hold the ball with both hands at chest level. Vigorously press the ball overhead with both hands until it flies into the air straight above you. Use your legs to help push the ball overhead. Catch the ball with both hands and then immediately throw it into the air again. Repeat.

One variation is the behind-the-neck catch. Stand with your feet shoulder-width apart and hold the ball behind your head with both hands. Vigorously press the ball overhead with both hands until it flies into the air straight above you. Use your legs to help push the ball overhead. Catch the ball behind your head with both hands

Ski box jump (a)

Ski box jump (b)

Ski box jump (c)

and then immediately throw it into the air again. Repeat. Don't do this exercise if you have shoulder problems. Start with a lightweight ball (two to five pounds) and progress to a heavier one.

Another variation is the waist-high catch. Stand with your feet shoulder-width apart and place your hands under the ball at waist level. Vigorously push the ball overhead with both hands until it flies into the air straight above you. Use your legs to help push the ball overhead. Catch the ball with both hands and then immediately throw it into the air again. Repeat. As you become accustomed to this exercise, jump into the air as you throw the ball; land and catch the ball; and repeat.

Medicine Ball or Shot-Put Throws

You can also develop power by throwing a medicine ball or shot in various ways. Exercises include overhead, underhand, and side-rotation throws.

The overhead throw involves throwing a medicine ball or shot-put over your head, behind you. Try to throw the object as far overhead as possible. Extend fully with the ankles, knees, hips, and arms, and jump as you throw the ball.

The front waist throw is an underhand throw initiated at the waist. Bend your knees. Lower the ball between your knees and throw the ball or shot-put in front of you.

For the waist throw to the side, hold the ball or shot-put in both hands. Rotate to the right and throw the object as far as possible by rotating in the opposite direction. Try to transfer your weight from the rear foot to the front foot during the throw. Repeat the exercise on the other side of the body.

Chest Passes

Chest passes develop the pushing muscles in the upper body. They also strengthen the muscles of the trunk and lower body.

Play catch with yourself (a)

Play catch with yourself (b)

The technique: Stand with one foot in front of the other, with knees bent slightly, approximately 6 to 10 feet from a partner. Hold the ball in both hands at chest level and throw it to your partner using a motion similar to a basketball chest pass. Your partner should catch the ball and immediately throw it back to you. The catching motion should blend with the throwing motion in a semicircular pattern. You can also do this exercise from a kneeling position if you want to isolate the upper-body muscles.

Overhead throw (a)

Overhead throw (b)

Medicine ball chest pass

Overhead Passes

This is an excellent exercise for developing power in your triceps and shoulder muscles. Beware of this exercise if you have shoulder problems.

The technique: Kneel facing your partner, approximately 6 to 10 feet apart. Hold the ball in both hands behind your head. Throw the ball forward over your head so that your partner catches it with arms extended overhead. Your partner then retracts the ball overhead and throws it back to you.

Medicine Ball Sit-Ups

Two athletes can do this exercise together, or you can do it by yourself with a spotter. Don't attempt to do this exercise until you have conditioned your abdominal and back muscles with standard exercises (crunches, back extensions, etc.). This exercise is not appropriate for people who have back pain.

The technique: Two athletes sit facing each other with knees bent, feet flat on the floor, and one person holding the medicine ball. Partners should be as close together as possible. Both people lean backward, with hands overhead, until their backs reach the floor. Then both sit up at the same time. As the person with the ball reaches the top of the sit-up, he or she tosses the ball to the other person. Repeat the exercise, with the ball being tossed back and forth at the top of each sit-up. The sequence for each person is as follows: Sit-up with ball, throw ball to partner, sit-up without ball, catch ball from partner, repeat.

To do this exercise with a spotter, follow the technique for the two-person sit-ups except that a spotter or coach stands three to five feet away. At the top of the sit-up, toss the ball to the spotter and complete the sit-up. When you return to the top of the sit-up, the spotter throws the ball for

you to catch. The sequence is as follows: sit-up with ball, throw ball to spotter, sit-up without ball, catch ball from spotter, repeat.

OTHER EXERCISES TO DEVELOP SPEED AND POWER

Variations of plyometric exercises are limited only by your imagination. Obviously, you can't include all the

Medicine ball sit-up (a)

Medicine ball sit-up (b)

Medicine ball sit-up (c)

exercises presented here in your exercise program. Choose those whose movements most closely resemble your favorite sports. In general, choose about 6 to 12 speed and power exercises and integrate them into a program that includes cardiovascular, strength, and flexibility exercises.

Remember, the gains you make from these exercises will not transfer automatically to increased power in sports. You have to practice the skill and gradually integrate your increased power into your movements. If you work consistently on sports skills and do exercises to increase strength and power, you will eventually become more powerful in your sport.

Sprint Starts

These are a top choice for developing power and acceleration capacity in the legs. The photo sequence shows proper sprint starting technique. The athlete in this sequence is a world-class sprinter. Notice the phenomenal extension he gets as he bursts from the blocks. Training to develop this kind of "explosive" strength may carry over to

other sports requiring power and speed.

When working on sprint starts, it's best to use starting blocks; however, they are not absolutely necessary. If you are a football player, do sprint starts from the football stance. If you are a tennis player, soccer player, or baseball player, do some of your starts from the ready position for your sport. The ready position is your waiting position before you initiate a movement.

"On your marks" position: Your feet are staggered 10 to 14 inches apart, with your front foot approximately 20 inches from the starting line. Try to relax in this position

"Set" position: Raise your back and hips. Your front leg bends about 90 degrees and your rear leg 120 degrees. Right-handed people generally start with the left foot forward. Your back is flat, and your hips are slightly higher than your shoulders. You contact the ground with your fingertips, which raises your shoulders as high as possible. Don't put too much weight on your fingertips.

Sprint start: on your marks (a)

Sprint start: get set (b)

Sprint start: go! (c)

"Go": Raise your shoulders so that you can direct force with your driving (front) leg through the length of your body. Drive the front leg fully so that your body forms a straight line from your hip to your heel. Push your rear foot hard against the block or ground as you drive your knee forward. As you drive forward, the arm on the side of the front foot drives straight forward, while the other arm drives straight backward. Both arms are bent approximately 90 to 110 degrees. Try to extend fully with your hips and knees and use your arms dynamically during the driving phases of the movement. After the start, run as fast as possible for three to five strides.

Begin with 3 sprint starts and progress to 10 to 20 starts as fitness increases. After a few weeks, have someone time your starts so that you can gauge your progress.

Harness Sprinting

Harness sprinting builds leg and core strength. It involves wearing a harness around your waist and pulling a weight sled, truck tire, or another person who's providing resistance. Vary the speed and resistance: the more resistance, the slower the speed, and vice versa.

Stadium Stairs

Running stairs is a tried-and-true technique for developing leg power. It overloads your body during the sprinting motion. The local football stadium is often a great place to do this exercise.

Find some unobstructed stairs that will support your weight. Beware of fields with old wooden seats that could collapse when you run on them. The number of repetitions will vary with the size of the stadium. Running up and down the stairs at a major university's football stadium will be much more difficult than at the local high school. As with other kinds of sprint exercises, start conservatively and build the intensity and duration as your fitness improves.

Variations of stadium stair running include running two steps at a time, hopping up the stairs on one or two

Harness sprinting

legs, and hopping up the stairs using a side-to-side motion. Most people should not hop down stairs because it is too dangerous. The latter is a good exercise for Alpine skiers. Advanced people can increase the resistance by doing stadium stair exercises while wearing a weighted vest. These are available at sporting goods stores and through track-and-field supply catalogs.

Be careful when running or hopping on stadium stairs, particularly when going down the stairs. You can easily lose your balance and get seriously injured. Stop if you find yourself losing your balance or equilibrium. Also, stair climbing may not be a good idea if you have kneecap pain. The exercise, particularly going down stairs, produces a lot of pressure on your kneecaps. If you have kneecap

pain the next day or several hours after running stadium stairs, cut down on your training volume or eliminate the exercises from your program.

Stair-climbing machines, while excellent for developing cardiovascular endurance, are less effective than running stadium stairs for developing lower-body power. Doing stadium stairs, you force your legs to extend vigorously during the push-off phase of the running stride and absorb shock as you land. This develops dynamic strength in your legs that is not possible using a stair-climbing machine, which requires minimal stride length and little or no impact.

High Knees, Fast Arms

This exercise is among the best for developing sprint power. It helps increase stride frequency, one of two

Stadium stairs

factors determining sprint speed (the other being stride length). Do this exercise on a grass field or wooden gym floor to minimize impact. This is a maximum-intensity exercise. I see athletes going through the motions on this exercise every day. It is better to do one set of 10 seconds at maximum effort than 10 sets of 20 seconds at 50 percent effort. This exercise works only if you do it at maximum intensity.

The technique: Simulating a sprint motion in a nearly stationary position, pump your arms and lift your knees as fast as possible. Try to complete 20 strides in only 10 yards. Begin with 3 repetitions (3 sets of 10 yards) and progress to 10 to 20 repetitions.

Bounding Strides

This exercise helps build stride length for sprinting. Rather than take many strides in a short distance, as in the preceding exercise, you attempt to take as few strides as possible over a longer distance.

The technique: Do this exercise on a grass field or running track over a distance of 50 to 100 yards. Stride as long as possible (i.e., take large steps), moving your arms vigorously in synchrony with your legs. Your strides should resemble bounding jumps. Begin with 2 or 3 repetitions and progress to 10 repetitions.

INTEGRATING POWER TRAINING INTO WORKOUTS

Power training requires the athlete to exercise at maximum intensity. This is the only way to overload the large, fast motor units. This training is very effective and will improve your power in sports, provided you also practice the skill. Because this training is extremely high intensity, there is a higher risk of injury. Also, it is easy to overtrain. Overtraining is an imbalance between training and recovery. Athletes get overtrained when they don't get

High knees, fast arms

Bounding strides (a)

Bounding strides (b)

enough rest between workouts or the workouts are too hard.

Start off gradually and progress slowly. Choose one or two of these exercises and add more as you get in better shape. Gauge the appropriateness of your workouts by how you feel the next day. If you are extremely sore for one or two days after a power workout, then you have done too much. In other words, listen to your body.

Peak-Power Weight Training

You can also use the peak-power training technique with weight training. This method involves lifting a relatively light weight as quickly as possible. Calculate your peak power output for five repetitions of an exercise. In general, use a weight that is 50 percent to 60 percent of the maximum weight you can lift for one repetition. Time how long it takes you to do five repetitions. Do the lift as rapidly as possible. It's essential to use good lifting technique with this method.

Calculate the peak-power workout weight for your lift. The example shown in Table 11.1 is for the bench press. In this example, the lifter can bench-press 300 pounds for one repetition. Begin with a weight that's 40 percent to 45 percent of your best one-rep lift. It's a good idea to use a rubber bounce pad on the bar to protect yourself from injury. Time how long it takes to bench-press five reps, lifting the weight as rapidly as possible. Don't cheat on the lift; go all the way down and all the way up. Repeat this procedure for weights that are 50, 60, and 70 percent of your one-rep maximum bench press. Your workout weight will be the one that renders the highest pounds per second.

In this example, peak power output was at 50 percent of maximum. Your workout weight should be 150 to 170 pounds. You would use more or less weight depending on the maximum weight you can do for your one rep. Do three to five sets of five repetitions at that weight, pushing the weight as quickly as possible. Increase your weight when you can do your sets in less than five to six seconds. This is a highly effective training technique that produces rapid gains in strength and power.

Table 11.1 CALCULATING TRAINING WEIGHT FOR PEAK-POWER TRAINING

Instructions: Do five timed reps at 45, 50, 60, and 70 percent of your one-rep maximum and calculate pounds per second.

Example: 1-rep max bench press = 300 pounds

Percent Max	Weight (pounds)	Reps	Total Weight for 5 Reps (pounds)	Time to Complete 5 Reps (seconds)	Weight per Second (total weight/time)
45	135	5	675	4.5	150
50	150	5	750	4.8	156.3 = peak power
60	180	5	900	6	150
70	210	5	1,050	8.5	123.5

12

Sports Nutrition

"Obstacles are those frightening things that become visible
when we take our eyes off our goals."
–Henry Ford

Food is critical for performance because it provides energy and nutrients for cells and tissues. Optimal nutrition not only prevents disease but also keeps the body working at maximum efficiency. Sound nutrition helps you perform better in sports and daily activities and helps keep you healthy and disease free.

We are flooded with dietary information seeking to improve our eating habits. Dietary labels on containers and packaging list the nutritional contents of the foods we eat. Diet books preach the latest weight-loss methods. Sports nutrition companies promote the newest formulas for improving performance. This barrage of often conflicting information is confusing. We need to clear up that confusion because good nutrition is fundamental for good health, appearance, and performance.

Poor diet is linked to many degenerative diseases. Proper diet can help prevent an array of health problems, such as coronary artery disease, some cancers, diabetes, and obesity. Dietary factors such as fat, fiber, and vitamins greatly affect your health, longevity, and well-being.

Most people want to have a healthy, lean-looking body. You will probably never achieve this goal unless you pay attention to your diet. If you eat calorie-dense, fatty foods, it will be difficult to develop the kind of body you want—no matter how much you exercise. Combine sensible eating and exercise habits to get the kind of body you want.

Sports and exercise performance depend on a good diet. The energy to run, jump, throw, and even rest comes from the foods we eat. Active people need a good diet to exercise and play sports effectively. Knowing what to eat and when can determine whether you are running on empty during the day or have plenty of energy to work and play.

Many active people search for a magic nutritional formula to help them feel and perform better and control their weight. Consequently, they often take food supplements and drugs in the hope of reaching their goals. The performance nutrition industry is extremely competitive and markets a wide variety of products that promise to build muscle, enhance performance, and help people attain the perfect body. How do you separate reality from hype?

This chapter presents an overview of nutritional principles for health and performance. Topics include the elements of the healthy, high-performance diet; diet and weight control; and food supplements and performance-enhancing drugs.

ESSENTIAL NUTRIENTS

The six types of essential nutrients you need in your diet are fats, carbohydrates, proteins, vitamins, minerals, and water. The body either doesn't produce these or makes them in insufficient quantities. You must include each component in your diet to stay alive and healthy.

The body gets energy from fats, carbohydrates, and proteins, while vitamins, minerals, and water help regulate the energy processes. Nutrients drive metabolism—the total of all the chemical reactions occurring in your body. Running, jumping, throwing, skiing, and walking require energy supplied by food. Proteins and fats are also used to make body structures such as muscle, bone, and cell membranes.

Energy

The ability to convert chemical energy from fuels to muscle energy (muscle contraction) largely determines exercise performance and physical fitness. As you deplete your body's energy stores, you fatigue rapidly, and performance decreases. Active people fight fatigue by taking in enough high-quality calories in their diet and replacing vital energy stores in muscles and the liver. Athletes work at high energy levels, so they need to eat a high-performance diet.

Fats provide the most energy, nine calories (also called kilocalories, abbreviated kcal) per gram, while carbohydrates and proteins each supply four calories per gram. Alcohol, which is not an essential nutrient, supplies seven calories per gram. During the past 15 years, experts have advised people to cut down on the fats they eat. High-fat diets, in addition to being extremely high in calories, increase the risk of a variety of diseases. Some new studies show that people lose weight faster on low-carbohydrate, high-fat, high-protein diets. While that may be true in the short run, these diets are inappropriate for people involved in sports or high-intensity exercise training.

The average adult needs about 2,200 calories per day. Adults who are physically active or larger than normal need more—2,800 calories or more for women and 3,400 calories for men. When you take in more calories than you use through metabolism or exercise, you will store the excess calories as fat.

Energy intake is important, even among people trying to lose weight. Starving yourself and overexercising can adversely affect your health, decrease performance, and make you feel miserable. When you're trying to lose weight, the best strategy is to decrease your caloric intake slightly and lose weight slowly. Weight-loss principles are discussed later in this chapter.

Most people take in more than enough energy to supply their needs. Overeating is a main reason so many people are overweight. However, underconsumption can be a problem in extremely active people. Nutritional studies of athletes show that the majority do not take in enough calories. Calories are the most important nutritional factor for exercise performance. Inadequate caloric intake can lead to loss of body weight and muscle mass, depletion of carbohydrate stores in the muscles and liver, and sometimes low blood sugar during training.

Fats

Fats are the most energy-rich food source. Fats—also called lipids—are mainly found in adipocytes (fat cells). You also store small amounts of fat in other cells, such as skeletal muscle. Many people try to carry as little fat as possible. However, it is far from being a useless tissue: it's the body's main energy-storage depot. It also protects and insulates your internal organs, composes parts of vital structures such as cell membranes, and serves as a building block for many important hormones. Dietary fats help you absorb some vitamins and serve as a vital energy source for most tissues in the body. In addition, they help regulate several essential body functions, such as blood pressure.

Among the several types of fats, the most important are triglycerides and cholesterol. Triglycerides are composed of glycerol and three fatty acids. Fatty acids are classified according to their structure as saturated, monounsaturated, or polyunsaturated. Fats are called saturated if they contain high amounts of saturated fatty acids. High-saturated-fat foods include meats, such as hamburger, steak, and lunch meats; cheese; butter; and whole milk.

Monounsaturated and polyunsaturated fats come from plants, such as olives, peanuts, corn, soybeans, and sunflowers. Palm and coconut oil, although from plant sources, are highly saturated. Food manufacturers can also "hydrogenate" vegetable fats, which involves adding hydrogen atoms to the fats, to make them saturated. They do this to improve the texture of food and to increase the shelf life of their products.

Very dangerous forms of fats are trans fats, which are mainly contained in solid or semisolid margarines and commercial cooking oils used in many processed foods. The liquid oils go through the hydrogenation process.

This makes the oils solid and helps preserve them. The trans fats made through this process increase cholesterol levels. The only way to avoid trans fats is to examine food labels and avoid foods that include "hydrogenated fat" and "partially hydrogenated fat." Nutritionists recommend that you avoid trans fats completely.

Most people consume 30 percent to 40 percent of their calories as fat. The body needs only a small fraction of this—about a tablespoon of vegetable oil a day. A high-fat diet increases serum cholesterol, a leading risk factor for coronary heart disease and some types of cancer. Nutritionists recommend that fat intake be less than 30 percent of the calories you eat; some recommend even lower levels.

Restrict the amount of saturated fats in your diet. Better fat sources include olive oil, which is high in monounsaturated fatty acids, and most kinds of fish (e.g., salmon, trout, and mackerel), which are high in omega-3 fatty acids. Omega-3 fatty acids are thought to reduce the risk of coronary heart disease. Consumer information on labels makes it relatively easy to track your fat intake.

The most telling item to look for on the label is percentage of calories from fat. (See Figure 12.1.) Try to stick with foods in which fat constitutes no more than 30 percent of the total calories. You don't have to be fanatical. Fats add flavor to food; a hearty meal in a French restaurant would hardly be the same without some fats. Moderation is the key. If one food or meal contains more fat than is desirable, balance it with food or a meal containing less than 30 percent fat. The overriding goal is to keep fat content in the diet at no more than 30 percent of the total calories.

Carbohydrates

Carbohydrates are the high-performance fuel. They are the most

KNOW THE DIFFERENT TYPES OF FAT

Saturated Fats

Foods high in saturated fats tend to raise blood cholesterol. These foods include high-fat dairy products (e.g., cheese, whole milk, cream, butter, and regular ice cream), fatty fresh and processed meats, the skin and fat of poultry, lard, palm oil, and coconut oil. Keep your intake of these foods low.

Dietary Cholesterol

Foods that are high in cholesterol also tend to raise blood cholesterol. These foods include liver and other organ meats, egg yolks, and dairy fats.

Trans-Fatty Acids

Foods high in trans-fatty acids likewise tend to raise blood cholesterol. These foods include those high in partially hydrogenated vegetable oils, such as many hard margarines and shortenings. Foods with a high amount of these ingredients include some commercially fried foods and some bakery goods.

Unsaturated Fats

Unsaturated fats (oils) do not raise blood cholesterol. Unsaturated fats occur in vegetable oils, most nuts, olives, avocados, and fatty fish like salmon. Unsaturated oils include both monounsaturated fats and polyunsaturated fats. Olive, canola, sunflower, and peanut oils are some of the oils high in monounsaturated fats. Vegetable oils such as soybean oil, corn oil, and cottonseed oil and many kinds of nuts are good sources of polyunsaturated fats. Some fish, such as salmon, tuna, and mackerel, contain omega-3 fatty acids, which are being studied to determine if they offer protection against heart disease. Use moderate amounts of food high in unsaturated fats, taking care to avoid excess calories.

Source: U.S. Department of Agriculture, "Nutrition and Your Health: Dietary Guidelines for Americans," Home and Garden Bulletin No. 232, fifth edition, 2000.

Start here →

Nutrition Facts

Serving Size 1 cup (228g)
Serving Per Container 2

Amount Per Serving	
Calories 250	Calories from Fat 110
	% Daily Value*
Total Fat 12g	**18%**
Saturated Fat 3g	**15%**
Cholesterol 30mg	**10%**
Sodium 470mg	**20%**
Total Carbohydrate 31g	**10%**
Dietary Fiber 0g	**0%**
Sugars 5g	
Protein 5g	
Vitamin A	4%
Vitamin C	2%
Calcium	20%
Iron	4%

Quick guide to % DV: 5% or less is low 20% or more is high

Limit these nutrients

Get enough of these nutrients

Footnote

* Percent Daily Values are based on a 2,000 calorie diet. Your Daily Values may be higher or lower depending on your calorie needs:

	Calories:	2,000	2,500
Total Fat	Less than	65g	80g
Sat Fat	Less than	20g	25g
Cholesterol	Less than	300mg	300mg
Sodium	Less than	2,400mg	2,400mg
Total Carbohydrate		300g	375g
Dietary Fiber		25g	30g

FIGURE 12.1 How to Read a Food Label

important energy source during exercise. Also, the brain, nervous system, and blood cells depend on them as their fuel source. Your capacity for exercise and mental processing will diminish quickly if you run out of this critical fuel.

Carbohydrates are classified as simple and complex. Simple carbohydrates contain only one or two sugar units per molecule, while complex carbohydrates consist of long chains of sugar molecules. Sweet-tasting foods, such as table sugar and honey, are examples of simple carbohydrates, while high-fiber foods, such as fruits, some vegetables, and grains, are complex carbohydrates. A diet high in dietary fiber is essential to good gastrointestinal health and the prevention of colon cancer. Nutritional experts recommend that you try to emphasize complex carbohydrates in your diet, but simple carbohydrates are

FOOD CHOICES LOW IN SATURATED FAT AND CHOLESTEROL AND MODERATE IN TOTAL FAT

Get most of your calories from plant foods such as grains, fruits, and vegetables. If you eat foods high in saturated fats for a special occasion, return to foods that are low in saturated fats the next day.

Fats and Oils

- Choose vegetable oils rather than solid fats (meat and dairy fats, shortening).
- If you need fewer calories, decrease the amount of fat you use in cooking and at the table.

Meat, Poultry, Fish, Shellfish, Eggs, Beans, and Nuts

- Choose two or three servings of fish, shellfish, lean poultry or other lean meats, beans, or nuts daily. Trim fat from meat and take skin off poultry. Eat dry beans, peas, or lentils often.
- Limit your intake of high-fat processed meats such as bacon, sausage, salami, bologna, and other cold cuts. Try the lower-fat varieties (check the nutrition facts label).
- Limit your intake of liver and other organ meats. Use egg yolks and whole eggs in moderation. Use egg whites and egg substitutes freely when cooking, since they contain no cholesterol and little or no fat.

Dairy Products

- Consume fat-free or low-fat milk, fat-free or low-fat yogurt, and low-fat cheese most often. Try switching from whole milk to fat-free or low-fat milk. This decreases the amounts of saturated fat and calories but keeps all other nutrients the same.

Prepared Foods

- Check the nutrition facts label to see how much saturated fat and cholesterol you get in a serving of prepared food. Choose foods lower in saturated fat and cholesterol.

Foods at Restaurants and Other Eating Establishments

- Choose fish or lean meats as suggested in the preceding entries. Limit ground meat and fatty processed meats, marbled steaks, and cheese.
- Limit your intake of foods with creamy sauces, and add little or no butter to your food.
- Choose fruits as desserts most often.

Source: U.S. Department of Agriculture, "Nutrition and Your Health: Dietary Guidelines for Americans," Home and Garden Bulletin No. 232, fifth edition, 2000.

also appropriate—particularly during recovery from exercise.

The body controls blood sugar levels by absorbing carbohydrates from the food you eat and by breaking down stored carbohydrates. The latter process is primary when you need energy quickly, such as during exercise. Hormones such as insulin, glucagon, and epinephrine (adrenaline) control blood sugar. These hormones activate when the energy level of your body changes, such as after you've eaten a meal or during exercise. While these hormones are critical to blood sugar regulation, they are ineffective unless they have fuels to work with. The body gets the carbohydrates it needs through the diet.

Carbohydrates are stored in cells as glycogen, which is a mass of blood sugar (glucose) units linked together. The liver and muscles store most of the body's glycogen. During exercise, the principal carbohydrate source for muscular work is muscle glycogen. You use approximately six times more muscle glycogen than blood sugar to run, ride a bicycle, or lift weights. Blood sugar fuels the nervous system. Motivation suffers without a well-functioning brain and nervous system—no matter how much glycogen you have in your muscles. You can't neglect blood sugar when considering which fuels your body will use during exercise. Muscle glycogen may provide most of the fuel for muscle movements, but the blood glucose supplies the brain and nervous system.

Blood sugar can also be manufactured in the liver from amino acids, lactate (lactic acid without the acid), and pyruvate. This process is called gluconeogenesis. Fuel sources in the bloodstream flow into the liver, where they are converted into blood sugar. Through this process and by breaking down liver glycogen, your body can maintain reasonably high levels of blood sugar, even during prolonged fasting.

During exercise, blood-sugar control processes allow blood sugar to increase. If you begin an exercise session with full glycogen stores in your liver, you can maintain elevated levels of blood sugar (compared with rest levels) for several hours of exercise before levels begin to decline.

Unfortunately, the liver's storage capacity is limited. When you're on a prolonged hard-training program and you don't consume enough calories or carbohydrates, liver glycogen stores can run low. Studies of athletes involved in heavy training show that because of poor diet, liver glycogen levels are often inadequate. High-carbohydrate diets are best for maintaining adequate glycogen stores in the liver. Eating a good breakfast is the best way of replenishing liver stores after the long night without any fuel intake.

Proteins

Proteins are the body's most basic structural material, making up much of muscle, bone, enzymes, some hormones, and cell membranes. Proteins are made of substances called amino acids. Of the 20 amino acids in foods, 9 are considered essential in the diet because the body can't make them. These essential amino acids are histidine, isoleucine, leucine, lysine, methionine, phenylalanine, theonine, tryptophan, and valine.

Protein supplements are popular with active people, particularly those who lift weights. However, most people take in much more protein than they need. The daily protein requirement is 0.8 gram of protein per kilogram of body weight. (A kilogram—abbreviated kg—equals about 2.2 pounds.) People who are extremely active may need slightly more protein. However, since most American athletes consume more than 1.5 grams of protein per kilogram of body weight, a protein deficit in the diet is rarely a problem. Active athletes need plenty of protein—about 1.5 grams per kilogram of body weight—because they must supply the demands for exercise and postexercise tissue building.

Proteins are important for people involved in endurance exercise. As noted, the liver can convert amino acids to blood sugar through gluconeogenesis. This term literally means making new glucose or blood sugar. Gluconeogenesis enables the body to maintain blood sugar during the hours in between meals. Amino acids, the building blocks of proteins, break down slowly and act like "time-released blood sugar tablets." Proteins in your meals help maintain blood sugar for many hours and prevent hunger sensations.

Amino acid use during exercise, particularly the branched-chain amino acids leucine, isoleucine, and valine, increases the longer and faster you exercise. Protein in your meals can help restore depleted amino acids.

Consumption of a protein supplement before weight training increases the rate at which amino acids travel into the muscle and speeds the rate at which muscles build new protein. Get into the habit of eating a protein energy bar (made by many companies) before weight training. It's a simple sports-nutrition tool that works.

Vitamins and Minerals

Americans spend more than one billion dollars per year on vitamin-mineral pills. Yet, the only common documented deficiency in the United States is iron deficiency. It appears that, with a couple of possible exceptions, anything more than a balanced diet and, perhaps, a basic vitamin pill is useless and a waste of money.

Vitamins act as coenzymes, meaning they work with enzymes to drive the body's metabolism, and aid in the production and protection of red blood cells. While vitamins are not produced in the body and must be consumed in the diet, they are required in extremely small amounts. Of all the body's vitamins, only vitamin C, thiamine, pyridoxine, and riboflavin are reduced by exercise. Of these, only vitamin C supplementation has been shown to improve performance, and that was in vitamin C–deficient adolescents.

Vitamin C supplementation has been a fertile area of debate since Linus Pauling suggested megadoses of the vitamin as a cure for the common cold in the 1970s. His contention has been extremely controversial, and, in general, medical studies have not supported his claims. However, recent studies have shown a link between vitamin C intake and immune function. This could be good news for anyone because reducing the downtime from illness can be just as effective as discovering a new ergogenic aid to enhance performance. It is certain that the debate regarding vitamin C and health will continue for many years.

Vitamin supplements will improve performance only if there is a nutritional deficiency. A moderate increase in vitamin C intake is safe, so it is not a bad idea to take a daily multi-vitamin supplement to compensate for an inadequate diet. Also, consuming additional vitamin C may be recommended in case it really does boost immune function. As long as you don't take excessive amounts of the vitamin, the extra vitamin C probably won't hurt. However, there does not appear to be any justification for the megadoses of vitamins taken by many athletes and active people.

Vitamins C and E may also help protect the body from destructive chemicals called free radicals, which are produced during normal metabolism. Free radicals cause aging, degenerative diseases, and breakdown of the immune system. Free radicals can be thought of as biological rust that attacks vital cell membranes and genes. Substances called antioxidants fight free radicals and help prevent aging and diseases such as hardening of the arteries (atherosclerosis). Vitamins C and E act as antioxidants that help eliminate free radicals and protect your body from their destructive effects. Scientists are just starting to learn about the relationship between vitamins and free radicals.

Water

Seventy percent of body weight is water. The average human body contains 11 gallons of water, which fills the cells, the spaces between the cells, and blood. Water helps distribute and disperse minerals, vitamins, amino acids, sugar, and many other nutrients throughout the cells. It participates in many chemical reactions, acts as a shock absorber in joints, and is critical for temperature regulation.

Dehydration is loss of body water. People can tolerate a 2 percent loss of water weight when the weather is cool but fatigue rapidly in hot weather. Replace fluids as you lose them, but do not drink so much water that you exceed the level of water loss. Take 30 to 60 grams of simple carbohydrates for each hour of exercise to maintain energy levels and prevent fatigue. The fluid-replacement beverage should contain electrolytes (e.g., sodium, potassium, and magnesium) if you're exercising for more than two hours. During recovery, weight lost through dehydration should be replaced before the next practice or competition. Thirst is a good measure of water needs at rest but may underestimate your needs during exercise in the heat.

In addition to drinking plain water, water found in the foods you eat—particularly fruits, vegetables, and liquids—will help keep you hydrated. While your body can make water through metabolism, 80 percent to 90 percent of daily water turnover comes from your diet. Recent studies showed that all nonalcoholic beverages—even coffee and colas containing caffeine—help replenish body water. You lose water every day in urine, sweat, feces, and evaporation from the lungs.

Your intake of water and salt affects your hydration level. Your body divides its water among cells, blood, and the area outside the cells. Dehydration upsets the balance and disrupts communications between different parts of the body, resulting in poor coordination and muscle stiffness. You also lose salt from your body when you sweat. This can cause muscle cramps because dehydration speeds muscle fatigue—the leading cause of cramps.

THE HEALTHY, HIGH-PERFORMANCE DIET AND THE FOOD GUIDE PYRAMID

The basic principles of good nutrition include eating a variety of foods, eating a balanced diet, and eating in moderation. It is difficult to improve upon sensible eating habits for maxi-mizing the effects of a fitness program and maintaining a trim, attractive body.

In 1995, the U.S. Department of Agriculture and the U.S. Department of Health and Human Services issued dietary guidelines for healthy Americans. The guidelines included a "food guide pyramid" that suggested the elements of a well-balanced diet. (See Figure 12.2.)

In September of 2002, the National Academy of Sciences issued new nutritional guidelines that allowed people to eat more monounsaturated fats, found in foods such as nuts, olive oil, and avocados.

The original food guide pyramid recommended that people avoid fats but eat plenty of carbohydrate-rich foods such as bread, cereal, rice, and pasta. The goal was to reduce the consumption of saturated fat, which raises cholesterol levels. Since then, researchers found that a high intake of refined carbohydrates such as white bread and white rice impairs the way the body handles sugars and causes insulin resistance. This can lead to a condition called metabolic syndrome, which involves elevated insulin levels; increased blood pressure, blood fats, and abdominal fat deposition; and blood clotting abnormalities. Replacing simple carbohydrates with healthy fats—monounsaturated or polyunsaturated—actually lowers the risk of heart disease.

The best diet for promoting health and weight control includes a variety of foods high in fruits, vegetables, whole grains, omega-3 fats (fish), nuts, olive oil, lean meats, poultry, and nonfat dairy products. Drink alcohol moderately or not at all, and avoid saturated and trans fats and excessive intake of simple sugars.

The healthy diet plays a critical role in any fitness-nutrition program. It provides all of the known nutrients, reduces the risk of coronary artery

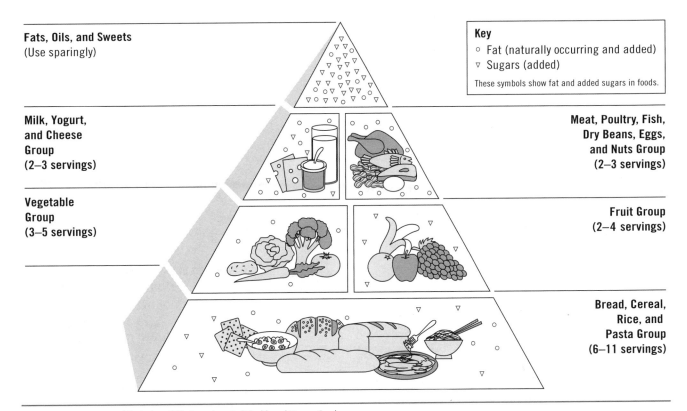

Fats, Oils, and Sweets
(Use sparingly)

Key
○ Fat (naturally occurring and added)
▽ Sugars (added)
These symbols show fat and added sugars in foods.

Milk, Yogurt, and Cheese Group
(2–3 servings)

Meat, Poultry, Fish, Dry Beans, Eggs, and Nuts Group
(2–3 servings)

Vegetable Group
(3–5 servings)

Fruit Group
(2–4 servings)

Bread, Cereal, Rice, and Pasta Group
(6–11 servings)

Source: U.S. Department of Agriculture/U.S. Department of Health and Human Services

FIGURE 12.2 Food Guide Pyramid

disease and some types of cancer, and provides enough energy to sustain a vigorous training program. The new nutritional recommendations from the National Academy of Sciences include the following:

- Emphasize weight control by exercising daily and not taking in too many calories.
- The bulk of the diet should consist of healthy fats (liquid vegetable oils such as olive, canola, soy, corn, sunflower, and peanut) and healthy carbohydrates (fruits, vegetables, and whole-grain foods such as whole-wheat bread, oatmeal, and brown rice).
- If both the fats and carbohydrates in your diet are healthy, you probably do not have to worry much about the percentages of total calories coming from each.
- Eat plenty of vegetables and fruits (six to eight servings per day).

- Eat moderate amounts of healthy sources of protein (nuts, legumes, fish, poultry, and eggs).
- Limit dairy consumption—other than nonfat dairy products—to one to two servings a day.
- Minimize the consumption of red meat, butter, refined grains (including white bread, white rice, and white pasta), potatoes, and sugar.

The food pyramid was designed to persuade people to eat fewer meat and dairy products containing cholesterol and saturated fats and eat more cereals, grains, fruits, and vegetables. The well-balanced diet suggested in the pyramid provides all known nutritional requirements and satisfies recommended daily allowances (RDA) for important nutrients. Because it is possible that all nutritional requirements have not been identified, people should consume a variety of foods from the basic food groups. Remember, all the food supplements in the world are not going to make up for a poor diet. You cannot get optimal nutrition from a pill!

Milk and milk products are principal sources of calcium, riboflavin, high-quality protein, carbohydrate, fat, and other assorted vitamins and minerals. Protein foods, such as meats, chicken, and fish, also supply iron, thiamine, riboflavin, niacin, phosphorus, and zinc. Avoid eating meats with a high fat content because they are associated with increased risk of heart disease.

The cereals and grains supply energy, thiamine, iron, niacin, and cellulose (fiber). These foods are critical for satisfying the energy requirements of a vigorous exercise program. Fruits and vegetables supply vitamins, minerals, and fiber. It is particularly important to eat dark green and deep yellow vegetables because of their high nutrient content and their possible influence in reducing the risk of certain types of cancer. Avoid foods with added sugar. These can contribute to problems with sugar metabolism and are a major source of excessive calories.

DIET, EXERCISE, AND WEIGHT CONTROL

The goal when losing weight is to maintain muscle mass and lose fat. This is not as easy as it sounds. Most people want instant results. People may try to lose weight any way they can—particularly girls and young women. Unfortunately, the results are rarely satisfactory when they try to lose weight rapidly.

Rapid weight loss causes muscle loss. When a person loses more than three pounds a week, 40 percent to 50 percent of the weight loss will be from lean body mass. The muscles are being used for food by the starving body. That's the last thing you need when you're trying to develop a fit, healthy-looking body.

Principles of Losing Weight for Active People

Weight loss is a worldwide obsession. Many people exercise in the hope of keeping the waistline under control. However, a program that depends solely on exercise—or solely on diet—is doomed to failure in the long run. You have to eat a healthy diet and exercise regularly if you are to achieve a fit, healthy-looking body.

The body's energy balance determines whether body fat increases, decreases, or remains the same. You gain fat when you eat more energy through meals than you burn through exercise and metabolism. While exercise is a big part of a weight-control program, a successful program demands caloric restriction. Exercise alone is rarely effective. Fat loss occurs when you take in less food than the energy you use.

The goal of a weight-control program should be to lose body fat and maintain the loss. Quick-loss programs often result in the loss of muscle tissue and do nothing to instill healthy long-term dietary habits that will maintain the new weight. Also, "yo-yo" diets are unhealthy and contribute to coronary heart disease. Following are several principles for losing body fat that will increase the chances of success for your weight-control program.

- **Stress fat loss.** Rapid weight loss from fad diets usually causes loss of muscle mass and water. Therefore, fat loss rather than weight loss should be the goal. Each pound of fat has 3,500 calories. The energy requirement of the average active person (depending on size, sex, and activity level) is typically between 2,000 and 5,000 calories per day. Even if you ate nothing and your body used only fat for energy, you would lose body fat slowly. Radical diets cause more than fat loss: you lose muscle and water too.

- **Lose weight slowly.** Lose no more than one kilogram (2.2 pounds) per week. More rapid weight loss results in the loss of muscle tissue. If you sustain a mild caloric deficit, you will lose fat. You lose little muscle or water this way. The weight stays off better. When you lose muscle, your body's metabolism slows. This reduces your need for food. When you go back on your normal diet, you gain weight rapidly because you no longer need as much food as before.

- **Stress a balanced diet.** The diet should be relatively high in complex carbohydrates and low in fat. Create a caloric deficit by combining caloric restriction with more exercise. Take in enough protein to help control appetite and maintain your muscles' needs. For active people, this is approximately 0.8 to 1 gram of protein per kilogram of body weight a day. Athletes need about 1.5 grams of protein per kilogram of body weight a day. You will lose muscle if you cut your calorie intake by too much, regardless of how much protein you take in.

- **Exercise is critical.** In a fall 2003 report, the National Academy of Sciences recommended that people exercise moderately for one hour a day. For the average person, the best exercises for losing weight include running, walking, and cycling. Your metabolism increases both during and after exercise, which causes you to burn calories at a faster rate all day long. Also, exercise helps main-

tain muscle mass, which is crucial for maintaining metabolic rate. If you can maintain your muscle mass during weight loss, you will be much more likely to maintain your new weight. The best exercises for promoting fat loss are prolonged-endurance exercises. However, intense exercise is also beneficial. High-intensity exercise—particularly weight training—increases your postexercise metabolism more than long, slow, endurance-type exercise. Studies have also shown that you break down fats faster during the postexercise period following a high-intensity exercise workout. High-intensity exercise also builds muscle mass more than endurance training. The bottom line is that both types of exercise are beneficial for weight control.

- **Monitor body composition.** Make sure that most of the weight loss is from a reduction in body fat rather than a reduction in lean body mass. The best way to do this is with an underwater weighing test, or Bodpod, which measures body composition by air displacement. These are widely available in university exercise physiology laboratories, health clubs, and medical facilities. Active people should know their body composition. If you don't have access to underwater weighing or a Bodpod, you can try other methods. Perhaps the best is skin-fold calipers. Almost every health club or high school physical education department has these. You can even buy plastic calipers from health-oriented magazines. Other popular choices are bioelectrical impedance and infrared methods. These techniques, while technologically advanced, are no more accurate than skin-fold calipers. Use these measurements as guides and rough indicators. The trained eye is often just as effective in evaluating body composition.

- **Avoid weight-loss aids.** The grocery and drugstore shelves are full of weight-loss products. Research has shown that these over-the-counter drugs are largely ineffective. Several appetite-suppressing drugs available by medical prescription are effective. However, according to the research, almost all the users gained back the weight they lost when they stopped taking the drugs. Also, the drugs were shown to have side effects, such as abnormal heart rhythms and insomnia. The best advice is to stay away from drugs that promise to help you lose weight. They probably don't work. If they do, they may damage your health. Only two drugs are approved for weight loss in the United States: orlistat and sibutramine. Both are expensive (about $100 a month), and both have side effects. Ephedrine-caffeine supplements were extremely popular for weight loss, but the Food and Drug Administration banned ephedra sales in April 2004.

The best strategy for body-composition management is to lose weight (fat) slowly. Change your body composition gradually so that you gain muscle and lose fat. Rapid weight loss causes you to lose muscle and also body water. This will impair your performance and not give you a healthy, fit-looking body.

Substances Taken to Aid Weight Control

Drugs used in weight control include those that suppress appetite, increase metabolic rate, affect the gastrointestinal tract, and control body water. As previously discussed, while some of these drugs may be temporarily effective, they can be dangerous and are not a satisfactory answer to long-term weight control.

The large variety and combination of supplements and drugs used by active people make it difficult to determine the efficacy of these practices or to predict the side effects. Numerous scientific reports describe catastrophic side effects from unsafe drug use and nutritional supplementation. Learn all you can about these supplements before taking them. You will get the best results by following a sensible diet and training program and avoiding dubious and potentially dangerous drugs and supplements.

13

Losing Weight: Weight Training, Aerobics, and Diet

"You must begin to think of yourself as becoming the person you want to be."
—David Viscott, physician, author, and radio personality

The key to weight loss is eating less and exercising more. This may sound simple, but even the experts can't agree on the best way to implement it. Some scientists state that people should exercise mildly for 30 minutes a day, while others contend that 60 minutes or more of aerobics and weight training is necessary. Some nutritionists say people should eat a low-calorie, balanced diet, while others say to eat fewer carbohydrates and more protein and fat.

DIET AND WEIGHT LOSS

For 25 years, the U.S. government urged us to eat less fat and more carbohydrates. The result: the obesity rate climbed from 14 percent of the population in 1971 to 30 percent today. The recommendations were based largely on scientific logic: Fat has more than twice the calories of carbohydrates per gram, and saturated fats contribute to hardening of the arteries and cancer. Also, eating carbs allows you to take in more food, which satisfies hunger and

prevents weight gain. Unfortunately, while people ate less fat, they ate more simple sugars, which can lead to obesity.

The low-fat recommendations in the 1970s coincided with the publication of the bestselling megahit *Dr. Atkins' Diet Revolution*, which advocated a diet low in carbohydrates and high in proteins and fats. Many health experts were appalled when the book was released and flabbergasted when it became a hit. They said that pushing diets high in fat and protein on the American public would promote obesity and heart disease and increase blood fats and the risk of kidney problems.

Two major clinical studies published in 2003 in the prestigious *New England Journal of Medicine* generated a national Atkins diet craze. They showed that overweight patients lost more weight on a low-carbohydrate diet than on a low-fat diet. The studies also showed that the Atkins diet reduced key risk factors for heart disease. Fats and proteins are in, and carbs are out!

In January of 2004, researchers from the University of Arkansas found opposite results: subjects given diets high in complex carbohydrates and low in fat (20 percent fat calories) and allowed to eat as much food as they wanted lost more weight than people on a diet higher in fat (40 percent fat calories). High-carb subjects who also exercised lost substantially more body fat than subjects in either diet group.

Whom do you believe? Incredibly, both are right. Under certain circumstances, you can lose weight on high-fat, high-protein diets or high-carbohydrate diets. It depends how much food you eat and whether you exercise. Another critical consideration is finding a plan that results in permanent weight loss and promotes health. This chapter will help separate the street noise from the street news regarding dieting and weight loss.

WHY AMERICANS ARE SO FAT

More than 65 percent of Americans are either overweight or obese. In some states, the obesity rates have increased by more than 100 percent in only three years. The Centers for Disease Control and Prevention (CDC) identified the obvious reasons for the obesity epidemic: Americans eat too much and don't get enough exercise.

A February 2004 CDC report showed that between 1971 and 2000, food intake increased from an average of 2,450 calories per day in men to 2,618 calories and increased from an average of 1,542 calories per day in women to 1,877 calories. The percentage of carbohydrates in the diet increased from 42 percent to 49 percent for men and increased from 45 percent to 52 percent for women, while fat intake decreased from 37 percent to 33 percent for men and decreased from 36 percent to 33

percent for women. The amount of fat (i.e., total grams) in the diet increased by nearly seven grams per day in women but decreased by five grams per day in men. People ate more calories—most from carbohydrates—but the same amount of fat.

In 1996, the U.S. surgeon general's office recommended that people exercise at moderate intensity for at least 30 minutes per day. That report noted that 50 percent of people didn't meet this requirement and only 12 percent did vigorous exercise regularly. Things haven't improved much. A report from the CDC in 2003 showed that Americans are doing even less exercise: nearly 55 percent of people fail to meet the 30-minute-per-day recommendation.

We're getting fatter every year but value the lean, muscular, athletic look. (See Figure 13.1.) The figure gives you a rough idea of how close you are to your ideal weight.

It's little wonder that low-carbohydrate diets that promise quick weight loss have taken the nation by storm. Most people want to lose weight the easy way—eat whatever they want and don't exercise. Unfortunately, having a fit, lean-looking body takes hard work. Relying on a fad diet may work in the short run, but most fad diets are unhealthy and will not give you the fit and healthy body you desire.

LOW-CARB DIET BASICS

Diets such as the Atkins, South Beach, and Protein Power are low in carbohydrates and high in proteins and fats. Low-carbohydrate diets in most research studies contain about 1,400 calories per day, 60 percent fat (94 grams per day), 10 percent carbohydrates (35 grams per day), and 30 percent protein (105 grams per day). The average American diet is 2,200

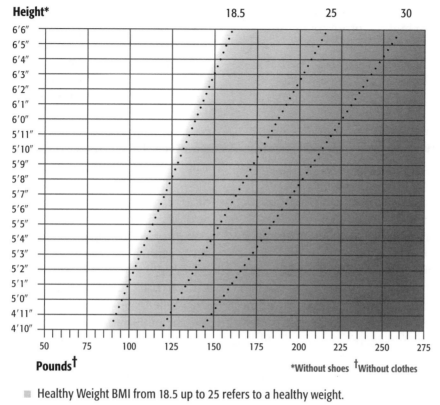

Height*   18.5   25   30

Pounds†   *Without shoes †Without clothes

- Healthy Weight BMI from 18.5 up to 25 refers to a healthy weight.
- Overweight BMI from 25 up to 30 refers to overweight.
- Obese BMI 30 or higher refers to obesity. Obese persons are also overweight.

Source: Report of the Dietary Guidelines Advisory Committee on the Dietary Guidelines for Americans, 2000, page 3.

FIGURE 13.1 BMI (Body Mass Index)
Are You at a Healthy Weight? BMI measures weight in relation to height. The BMI ranges shown above are for adults. They are not exact ranges of healthy and unhealthy weights. However, they show that health risk increases at higher levels of overweight and obesity. Even within the healthy BMI range, weight gains can carry health risks for adults.
Directions: Find your weight on the bottom of the graph. Go straight up from that point until you come to the line that matches your height. Then look to find your weight group.

calories per day, 35 percent fat (85 grams per day), 50 percent carbohydrates (275 grams per day), and 15 percent protein (83 grams per day). Compared with normal diets, the Atkins-type diets contain about the same fat intake but much less carbohydrate and more protein.

The scientific basis of low-carbohydrate diets is that the body prefers to use carbohydrates as fuel and save fats for emergencies. Millions of years of development encouraged our genes to maintain and preserve fat stores. In other words, the body makes it easy to store fat but makes it difficult to lose it. This made sense in the time of the cavemen: they could survive for days on their fat stores if they couldn't find any food.

Our genes controlling metabolism and fat storage are identical to those of our ancient ancestors. However, prehistoric humans didn't have processed foods with sugar dumped in everything they ate, nor did they have junk foods or pie shops in every cave. Their diets were high in protein, fat, and complex carbohydrates.

The problem with sugar is that it stimulates insulin. The pancreas secretes this hormone in response to high blood-sugar levels. Insulin is essential for transporting sugar into the cells, but it also promotes fat storage. Insulin stimulates fat storage in fat cells by turning off a chemical called hormone-sensitive lipase, which breaks down fat so the body can't use it as a fuel. It also increases the concentration of a chemical called acetyl CoA carboxylase, which stimulates fat storage. A major goal of low-carbohydrate diets is to keep insulin release to a minimum. This allows your body to use more fat for energy and helps you lose weight.

Scientists have criticized the Atkins diet since the '70s because there were no well-controlled clinical studies testing the weight-loss plan. However, as noted earlier, two studies published in the *New England Journal of Medicine* in 2003 showed that the Atkins diet helped people lose more weight than people following the government's food pyramid diet. Surprisingly, the Atkins diet reduced markers of heart disease, such as blood triglycerides and insulin resistance.

The first study, from Philadelphia Veterans Affairs Medical Center, found that people who ate a low-carbohydrate diet lost an average of 13 pounds, while those who ate a low-fat diet lost an average of only 4 pounds. Also, the Atkins diet appeared to reduce the risk of heart disease: blood fats decreased, while insulin sensitivity (a primary factor in obesity and heart disease) improved. One problem with the study is that nearly 50 percent of the subjects dropped out, with a strong trend toward more dropouts in the Atkins group.

The second study, from the University of Pennsylvania School of Medicine, found that weight loss was markedly higher in people who followed the Atkins diet than in a group eating a low-fat diet—at 3 months (6.8 percent weight loss versus 2.7 percent) and at 6 months (7.0 percent versus 3.2 percent) but not at 12 months (4.4 percent versus 2.5 percent)—still comparatively better. As with the first study, the Atkins followers showed marked improvements in heart disease risk factors—increased good cholesterol (HDL), decreased triglycerides, and improved ability to control blood sugar (glucose tolerance).

People lose weight on low-carbohydrate diets mainly because they take in fewer calories than they use through metabolism and physical activity. Also, though, they lose more water than fat during the first few weeks of the diet, so they quickly regain the weight when they stop dieting.

While the diets help speed fat use, caloric balance (food in versus energy out) mainly determines if you lose weight. People who don't exercise must take in a maximum of 1,400 to 1,500 calories per day if they want to lose weight. These diets have several major weaknesses: (1) It's difficult to maintain a vigorous exercise program on a low-carb diet because carbohydrates are the main fuel during exercise above 65 percent of maximum effort. (2) Limiting complex carbohydrates—particularly fruits and vegetables—may have long-term health consequences because of deficiencies in vitamins E and A, thiamine, vitamin B6, folate, calcium, zinc, magnesium, potassium, and fiber. (3) The diet disturbs acid-base balance, which weakens bones and promotes kidney stones. (4) High-protein diets promote intake of unhealthy amounts of cholesterol, fat, saturated fat, and protein.

HIGH-CARBOHYDRATE, LOW-FAT DIETS

Low- to moderate-fat diets have been popular since the 1970s and are promoted in successful programs and diet books such as Weight Watchers, the food guide pyramid, *The Dash Diet*, *Dr. Dean Ornish's Program for Reversing Heart Disease*, *Eat More, Weigh Less*, and *The New Pritikin Program*. As with low-carbohydrate diets, people lose weight on low-fat diets because they take in fewer calories than normal. Low-fat and moderate-fat weight-loss diets usually contain about 1,400 to 1,500 calories per day, 10 percent to 30 percent fat (16 to 40 grams per day), 60 percent to 75 percent carbohydrates (218 to 271 grams per day), and 15 percent to 20 percent protein (54 to 72 grams per day). The diets may also lead to lifestyle modification, such as decreased fat and food intake and increased exercise.

Dr. Dean Ornish, from the University of California, San Francisco, Medical School, advocates a diet low in fat and high in complex carbohydrates. He agrees that we are eating too many simple sugars but disagrees that the answer is to eat more fat and protein. Rather, we should eat more complex carbohydrates such as whole wheat, brown rice, and legumes (beans).

University of Arkansas for Medical Sciences researchers found that men and women lost weight and body fat on a complex-carbohydrate, low-fat diet that let them eat as much food as they wanted. A group that exercised and ate a high-carb diet lost even more fat during the 12-week study. The study showed that diets high in complex carbohydrates—vegetables, fruits, and whole grains—are high in fiber and less calorie-dense, so they have more volume per calorie. Eating diets high in complex carbs satisfies hunger and provides the energy to exercise vigorously so that you can burn more calories all day and night.

Humans convert very little carbohydrate into fat. Body fat reflects how much fat you eat and how much fat you use for fuel. With the Atkins diet, reducing carbohydrate intake suppresses appetite, so you eat fewer calories and lose weight. This is a quick fix for rapid weight loss, but it is not consistent with a healthy lifestyle.

Complex carbohydrates are high in fiber, which slows their digestion and prevents a rapid increase in blood sugar. Their bulk fills you up before you eat too much. Also, they contain many nutrients that help prevent heart disease, cancer, and cell aging. Harvard scientists—in a study of nearly 60 thousand people published in 2002—found that women who ate diets high in fruits, vegetables, whole-grain breads, cereals, fish, and low-fat dairy products lived longer than those who ate few of these foods. The study showed that eating a variety of healthy foods was more important than avoiding unhealthy foods. These results probably apply to men, too.

Simple sugars are another matter. High-sugar soft drinks, for example, can account for much of the increased carbohydrate intake during the past 30 years. The high-calorie drinks do not satisfy hunger very well, so your total calorie intake mushrooms.

SUCCESSFUL "LOSERS"

People wanting to lose weight should look at the habits of people who successfully lost weight and kept it off. The National Weight Control Registry—established by scientists from the University of Colorado Health Sciences Center, in Denver—includes more than 2,900 people who lost an average of 66 pounds and maintained the required minimum weight loss of

30 pounds for an average of five years. The profiles of these people are remarkably similar: they exercised for 60 to 90 minutes per day and cut down on calories and fat intake. Nearly 80 percent ate breakfast every day. Fewer than 1 percent of these successful "losers" followed low-carbohydrate Atkins-type diets.

EXERCISE IS CRITICAL FOR SUCCESSFUL WEIGHT LOSS

The goal of a weight-loss program should be to achieve and maintain a healthy weight and look good. You can't do this without exercise—and the more intense, the better. You lose fat by using more calories than you take in. Intense exercise causes you to burn plenty of calories during exercise and to burn more calories and fat after the exercise is over. So, when trying to lose fat, work harder and burn more calories.

Again, intense exercise increases fat use after the exercise is over. You use the readily available carbs during intense exercise and then switch to fats during recovery. The body uses more fats as fuel after an intense workout than after an easy one. Run for an hour at 70 percent to 80 percent of maximum effort and you get a post-exercise calorie-burning bonus of nearly 100 calories.

The benefits of intense exercise have been supported by a series of studies conducted for more than 10 years at Laval University, in Canada. People who trained intensely had more muscle and less fat than those who exercised at lower intensities. People exercising more intensely lost much more body fat, even though they exercised for less time, than people who trained moderately.

Researchers from Duke University—led by Dr. Cris Slentz—found similar results in a study published in January 2004. The eight-month study showed that people could lose weight through exercise alone—without dieting. (The average energy intake was slightly more than 2,000 calories per day.) People who exercised intensely lost much more fat than those who trained moderately. Even moderate-intensity exercise caused some fat loss.

The healthiest and best long-term diet-and-exercise plan for weight loss and wellness is to avoid saturated fats, simple sugars, and excessive alcohol consumption. Eat a variety of foods, emphasizing vegetables, fruits, whole grains, lean meats, fish, and low-fat or nonfat dairy products. Most important, exercise for 60 to 90 minutes a day, and train with weights two or three days per week. Forget about fad diets, eat healthy foods and exercise, and you will maintain a healthy weight.

WEIGHT TRAINING AND WEIGHT LOSS

Muscles are extremely active tissues. At rest, they burn calories continuously. When muscles contract, they really turn up the heat. During exercise, muscle metabolism can increase as much as 15 to 20 times above rest levels. Scientists, using a technique called direct calorimetry (which estimates metabolic rate by measuring heat loss), found that the body's heat-generating capacity is directly proportional to muscle mass. The more muscle you have, the greater your metabolic rate. The best way to stoke your metabolic fire is to add muscle and then keep your new tissue active.

There are right and wrong ways to lose weight. Think of what happened to your girlfriend after she lost 20 or 30 pounds. Did she look healthy and athletic, or did she appear gaunt and drawn, with a lot of excess skin? Probably, she looked terrible, more like a patient with anorexia than the picture of health. And, to make matters worse, she probably gained back all the weight and then some within six to eight months.

Her problem: a good portion of her lost weight was muscle tissue. Losing muscle slows metabolism, which makes it difficult to maintain fat loss. She dug herself into an energy-deficit hole that made weight gain inevitable. Don't fall into the same trap that your girlfriend did. Build muscle through weight training, and you will find it much easier to lose weight and keep it off.

YO-YO DIETING: TIME FOR A CHANGE

Many people spend their lives on yo-yo diets—endless cycles of losing weight and gaining it back. They are suckers for any crackpot diet that comes along. Sometimes they restrict calories; other times, fat; and still other times, carbohydrates. In the short run, these people often lose some weight, but they usually gain it back and then some.

Americans are clearly losing the "battle of the bulge." Recent studies by the CDC show that more than half of Americans are obese or overweight. What is most alarming is that the population obesity rate has increased a whopping 50 percent since 1991. While we don't totally understand the reasons for the obesity explosion, lack of exercise and excess calories in the diet are at the core of the problem.

PHAT (PRETTY, HOT, AND TEMPTING) INSTEAD OF FAT

When are the busiest times of the year in the gym? The beginning of January and a month or two before summer.

Why? Because people want to lose fat so they can look better (i.e., PHAT). After New Year's Eve, they have to make amends for a month of overeating. Just before summer, they realize that they will soon have to display their less-than-perfect bodies on nearby beaches and in vacation spots around the world. Sure, they want to be healthier, but health takes a backseat to looks every time. If they can combine good health and looks, all the better.

Caloric restriction (usually without exercise) is by far the most popular weight-loss strategy in America. Unfortunately, people lose muscle mass as well as fat. Most studies show that if you lose 20 pounds from a weight-loss diet without exercise, nearly 30 percent of the weight loss will be from muscle.

Sure, you lost weight. But, have you gotten closer to your goal of looking better in a swimsuit or sexier in your clothes? Not by a long shot. More typically, you look as if you have just recovered from an extended bout with the flu.

What if you could lose weight but look better? That's what you want, right? Scientific studies have shown that this is not only possible but also probably the key to permanent weight loss. With the right diet-and-exercise program, you can maintain almost all your muscle mass, even when you lose substantial amounts of weight.

Dr. William Kraemer and colleagues from Penn State University and Ball State University found that people who combined caloric restriction with a weight-training and aerobic exercise program maintained muscle mass while making sizable improvements in strength, body composition, and aerobic capacity.

The study included three groups: subjects who dieted but didn't exercise, those who dieted and did aerobic exercise, and those who dieted and did aerobics and weight training. In 12 weeks, members of each group lost the same amount of weight, about 20 pounds. The big difference among groups was the amount of muscle lost. People who dieted without exercising lost nearly seven pounds of muscle. Those who dieted and did aerobics lost more than four pounds of muscle. Only members of the group who dieted while also lifting weights and doing aerobics maintained their muscle mass. They lost only about one-half pound of muscle, even though they lost a substantial amount of body weight. The bottom line from this study: when you add weight training and aerobics to your weight-loss program, you lose more fat and less muscle.

Not all studies agree with Kraemer's research. Other investigators have shown that adding weight training to a weight-loss diet program makes no contribution to maintaining muscle mass or improving overall body composition. Why was Kraemer's group successful while other researchers came up empty-handed? Kraemer's study carefully controlled the exercise intensity. Personal trainers made sure that people actually did the work.

Look around in any health club. Some people spend more time socializing than working hard. You can't build muscle and lose fat by looking at yourself in the mirror or talking to your friend on the next machine. Push yourself when you do resistive or aerobic exercises. You don't have to exercise for hours and hours, but you do need to be serious about your program.

THE JOYS OF MUSCLE MASS

Until recently, health experts downplayed resistive exercise as a principal component in a health-promotion program. However, many recent studies have demonstrated that this type of exercise deserves a central place in your fitness and weight-control program.

People with more muscle have a higher metabolic rate. While metabolic rate drops during rapid weight loss—regardless of whether you maintain muscle mass—over the long term, maintaining muscle mass seems to be the most significant factor in determining if you can keep the weight off. As discussed, you are certainly going to look better if, after losing weight, you have maintained your muscle mass. People on "yo-yo" weight-control programs tend to lose muscle mass during periods of weight loss and replace it with fat during periods of weight gain.

Muscle is critical for quality of life. People who lose a lot of muscle mass during a weight-loss program usually lose some fitness. They can't do as much physically, so their performance declines when they're skiing, playing golf, hitting a tennis ball, or carrying groceries.

Muscle holds a lot of your body water and is essential for regulating body temperature. Losing muscle mass during a weight-loss program robs your body of its precious water stores. Having less body water means you will have more trouble regulating heat and body temperature. Muscle water loss also decreases your blood volume, which can impair endurance capacity.

Finally, muscle mass is critical to bone health. Many studies show that muscle and bone strength are highly related. Women—and men to a lesser extent—lose bone mass with age. Maintaining muscle strength and mass helps prevent age-related loss of bone mass and life-threatening fractures.

THE FINAL FRONTIER OF FAT MANAGEMENT

Unfortunately, building muscle is not the magic bullet for weight management. It helps, but it is not the total answer. Most studies, including Kraemer's, show that you lower your metabolic rate whenever you lose weight, regardless of whether you maintain muscle. Maintaining muscle mass certainly prevents some of the decrease, but not all. This has confused researchers and is the subject of intense study. If muscle mass is closely linked to metabolic rate, why is metabolism depressed even when you maintain muscle mass?

The answer lies in the complex genetic controls of body weight and fat stores. Your body maintains a balance in its tissues to survive. When you remove fat from fat cells, you disturb their balance. They initiate complex physiological control mechanisms to maintain the biological status quo. Over the short term, increased muscle mass cannot compensate fully for these natural controls. However, over the long term, the natural links between muscle mass and metabolic rate most likely reestablish themselves.

Losing fat while gaining muscle is the key to looking good in your clothes or swimsuit. If you want to lose weight and improve your appearance, your direction is clear: eat less, but include weight training and aerobics in your program. If you don't do resistive exercises while trying to lose weight, you are going to lose muscle mass and will not get the results you want.

14

Ergogenic Aids: Drugs and Supplements

"I really lack the words to compliment myself today."
—Alberto Tomba, downhill skiing legend

Substances taken to enhance performance are called ergogenic aids. Active people consume a wide variety of drugs and nutritional supplements in the quest for improved performance and the "perfect body." They take these substances to (1) enhance muscle hypertrophy (growth), (2) speed recovery and prevent the effects of overtraining, (3) increase training intensity and aggressiveness, and (4) control fat, body water, and appetite.

Sports, fitness, and bodybuilding have become popular, high-profile activities. Several bodybuilding champions have become international film stars (one became governor of California), and many make a lot of money endorsing athletic food supplements. Many bodybuilding and fitness magazines serve as promotional vehicles for a plethora of products of questionable value. As an aware, educated consumer of fitness products, you should be able to separate fact from fiction in evaluating "performance-enhancing" drugs and food supplements. This chapter reviews some of the more popular drugs and food supplements touted to improve appearance and performance.

Many of the drugs and supplements used by athletes and other active people to improve performance and appearance are banned for use in amateur and professional sports, and some are illegal. Table 14.1 summarizes the supposed effects, actual effects, and potential side effects of some of the best-known of these aids.

Research tells us little about the effectiveness and long-term health effects of these substances. You should be aware of the latest information about these substances and be careful of what you put in your body.

ANABOLIC-ANDROGENIC STEROIDS

Anabolic refers to tissue building, while androgenic refers to the development of male sexual characteristics. People take anabolic steroids in the hope of gaining weight, muscle size, strength, power, speed, endurance, and aggressiveness. In the United States in 1990, the Anabolic Steroid Control Act classified anabolic steroids as Schedule III substances (highly controlled). The

Table 14.1 POPULAR SUPPLEMENTS AND DRUGS USED BY ATHLETES TO IMPROVE PERFORMANCE

Substance	Supposed Effects	Actual Effects	Potential Side Effects
Adrenal androgens: DHEA and androstenedione	Increased testosterone, muscle mass, and strength; decreased body fat	Increased testosterone, strength, and muscle mass in older subjects; no effects in younger subjects	Gonadal suppression, prostate hypertrophy, gynecomastia, and masculinization in women
Amino acids	Increased muscle mass	No effects if protein intake is adequate; timing may promote hypertrophy	Minimal side effects
Anabolic steroids	Increased muscle mass, strength, power, psychological aggression, and capacity for high-intensity exercise	Increased muscle mass, strength, power, psychological aggression, and capacity for high-intensity exercise	Minor to severe: gonadal suppression, liver disease, heart disease, prostate disease, acne, gynecomastia, and masculinization and precocious puberty in children
Chromium picolinate	Increased muscle mass; decreased fat	No effects on muscle mass or fat	Moderate doses safe; high doses may cause DNA damage
Creatine monohydrate	Increased muscle mass, strength, and power	Increased muscle mass, strength, and power in some types of high-intensity exercise	Minimal side effects; some reports of muscle cramping; long-term effects unknown
Ephedrine (usually combined with caffeine)	Decreased body fat; increased training intensity	Decreased appetite; increased energy level	Insomnia, nervousness, and heart arrhythmias
Ginseng	Decreased physical and emotional stress; increased maximal oxygen consumption	No effects on performance	No serious side effects; high doses can cause high blood pressure, nervousness, and insomnia
Growth hormone	Increased muscle mass, power, and strength; decreased body fat	Increased muscle mass and strength; decreased body fat	Diabetes, acromegaly, enlarged heart, and carpal tunnel syndrome
HMB (beta-hydroxy-beta-methylbutyrate)	Increased muscle mass, power, and strength; decreased body fat	Increased muscle mass and strength; decreased body fat	No reported side effects; long-term effects unknown
Metabolic-optimizing meals for athletes	Increased muscle mass and energy supply; decreased body fat	No proven effects beyond normal meals	No reported side effects
Protein	Increased muscle mass	No effects if protein intake is adequate; taking before workout may promote muscle hypertrophy	Excessive intake can be dangerous in people with kidney or liver disease

law gave the Drug Enforcement Administration power to restrict the importation, exportation, distribution, and dispensing of anabolic steroids. This has led to a thriving "black market" for illegal anabolic steroids in the United States.

Anabolic steroids increase protein synthesis, which enhances lean body mass. They bind with receptor molecules in the cells, which stimulate the cells to make proteins. They also interfere with the activity of hormones that break down tissue after exercise, which helps steroid users recover more quickly. Anabolic steroids may also increase aggressiveness, which allows athletes to train harder. Recent studies show that steroids work better at higher dosages (more than 400 milligrams a week of testosterone). Unfortunately, the incidence of side effects increases with dosage.

How Steroids Work in the Body

Steroids primarily operate in the following ways:

- **Increase the size of muscle cells:** Steroids make muscles larger and increase strength, power, speed, and endurance.
- **Increase speed of calcium release:** Power athletes ranging from baseball players to Olympic lifters have long appreciated the effects of steroids on quickness and power. Calcium triggers muscle contraction. Steroids increase the speed of calcium release and make the muscle cells more sensitive to calcium. This means that the muscles contract faster and more powerfully.
- **Increase androgen receptor activity:** Steroids work by binding to androgen receptors in the tissues. Then the steroid-receptor enters the cell nucleus and triggers the cell to make new proteins. In the past, scientists said that taking high doses

of steroids was ineffective because there weren't enough androgen receptors to accommodate the high levels of testosterone—the hormone couldn't work if it didn't have a receptor to bind. The activity of the receptor increases in the face of high blood levels of testosterone. Also, intense weight training increases receptor number and activity. Heavy training and high doses of testosterone combine to promote muscle growth.

Receptor density has been found to be greater in the upper body than in the lower body. This suggests that steroids may be more effective for increasing strength and muscle mass of the pecs over the quads.
- **Anticatabolic effects:** Muscle growth occurs when protein synthesis in the muscle exceeds breakdown. Hormones called corticosteroids are secreted during and after exercise and promote muscle breakdown. If you can slow breakdown after a workout, you can make gains by having only a small amount of net protein synthesis. Animal studies show that anabolic steroids can cross-bind with corticosteroid binding sites, which prevents muscle breakdown. These hormones are catabolic, which means they cause protein breakdown. High doses of steroids may promote cross-binding, but not all studies show that steroids have anticatabolic effects.
- **Trigger growth hormone and muscle growth factors:** Steroids trigger the release of growth hormone from the brain and IGF-1 (muscle growth factor) from the liver. They do this only when the weekly dosage of anabolic steroids equals a minimum of 400 milligrams. IGF-1 and GH (growth hormone) are highly anabolic. Athletes have not seen significant gains by taking GH by itself. The

gains are more impressive when the drugs are combined with anabolic steroids.

- **Psychological effects:** You can't be a great athlete—or a great anything —if you can't control your mind. Recent studies suggest that "roid rage" is a myth—in most people. Anabolic steroids do affect euphoria, energy, and sexual arousal, which could have powerful effects on the desire and motivation to train hard. High blood testosterone increases androgen receptors in the brain— just as it does in muscle. Steroids increase certain brain chemicals, such as serotonin, GABA, and acetyl- choline, which could help psych you up and encourage you to train harder. These chemicals are impor- tant for communications between brain cells and general arousal of the brain.

Health Risks of Anabolic Steroids

Side effects include liver toxicity and tumors—with oral steroids; decreased high-density lipoproteins (good choles- terol); cardiac arrhythmia (abnormal heart rhythms); reduced sperm count; lowered testosterone production; high blood pressure; increased risk of AIDS (due to shared needles); depressed immune function; glucose intolerance; psychological disturbances; masculin- ization in women and children; prema- ture closure of the bone growth centers; and an increased cancer risk. Steroids can also make adolescent acne much worse in young men and women. Severe side effects of anabolic steroid use have been reported in athletes, including myocardial infarc- tion (heart attack), ventricular tachy- cardia (accelerated heart rate), liver cancer, and severe psychiatric distur- bances. Athletes may be particularly prone to side effects because they often take high dosages of the drugs for prolonged periods.

New research makes clear that athletes must take high doses of steroids if they want significant effects. There is no purely anabolic steroid; androgen receptors exist in most of the tissues in the body, including the heart and prostate gland—all have sexual side effects. Taking extremely high doses of steroids may be setting the stage for heart enlargement and even- tual heart failure as well as prostate enlargement and cancer. Also, high doses of steroids increase IGF-1, a potent growth stimulator of muscle and cancer cells. Steroid users from the 1970s and '80s have not been dying in large numbers from cancer and heart disease. However, they didn't take the same amount of steroids that modern athletes do.

GROWTH HORMONE (GH)

Growth hormone is popular with athletes, who use it to increase muscle mass and strength. Reports in the news media suggest that, as with anabolic steroids, its use has filtered down to nonathletes interested in improving their appearance. The development of recombinant human growth hormone (GH made using gene technology) has made the hormone more widely avail- able. Nevertheless, growth hormone is extremely expensive and can cost athletes $1,000 or more per month.

GH speeds the rate at which proteins enter muscle cells, which increases their growth rate. It also stimulates insulin-like growth factor. In addition, GH mobilizes fats from the fat cells, so the drug is used as well to help control body composition.

Studies of growth hormone in humans have shown no beneficial effects on muscle or performance. Animal studies found that GH admin- istration stimulates muscle growth. Observations in athletes suggest that

GH is highly anabolic in elite body-builders who train intensely. However, the side effects can be severe.

Prolonged GH administration may result in low blood sugar, elevated insulin levels, heart enlargement, and elevated blood fats. Long-term use could also lead to acromegaly, characterized by enlarged bones in the head, face, and hands; cardiomyopathy (heart inflammation and destruction of heart muscle cells); peripheral nerve damage; weakening of the bones (osteoporosis); arthritis; heart disease; insulin resistance; and carpal tunnel syndrome. These side effects occur at higher doses.

Some athletes also take drugs that increase the secretion of natural growth hormone. These drugs include propranolol, vasopressin, clonidine, and levodopa. There is no evidence that these practices enhance muscle hypertrophy.

INSULIN-LIKE GROWTH FACTOR (IGF-1)

The use of recombinant IGF-1, also called somotomedin C, has recently become popular among athletes. IGF-1 production is stimulated by growth hormone. The hormone is released mainly by the liver but may also be secreted by the testes, fat cells, bones, and heart. It is an extremely anabolic (muscle-building) hormone. The side effects are thought to be similar to those of growth hormone. The long-term effects are unknown.

DEHYDROEPIANDROSTERONE (DHEA) AND ANDROSTENEDIONE

DHEA and androstenedione (andro) are relatively weak androgen hormones that are produced mainly in the adrenal glands. They are broken down

to testosterone, which explains their popularity with athletes. DHEA is widely available in health food stores and supermarkets, but the Food and Drug Administration (FDA) no longer recognizes andro as a food supplement, so it is available only by prescription.

Athletes take these hormones to stimulate muscle hypertrophy and lose weight. In one study, administration of DHEA or androstenedione in middle-aged and older adults was shown to improve energy levels and increase muscle mass, mental acuity, and immune function. However, these subjects had blood levels of the hormone at least 20 percent below the average level of a 20-year-old. These hormones may boost performance by increasing blood testosterone levels.

In another study, high doses of DHEA (1,600 milligrams per day) in young men led to a reduction in HDL cholesterol (good cholesterol). However, in elderly subjects, DHEA reduced LDL (bad cholesterol) and had no effect on HDL. Doses of 150 to 300 milligrams per day increase testosterone levels. This could lead to masculinization in women and interfere with hormone controls in both sexes.

Androstenedione administration could have similar side effects. These "pro-hormones" could have the same side effects in young people as testosterone: stunted growth, skin problems, interference with normal sex hormones, and psychological disorders. Women should avoid them because they could interfere with the menstrual cycle and cause reproductive and bone problems.

INSULIN

Some active people take insulin injections to promote muscle hypertrophy. Insulin promotes carbohydrate and fat storage and speeds protein synthesis. It helps build muscle by enhancing amino acid transport into cells, increasing the rate of incorporation of amino acids into protein, and suppressing protein breakdown. The effects of insulin supplements on muscle size and strength are unknown. The most serious side effect of bodybuilders taking insulin shots before exercise is insulin shock, a condition in which blood sugar reaches dangerously low levels.

CLENUBUTEROL

This drug is used medically to treat asthma. Athletes take it to prevent muscle atrophy, increase lean body mass, and decrease body fat. Beneficial effects have been shown in animals, but few studies have been done in humans. Side effects include insomnia, abnormal heart rhythm, anxiety, depressed appetite, and nausea. More serious side effects include enlarged heart, heart failure, and heart attack. This drug is easy to get, but its side effects can be serious.

MYOSTATIN

IGF-1 and myostatin are two chemicals within muscle that help regulate muscle growth. Control systems in the body almost always have checks and balances. For example, insulin helps store carbohydrates, while glucagon (carbohydrates stored in muscle and liver) moves carbs out of cells and into the blood. Muscle has its checks and balances, too. While IGF-1 stimulates muscle growth, myostatin prevents growth. French researchers studied the balance between these two chemicals in growing chickens bred to have large breasts (the pectoralis major muscles). During growth, the chickens bred for larger chest muscles showed an increase in IGF-1 and a decrease in

myostatin, which coincided with a rapid increase in muscle. Scientists have been working on drugs that will promote protein synthesis in muscle by increasing IGF-1 and decreasing myostatin. They hope to increase meat yields in cows, pigs, chickens, and sheep. The drugs are of obvious interest to bodybuilders and power athletes.

OTHER SUBSTANCES

Other substances sometimes used as ergogenic aids include human chorionic gonadotropin (HCG), periactin, conjugated linoleic acid (CLA), vanadyl sulfate, dibencozide, and organ extracts. These agents are much less popular, and their effectiveness is questionable.

AGENTS AND TECHNIQUES TO IMPROVE OXYGEN TRANSPORT CAPACITY

In 1972, Swedish scientists published a paper on the effects of transfusion on oxygen transport capacity. The test subjects increased maximal oxygen consumption and exercise capacity by more than 10 percent. This study served as the basis for "blood doping." Several runners were suspected of using blood doping to win Olympic medals. The procedure involved withdrawing two units of blood (800 milliliters), storing it for one to two months while the body restored the lost blood cells, and then reinfusing it in the athlete. The extra blood induced a large increase in oxygen-carrying capacity.

In the mid-1980s, scientists developed a synthetic erythropoietin (EPO) that stimulated the bone marrow to produce red blood cells. During the early years, many deaths were associated with its use. Synthetic EPO is extremely popular with endurance athletes such as cyclists, runners, cross-country skiers, and swimmers. Stimulating the bone marrow to produce new red blood cells increases the ability to deliver oxygen to the muscles and can increase exercise capacity by 10 percent or more. There is a test to detect EPO use, but it is not totally effective. EPO is banned in Olympic, college, and some professional sports.

In medicine, EPO is used to treat anemia (low red blood cell count). Worldwide sales of the drug approached $3 billion in 2004. More than 180 patients who used EPO have developed a mysterious and potentially deadly blood disease called aplasia, an autoimmune condition in which the body destroys its tissues. This comes as bad news to the many endurance athletes, particularly at the elite levels, for whom EPO is the performance-enhancing drug of choice. EPO users also risk stroke and heart attack.

AGENTS TAKEN TO SPEED RECOVERY

The primary purposes of taking agents to speed recovery are to replenish depleted body fuels (e.g., for creatine phosphate: creatine supplementation; for muscle and liver glycogen: glucose and lactate polymers) and serve as sources for postexercise protein synthesis (i.e., amino acids).

Creatine Monohydrate
Creatine monohydrate (creatine) is among the most popular and widely used supplements among athletes. They take these supplements to build strength and muscle mass, enhance recovery, and improve exercise capacity.

Creatine feeding increases the creatine phosphate content of the muscle by about 20 percent. Creatine phosphate is a high-energy chemical that is used to maintain adenosine triphosphate (ATP) levels. ATP supplies the energy for most physiological functions in the body. Taking creatine supplements increases the capacity for intense exercise. The most effective dosage of creatine is two to five grams (about one teaspoon) per day. Taking more than that causes no further increase in total muscle creatine. In more than thirty studies, creatine supplementation improved performance in short-term, high-intensity, repetitive exercise, which might make it a valuable supplement for active people. It may improve performance by augmenting the availability of creatine phosphate and possibly regulating the rate of muscle sugar breakdown. It may increase muscle-building capacity during resistive exercise by allowing more-intense training.

Creatine has been linked to diarrhea, dehydration, muscle cramping, and muscle strains. However, in more than 30 studies—some conducted for as long as three years—creatine use was shown to have no side effects. The often-cited links between creatine and dehydration and cramps have been refuted repeatedly by scientific studies. Moreover, college football players who took creatine monohydrate supplements (5 to 20 grams per day for up to five years) showed no evidence of kidney or liver damage based on the results of standard blood tests.

Beta-hydroxy-beta-methylbutyrate (HMB)
HMB is a breakdown product of the amino acid lysine. Combining all the studies on HMB shows that the supplement increased net lean mass by 0.28 percent per week and increased strength by 1.40 percent per week. Other studies show that taking HMB with creatine monohydrate caused

greater improvements in muscle mass and strength than taking either one alone. The few studies on the side effects of HMB suggest that the supplement is safe.

Amino Acid and Polypeptide Supplements

Athletes take amino acid and polypeptide supplements to accelerate muscle development, decrease body fat, and stimulate the release of growth hormone. There is little scientific proof to support amino acid or polypeptide supplementation. The protein requirement for active people is not much higher than that for sedentary individuals—0.8 gram to 1.5 grams of protein per kilogram of body weight per day—so the rate of amino acid absorption from the gastrointestinal tract is not significant. Also, substituting amino acid or polypeptide supplements for protein-rich foods may cause deficiencies in important nutrients, such as iron and the B vitamins.

The timing of protein and amino acid feeding may be important for stimulating muscle growth. Radioactive tracer studies—which can follow the metabolism of various fuels—found that taking a protein supplement either 30 minutes before weight training or immediately after speeds the movement of amino acids into muscle and stimulates protein synthesis (i.e., makes new muscle tissue faster). There is only one study showing that this technique improves performance or increases muscle size.

Other Substances

Consuming carbohydrate beverages, such as Gatorade, during and immediately following exercise enhances recovery from intense training, speeding the replenishment of liver and muscle glycogen. The use of other substances to speed recovery, such as vitamin C, N-acetyl-L-cysteine (NAC), and inosine, is not currently supported by positive research findings.

SUBSTANCES TAKEN TO INCREASE AGGRESSIVENESS AND TRAINING INTENSITY

Serious exercisers often spend several hours per day training for their favorite activities. Monotony and fatigue sometimes make it difficult to achieve significant improvement. Many athletes therefore use stimulants to help them train harder and combat fatigue.

Amphetamines

Some athletes and other active people take amphetamines to prevent fatigue and to increase confidence and training intensity. Examples of amphetamines include Benzedrine, Dexedrine, dexamyl, and methedrine. These drugs act by stimulating the nervous system. Effects include increased blood pressure, heart rate, arousal, wakefulness, and confidence, and the feeling of an enhanced capability to make decisions.

Studies show that the drugs mask fatigue but have not consistently shown that they increase endurance performance. Most studies have shown increases in static strength but mixed results in muscle endurance. Amphetamines appear to aid power-oriented movement skills in activities that employ constant motor patterns such as the shot put and hammer throw, and theoretically, they could provide some benefit to bodybuilders and weight lifters by allowing them to train harder.

Amphetamines can cause severe neural and psychological effects. These include aggressiveness, paranoia, hallucinations, compulsive behavior, restlessness, and irritability. They also can cause arrhythmias, hypertension, and angina (heart-related chest pain). They are highly addictive and dangerous.

Caffeine

Caffeine—found in coffee, cola, tea, and chocolate—is a favorite stimulant of active people. It stimulates the central nervous system by causing the release of adrenaline (epinephrine). In athletics, caffeine is used as a stimulant and as a fatty acid mobilizer. While there is some evidence that caffeine may improve endurance, the drug does not appear to enhance short-term maximal exercise capacity.

The diuretic and cardiac-stimulatory properties of this substance can combine to increase the risk of arrhythmias, such as ventricular ectopic beats and paroxysmal atrial tachycardia (potentially dangerous heart rhythms). Caffeine can also cause insomnia and is addicting. Caffeine was removed from the Olympic doping control list in early 2004.

Other Agents

Other agents used by active people to enhance training intensity include cocaine, ephedrine, modafinil (Provigil), and ginseng. Cocaine use is not thought to be widespread in athletes, but some athletes reportedly use it to increase training intensity. Ephedrine, a weak stimulant, is widely used by athletes during workouts. Studies have shown that despite a slight stimulating effect on blood pressure and on exercise and recovery heart rates, ephedrine had no effect on physical work capacity. Ephedrine and ephedra supplements have become controversial and have been associated—rightly or wrongly—with the deaths of several professional athletes. Ephedra was banned by the FDA in April 2004. Provigil is a medication used to treat

excessive daytime sleepiness (narcolepsy). It acts as a minor stimulant and may improve concentration. It was recently added to the Olympic banned drug list. Ginseng is also popular with athletes, but there is little evidence to support its use as an ergogenic aid.

SUBSTANCES TAKEN TO AID WEIGHT CONTROL

Drugs used in weight control include those that suppress appetite, thermogenic drugs, drugs affecting the gastrointestinal tract, and diuretics to control weight and increase muscle definition. Gymnasts, dancers, figure skaters, and weight-class athletes, among others, use a variety of techniques to decrease body fat. They may do this immediately before a contest or chronically because of the requirements of the sport.

Appetite-suppressing drugs work by acting on brain receptors and chemicals that control food intake. Thermogenic drugs affect metabolic rate. Gastrointestinal drugs attempt to affect nutrient absorption. Other agents with questionable effectiveness and desirability include human chorionic gonadotropin, growth hormone, glucagon, progesterone, and biguanides. These substances affect metabolism and appetite control, but have not, as yet, passed scientific trials.

Appetite suppressants include amphetamines, ephedrine, sibutramine, diethylpropion, fenfluramine, and phenylpropanolamine. While these drugs depress appetite and cause weight loss, some have serious side effects. Amphetamines, for example, as noted, are highly addictive and can cause cardiac arrhythmias and impair temperature regulation.

Thermogenic drugs include thyroid hormone, ephedrine, and dinitrophenol. Thyroid hormones were commonly used in the 1970s. They reduce lean body mass and cause an increased incidence of cardiac arrhythmias. Ephedrine and beta-agonists have been suggested as useful agents, but more research is necessary to establish their effectiveness. Uncoupling agents, such as dinitrophenol, are toxic at effective dosages and are associated with neuropathy (nerve damage) and cataracts (eye damage).

Drugs affecting the gastrointestinal tract include orlistat, dietary fiber, and sucrose polyester. Orlistat—one of two weight-loss prescription drugs approved in the United States (sibutramine is the other)—partially blocks fat absorption. While effective, it has side effects—such as abdominal cramping and oily stools—that are unacceptable to many people. Dietary fiber causes gastrointestinal distention and may restrict energy intake. Limited clinical trials suggest that including fiber supplements may aid weight loss. Sucrose polyester (olestra) is a new diet ingredient of some promise. This substance cannot be digested and can be substituted for fats in the diet. The few studies on olestra have shown conflicting results.

The combination of ephedrine and caffeine is an effective weight-loss agent—comparable to either orlistat or sibutramine. However, the supplements are controversial. As discussed previously ephedra is no longer legally sold as a supplement.

Diuretics

Before a contest, many bodybuilders attempt to accentuate their muscle definition by using diuretics, potassium supplements, and low-calorie diets. Some bodybuilders also take potassium supplements to promote fluid retention in their muscle cells, thus increasing muscle size. Athletes combine these practices with very low-calorie diets and dehydration in the quest for leanness.

There is no evidence that these unhealthy practices improve performance in bodybuilding. Serious complications have developed from these practices, including rhabdomyolysis (muscle destruction, suggested by elevated serum creatine kinase and phosphorus), hypotension (low blood pressure), marked hemoconcentration (loss of blood fluid), hyperkalemia (potassium increase due to the use of potassium-sparing diuretics and potassium supplements), cardiac arrhythmias, and heart failure.

SUPPLEMENTS AND YOUR EXERCISE PROGRAM

Be careful what you put in your body. Most supplements and drugs either don't work or have potentially dangerous side effects. It's always best to seek the advice of a health professional before using supplements.

WEIGHT-TRAINING EXERCISES FOR MACHINES FROM SELECTED MANUFACTURERS

Company	Legs	Arms	Shoulders and Chest	Torso
Atlantis	Butt Machine	Arm Curl	Chest Press	Cross Over
	Donkey Calf	Preacher Curl	Deltoid Raise	Lat Pull-Down
	Leg Abduction	Triceps Extension	Incline Press	Low-Back Extension
	Leg Adduction	Triceps Push-Down	Pec Deck	Pull-Over Row
	Leg Curl		Real Delt	
	Leg Extension		Rotator Cuff	
	Leg Press		Shoulder Press	
	Total Hip			
Body Master	Abductor	Arm Curl	Chest Press Incline	Abdominal
	Adductor	Overhead	Chest Press Vertical	Abdominal Crunch
	Glute Trainer	Triceps Extension	Lateral Raise	Lat Pull-Down
	Leg Curl	Triceps Press	Seated Pec Deck	Low-Back Extension
	Leg Extension		Vertical Shoulder Press	Low Row
	Seated Leg Curl			Rowing
	Standing Calf			
	Standing Leg Curl			
	Super Leg Curl			
	Super Leg Extension			
	Super Leg Press			
Cybex	Hip Abduction	Arm Curl	Chest Press	Ab Crunch
	Hip Adduction	Triceps Extension	Incline Press	Pull-Down
	Leg Extension		Overhead Press	Torso Rotation
	Leg Press			
	Prone Leg Curl			
	Rotary Calf			
	Seated Leg Curl			
Hammer	Abductor	Behind Neck Press	Bench Press	Behind Neck Pull-Down
	Adductor	Bench Press	Flat Back Chest	Bilateral Row
	Calf	Flat Back Chest	Iso Wide Chest	Dead Lift
	H Squat	Front Military Press	Lateral Raise	Front Pull-Down
	Iso Leg Curl	Incline Press	Rear Deltoid	High Row
	Iso Leg Extension	Iso Behind Neck	Rotator Cuff	Iso Pull-Over

WEIGHT-TRAINING EXERCISES FOR MACHINES FROM SELECTED MANUFACTURERS
(continued)

Company	Legs	Arms	Shoulders and Chest	Torso
Hammer	Lateral Leg Press Leg Curl Leg Extension Leg Press Seated Calf Raise Seated Leg Curl	Iso Incline Press Iso Wide Chest Seated Biceps Seated Triceps	Seated Dip	Low Row Pull-Over Row Shrug
Icarian	Leg Curl Leg Extension Leg Press	Camber Curl Triceps Push-Down	Incline Pec Deck Shoulder Press Vertical Chest Press	Ab Crunch Low Back Extension Seated Row
Life Fitness	Calf Raise Leg Abduction Leg Adduction Leg Curl Leg Extension Leg Press Seated Leg Curl	Biceps Curl Triceps Extension	Chest Press Incline Press Lateral Raise Pec Deck Fly Seated Raise Shoulder Press	Ab Crunch Lat Pull-Down Low Back Extension Seated Row Shoulder Pull-Over
Magnum	Glute/Ham Leg Abduction Leg Adduction Leg Curl Leg Extension Leg Press Multi Hip Seated Calf	Arm Curl Biangular Arm Curl Triceps Extension Triceps Push-Down	Bench Press Bilateral Chest Lateral Raise Pec Real Delt Shoulder Press Vertical Bench Press	Biangular Lat Row Cable Crossover Lat Pull-Down Rogers Row Rotary Back Upper Back

REFERENCES

Aagaard, P., J. Andersen, P. Dyhre-Poulsen, A.M. Leffers, A. Wagner, S. Magnusson, J. Halkjaer-Kristensen, and E. Simonsen. A mechanism for increased contractile strength of human pennate muscle in response to strength training: Changes in muscle architecture. *Journal of Physiology* 534 (2001): 613–623.

Ahtiainen, J. P., A. Pakarinen, M. Alen, W. J. Kraemer, and K. Hakkinen. Muscle hypertrophy, hormonal adaptations, and strength development during strength training in strength-trained and untrained men. *European Journal of Applied Physiology* 89 (2003): 555–563.

Bahr, R., and O. M. Sejersted. Effect of intensity of exercise on excess postexercise O_2 consumption. *Metabolism* 40 (1991): 836–841.

Bayramoglu, M., M. N. Akman, S. Kilinc, N. Cetin, N. Yavuz, and R. Ozker. Isokinetic measurement of trunk muscle strength in women with chronic low-back pain. *American Journal of Physical Medicine and Rehabilitation* 80 (2001): 650–655.

Berger, R. A. Application of research findings in progressive resistance exercise to physical therapy. *Journal of the Association for Physical and Mental Rehabilitation* 19 (1965): 200–203.

———. Effect of varied weight-training programs on strength. *Research Quarterly* 33 (1962): 168–181.

———. Response to "Berger in retrospect: Effect of varied weight-training programs on strength." *British Journal of Sports Medicine* 37 (2003): 372–373.

Bhasin, S., L. Woodhouse, and T. W. Storer. Proof of the effect of testosterone on skeletal muscle. *Journal of Endocrinology* 170 (2001): 27–38.

Bhasin, S., T. W. Storer, N. Berman, K. E. Yarasheski, B. Clevenger, J. Phillips, W. P. Lee, T. J. Bunnell, and R. Casaburi. Testosterone replacement increases fat-free mass and muscle size in hypogonadal men. *Journal of Clinical Endocrinology and Metabolism* 82 (1997): 407–413.

Bohannon, R. W. Measuring knee extensor muscle strength. *American Journal of Physical Medicine and Rehabilitation* 80 (2001): 13–18.

Bosco, C., R. Colli, R. Bonomi, S. P. von Duvillard, and A. Viru. Monitoring strength training: Neuromuscular and hormonal profile. *Medicine and Science in Sports and Exercise* 32 (2000): 202–208.

Brooks, G., T. Fahey, and K. Baldwin. *Exercise Physiology: Human Bioenergetics and Its Applications*. New York: McGraw-Hill, 2005 (fourth ed.).

Brooks, G., and J. Mercier. The balance of carbohydrate and lipid utilization during exercise: The crossover concept (brief review). *Journal of Applied Physiology* (1994) 80: 2253–2261.

Burke, D. G., P. D. Chilibeck, G. Parise, D. G. Candow, D. Mahoney, and

M. Tarnopolsky. Effect of creatine and weight training on muscle creatine and performance in vegetarians. *Medicine and Science in Sports and Exercise* 35 (2003): 1946–1955.

Centers for Disease Control and Prevention. Prevalence of physical activity, including lifestyle activities among adults—United States, 2000–2001. *Morbidity and Mortality Weekly Report* 52 (2003): 764–769.

Chandler, T. J., G. D. Wilson, and M. H. Stone. The effect of the squat exercise on knee stability. *Medicine and Science in Sports and Exercise* 21 (1989): 299–303.

Cohen, R. I., K. Marzouk, P. Berkoski, C. P. O'Donnell, V. Y. Polotsky, and S. M. Scharf. Body composition and resting energy expenditure in clinically stable, non-weight-losing patients with severe emphysema. *Chest* 124 (2003): 1365–1372.

Cordo, P. J., V. S. Gurfinkel, T. C. Smith, P. W. Hodges, S. M. Verschueren, and S. Brumagne. The sit-up: Complex kinematics and muscle activity in voluntary axial movement. *Journal of Electromyography and Kinesiology* 13 (2003): 239–252.

Cronin, J., P. J. McNair, and R. N. Marshall. The effects of bungee weight training on muscle function and functional performance. *Journal of Sports Sciences* 21 (2003): 59–71.

———. Velocity specificity, combination training, and sport-specific tasks. *Journal of Science and Medicine in Sport* 4 (2001): 168–178.

Cussler, E. C., T. G. Lohman, S. B. Going, L. B. Houtkooper, L. L. Metcalfe, H. G. Flint-Wagner, R. B. Harris, and P. J. Teixeira. Weight lifted in strength training predicts bone change in postmenopausal women. *Medicine and Science in Sports and Exercise* 35 (2003): 10–17.

Duncan, G. E., M. G. Perri, D. W. Theriaque, A. D. Hutson, R. H. Eckel, and P. W. Stacpoole. Exercise training, without weight loss, increases insulin sensitivity and postheparin plasma lipase activity in previously sedentary adults. *Diabetes Care* 26 (2003): 557–562.

Foster, G. D., H. R. Wyatt, J. O. Hill, B. G. McGuckin, C. Brill, B. S. Mohammed, P. O. Szapary, D. J. Rader, J. S. Edman, and S. Klein. A random trial of a low-carbohydrate diet for obesity. *New England Journal of Medicine* 348 (2003): 2082–2090.

Gabriel, D. A., J. R. Basford, and K. N. An. Neural adaptations to fatigue: Implications for muscle strength and training. *Medicine and Science in Sports and Exercise* 33 (2001): 1354–1360.

Gorostiaga E. M., M. Izquierdo, P. Iturralde, M. Ruesta, and J. Ibanez. Effects of heavy-resistance training on maximal and explosive force production, endurance, and serum hormones in adolescent handball players. *European Journal of Applied Physiology and Occupational Physiology* 80 (1999): 485–493.

Hakkinen, K. Neuromuscular and hormonal adaptations during strength and power training: A review. *Journal of Sports Medicine and Physical Fitness* 29 (1989): 9–26.

Hakkinen, K., and A. Pakarinen. Acute hormonal responses to two different fatiguing heavy-resistance protocols in male athletes. *Journal of Applied Physiology* 74 (1993): 882–887.

Hakkinen, K., W. J. Kraemer, R. U. Newton, and M. Alen. Changes in electromyographic activity, muscle fiber, and force production characteristics during heavy resistance/ power strength training in middle-aged and older men and women. *Acta Physiologica Scandinavica* 171 (2001): 51–62.

Hakkinen, K., A. Pakarinen, W. J. Kraemer, A. Hakkinen, H. Valkeinen, and M. Alen. Selective muscle hypertrophy, changes in EMG and force, and serum hormones during strength training in older women. *Journal of Applied Physiology* 91 (2001): 569–580.

Haupt, H. A. Upper-extremity injuries associated with strength training. *Clinics in Sports Medicine* 20 (2001): 481–490.

Hays, N. P., R. D. Starling, X. Liu, D. H. Sullivan, T. A. Trappe, J. D. Fluckey, and W. J. Evans. Effects of an ad libitum low-fat, high-carbohydrate diet on body weight, body composition, and fat distribution in older men and women: A randomized controlled trial. *Archives of Internal Medicine* 164 (2004): 210–217.

Isear, J. A., Jr., J. C. Erickson, and T. W. Worrell. EMG analysis of lower-extremity muscle-recruitment patterns during an unloaded squat. *Medicine and Science in Sports and Exercise* 29 (1997): 532–539.

Izquierdo, M., K. Hakkinen, J. Ibanez, M. Garrues, A. Anton, A. Zuniga, J. L. Larrion, and E. M. Gorostiaga. Effects of strength training on muscle power and serum hormones in middle-aged and older men. *Journal of Applied Physiology* 90 (2001): 1497–1507.

Jenkins, D. J. A., C. W. C. Kendall, L. S. A. Augustin, S. Franceschi, M. Hamidi, A. Marchie, A. L. Jenkins, and M. Axelsen. Glycemic index: Overview of implications in health and disease. *American Journal of Clinical Nutrition* 76 (2002): 266S–273S.

Jensen, M. D. Androgen effect on body composition and fat metabolism. *Mayo Clinic Proceedings* 75 (2000): S65–S68; discussion S68–S69.

Jiang, B., A. Gower, G. R. Hunter, A. Goodman, C. L. McLafferty Jr., and R. J. Urban. Mechanical load increases muscle IGF-1 and androgen receptor mRNA concentrations in humans. *American Journal of Physiology, Endocrinology and Metabolism* 280 (2001): E383–E390.

Joseph, L. J., T. A. Trappe, P. A. Farrell, W. W. Campbell, K. E. Yarasheski, C. P. Lambert, and W. J. Evans. Short-term moderate weight loss and resistance training do not affect insulin-stimulated glucose disposal in postmenopausal women. *Diabetes Care* 24 (2001): 1863–1869.

Jowko, E., P. Ostaszewski, M. Jank, J. Sacharuk, A. Zieniewicz, J. Wilczak, and S. Nissen. Creatine and beta-hydroxy-beta-methylbutyrate (HMB) additively increase lean body mass and muscle strength during a weight-training program. *Nutrition* 17 (2001): 558–566.

Klem, M. L., R. R. Wing, M. T. McGuire, H. M. Seagle, and J. Hill. A descriptive study of individuals successful at long-term maintenance of substantial weight loss. *American Journal of Clinical Nutrition* 66 (1997): 239–246.

Kraemer, W. J., S. J. Fleck, J. E. Dziados, E. A. Harman, L. J. Marchitelli, S. E. Gordon, R. Mello, P. N. Frykman, L. P. Koziris, and N. T. Triplett. Changes in hormonal concentrations after different heavy-resistance exercise protocols in women. *Journal of Applied Physiology* 75 (1993): 594–604.

Lamont, L. S., A. J. McCullough, and S. C. Kalhan. Gender differences in the regulation of amino acid metabolism. *Journal of Applied Physiology* 95 (2003): 1259–1265.

Liow, D. K., and W. G. Hopkins. Velocity specificity of weight training for kayak sprint performance. *Medicine and Science in Sports and Exercise* 35 (2003): 1232–1237.

Marniemi, J., E. Kronholm, S. Aunola, T. Toikka, C. E. Mattlar, M. Koskenvuo, and T. Ronnemaa. Visceral fat and psychosocial stress in identical twins discordant for obesity. *Journal of Internal Medicine* 251 (2002): 35–43.

Marx, J. O., N. A. Ratamess, B. C. Nindl, L. A. Gotshalk, J. S. Volek, K. Dohi, J. A. Bush, A. L. Gomez, S. A. Mazzetti, S. J. Fleck, K. Hakkinen, R. U. Newton, and W. J. Kraemer. Low-volume circuit versus high-volume periodized resistance training in women. *Medicine and Science in Sports and Exercise* 33 (2001): 635–643.

McCarthy, M. E. Getting a lift from lifting: Weight training can effectively improve strength, mobility, and, ultimately, independence for even very old and frail adults. *Provider* 29 (2003): 36–38.

McGuire, M. T., R. R. Wing, M. L. Klem, W. Lang, and J. O. Hill. What predicts weight regain among a group of successful weight losers? *Journal of Consulting and Clinical Psychology* 67 (1999): 177–185.

Medbo, J. I., E. Jebens, H. Vikne, P. E. Refsnes, and P. Gramvik. Effect of strenuous strength training on the Na-K+ pump concentration in skeletal muscle of well-trained men. *European Journal of Applied Physiology* 84 (2001): 148–154.

Michels, K. B., and A. Wolk. A prospective study of variety of healthy foods and mortality in women. *International Journal of Epidemiology* 31 (2002): 847–854.

Mirmiran, P., F. Mohammadi, N. Sarbazi, S. Allahverdian, and F. Azizi. Gender differences in dietary intakes, anthropometrical measurements, and biochemical indices in an urban adult population: The tehran lipid and glucose study. *Nutrition, Metabolism, and Cardiovascular Diseases* 13 (2003): 64–71.

Morley, J. E., R. N. Baumgartner, R. Roubenoff, J. Mayer, and K. S. Nair. Sarcopenia. *Journal of Laboratory and Clinical Medicine* 137 (2001): 231–243.

Mujika, I., and S. Padilla. Muscular characteristics of detraining in humans. *Medicine and Science in Sports and Exercise* 33 (2001): 1297–1303.

Munson, B. L. Myths and facts . . . about ephedrine use. *Nursing* 33 (2003): 81.

Nindl, B. C., E. A. Harman, J. O. Marx, L. A. Gotshalk, P. N. Frykman, E. Lammi, C. Palmer, and W. J. Kraemer. Regional body composition changes in women after six months of periodized physical training. *Journal of Applied Physiology* 88 (2000): 2251–2259.

Petrofsky, J. S., and M. Laymon. The effect of previous weight training and concurrent weight training on endurance for functional electrical stimulation cycle ergometry. *European Journal of Applied Physiology* 91 (2004): 392–398.

Pipe, A. Effects of testosterone precursor supplementation on intensive weight training. *Clinical Journal of Sport Medicine* 11 (2001): 126.

Porter, M. M. The effects of strength training on sarcopenia. *Canadian Journal of Applied Physiology* 26 (2001): 123–141.

Roberts, S. S. Simple steps to fitness. Secrets of strength. Strength training is as important to weight loss and fitness as aerobic exercise is, but many people ignore it. Here's how to get started. *Diabetes Forecast* 55 (2002): 98–100.

Roemmich, J. N., and A. D. Rogol. Exercise and growth hormone: Does one affect the other? *Journal of Pediatrics* 131 (1997): S75–S80.

Ross, R., and I. Janssen. Physical activity, total and regional obesity: Dose-response considerations. *Medicine and Science in Sports and Exercise* 33 (2001): S521–S527; discussion S528–S529.

Rossi, A. B., and A. L. Vergnanini. Cellulite: A review. *Journal of the European Academy of Dermatology and Venereology* 14 (2000): 251–262.

Roth, S. M., G. F. Martel, F. M. Ivey, J. T. Lemmer, B. L. Tracy, E. J. Metter, B. F. Hurley, and M. A. Rogers. Skeletal muscle satellite-cell characteristics in young and older men and women after heavy-resistance strength training. *Journals of Gerontology: Series A, Biological Sciences and Medical Sciences* 56 (2001): B240–B247.

Samaha, F. F., N. Iqbal, P. Seshadri, K. L. Chicano, D. A. Daily, J. McGrory, T. Williams, M. Williams, E. J. Gracely, and L. Stern. A low-carbohydrate as compared with a low-fat diet in severe obesity. *New England Journal of Medicine* 348 (2003): 2074–2081.

Sartorio, A., C. L. Lafortuna, M. Massarini, and C. Galvani. Effects of different training protocols on exercise performance during a short-term body-weight reduction program in severely obese patients. *Eating and Weight Disorders* 8 (2003): 36–43.

Schmidt, W. D., C. J. Biwer, and L. K. Kalscheuer. Effects of long- versus short-bout exercise on fitness and weight loss in overweight females.

Journal of the American College of Nutrition 20 (2001): 494–501.

Schoenfeld, B. Repetitions and muscle hypertrophy. *Strength and Conditioning Journal* 22 (2000): 67–69.

Shrier, I., D. Feldman, J. Klvana, M. Rossignol, and L. Abenhaim. Comparison between tests of fatigue and force for trunk flexion. *Spine* 28 (2003): 1373–1378.

Slentz, C. A., B. D. Duscha, J. L. Johnson, K. Ketchum, L. B. Aiken, G. P. Samsa, J. A. Houmard, C. W. Bales, and W. Kraus. Effects of the amount of exercise on body weight, body composition, and measures of central obesity. *Archives of Internal Medicine* 164 (2004): 31–39.

Stubbs, R. J., N. Mazlan, and S. Whybrow. Carbohydrates, appetite, and feeding behavior in humans. *Journal of Nutrition* 131 (2001): 2775S–2781S.

Suzuki, J., R. Tanaka, S. Yan, R. Chen, P. T. Macklem, and B. Kayser. Assessment of abdominal muscle contractility, strength, and fatigue. *American Journal of Respiratory and Critical Care Medicine* 159 (1999): 1052–1060.

Szasz, A., A. Zimmerman, E. Frey, D. Brady, and R. Spalletta. An electromyographical evaluation of the validity of the two-minute sit-up section of the army physical fitness test in measuring abdominal strength and endurance. *Military Medicine* 167 (2002): 950–953.

Tesch, P. A., E. B. Colliander, and P. Kaiser. Muscle metabolism during intense, heavy-resistance exercise. *European Journal of Applied Physiology* 55 (1986): 362–366.

Trappe, S. W., T. A. Trappe, G. A. Lee, and D. L. Costill. Calf muscle strength in humans. *International Journal of Sports Medicine* 22 (2001): 186–191.

Tremblay, A., J. Després, C. Leblanc, C. L. Craig, B. Ferris, T. Stephens, and C. Bouchard. Effect of intensity of physical activity on body fatness and fat distribution. *American Journal of Clinical Nutrition* 51 (1990): 153–157.

Tremblay, A., J. Simoneau, and C. Bouchard. Impact of exercise intensity on body fatness and skeletal muscle metabolism. *Metabolism* 43 (1994): 814–818.

Treuth, M. S., G. R. Hunter, and M. Williams. Effects of exercise intensity on 24-h energy expenditure and substrate oxidation. *Medicine and Science in Sports and Exercise* 28 (1996):1138–1143.

Trudeau, F., R. J. Shephard, F. Arsenault, and L. Laurencelle. Tracking of physical fitness from childhood to adulthood. *Canadian Journal of Applied Physiology* 28 (2003): 257–271.

Weltman A., J. P. Després, J. L. Clasey, J. Y. Weltman, L. Wideman, J. Kanaley, J. Patrie, J. Bergeron, M. O. Thorner, C. Bouchard, and M. L. Hartman. Impact of abdominal visceral fat, growth hormone, fitness, and insulin on lipids and lipoproteins in older adults. *Metabolism* 52 (2003): 73–80.

Wing, R. R., and J. O. Hill. Successful weight-loss maintenance. *Annual Review of Nutrition* 21 (2001): 323–341.

Woods, S. C., K. Gotoh, and D. J. Clegg. Gender differences in the control of energy homeostasis. *Experimental Biology and Medicine* 228 (2003): 1175–1180.

Wretenberg, P., Y. Feng, and U. P. Arborelius. High- and low-bar squatting techniques during weight training. *Medicine and Science in Sports and Exercise* 28 (1996): 218–224.

INDEX

Page numbers followed by *f* indicate that the referent appears in a figure on that page; page numbers followed by *t* indicate that the referent appears in a table on that page.